D1382877

Fraud Auditing and Forensic Accounting

Fraud Auditing and Forensic Accounting

Fourth Edition

TOMMIE W. SINGLETON
AARON J. SINGLETON

John Wiley & Sons, Inc.

Copyright © 2010 by John Wiley & Sons, Inc. All rights reserved.

Published by John Wiley & Sons, Inc., Hoboken, New Jersey.
Published simultaneously in Canada.

No part of this publication may be reproduced, stored in a retrieval system, or transmitted in any form or by any means, electronic, mechanical, photocopying, recording, scanning, or otherwise, except as permitted under Section 107 or 108 of the 1976 United States Copyright Act, without either the prior written permission of the Publisher, or authorization through payment of the appropriate per-copy fee to the Copyright Clearance Center, Inc., 222 Rosewood Drive, Danvers, MA 01923, (978) 750-8400, fax (978) 646-8600, or on the Web at www.copyright.com. Requests to the Publisher for permission should be addressed to the Permissions Department, John Wiley & Sons, Inc., 111 River Street, Hoboken, NJ 07030, (201) 748-6011, fax (201) 748-6008, or online at http://www.wiley.com/go/permissions.

Limit of Liability/Disclaimer of Warranty: While the publisher and author have used their best efforts in preparing this book, they make no representations or warranties with respect to the accuracy or completeness of the contents of this book and specifically disclaim any implied warranties of merchantability or fitness for a particular purpose. No warranty may be created or extended by sales representatives or written sales materials. The advice and strategies contained herein may not be suitable for your situation. You should consult with a professional where appropriate. Neither the publisher nor author shall be liable for any loss of profit or any other commercial damages, including but not limited to special, incidental, consequential, or other damages.

For general information on our other products and services or for technical support, please contact our Customer Care Department within the United States at (800) 762-2974, outside the United States at (317) 572-3993 or fax (317) 572-4002.

Wiley also publishes its books in a variety of electronic formats. Some content that appears in print may not be available in electronic books. For more information about Wiley products, visit our web site at www.wiley.com.

Library of Congress Cataloging-in-Publication Data:

Singleton, Tommie.
Fraud auditing and forensic accounting/Tommie W. Singleton, Aaron J. Singleton. – 4th ed.
p. cm.
Rev. ed. of: Fraud auditing and forensic accounting. 3rd ed. 2006.
Includes index.
ISBN 978-0-470-56413-4; ISBN 978-0-470-87748-7 (ebk);
ISBN 978-0-470-87790-6 (ebk); ISBN 978-0-470-87791-3 (ebk)
1. White collar crime investigation–United States. 2. Forensic accounting–United States. 3. Fraud investigation–United States. I. Singleton, Aaron J., 1980- II. Fraud auditing and forensic accounting. III. Title.
HV8079.W47B65 2010
364.16'3—dc22
2010013504

Printed in the United States of America

10 9 8 7 6 5 4 3 2 1

Contents

Preface xi

Acknowledgments xiii

Chapter 1: Background of Fraud Auditing and Forensic Accounting **1**

Introduction 1
Brief History of Fraud and the Antifraud Profession 3
The Fraud Cycle 7
Review of Technical Literature 9
Forensic Accountant and Audits 11
Forensic Accountants 20
Fraud Auditors 25
Keys to Effective Fraud Investigation 31
The Antifraud Professional's Career 33
Summary 36
Notes 37

Chapter 2: Fraud Principles **39**

Introduction 39
Definition: What Is Fraud? 40
Synonyms: Fraud, Theft, and Embezzlement 42
Classic Fraud Research 42
Fraud Triangle 44
Scope of Fraud 47
Profile of Fraudsters 49
Who Is Victimized by Fraud Most Often? 53
Fraud Taxonomies 54
Fraud Tree 62
Evolution of a Typical Fraud 65
Summary 68
Notes 69

Chapter 3: Fraud Schemes **71**

Introduction 71
ACFE Fraud Tree 73
Financial Statement Schemes 80
Corruption Schemes 83
Asset Misappropriation Schemes 84
Summary 94
Notes 94

Chapter 4: Red Flags **95**

Introduction 95
Professional Standards 97
Common Red Flags 99
Specific Red Flags 101
Fraud Detection Model 110
Summary 111
Notes 112

Chapter 5: Fraud Risk Assessment **113**

Introduction 113
Technical Literature and Risk Assessment 114
Risk Assessment Factors 115
Risk Assessment Best Practices 119
Risk Management Checklists and Documentation 125
Summary 129
Notes 129

Chapter 6: Fraud Prevention **131**

Introduction 131
Prevention Environment 132
Perception of Detection 135
Classic Approaches 137
Other Prevention Measures 139
Accounting Cycles 141
Summary 143
Notes 143

Chapter 7: Fraud Detection 145

Introduction 145
Fraud Detection Axioms 146
Common Detection Methods 146
Specific Detection Methods 149
Summary 155
Appendix 7A: Beneish's Ratios 156

Chapter 8: Fraud Response 157

Introduction 157
Fraud Policy 157
Fraud Response Team 160
Recovery 164
Summary 165
Notes 166
Appendix 8A: ACFE Sample Fraud Policy 167
Appendix 8B: Sample Fraud Policy Decision Matrix 172

Chapter 9: Computer Crime 175

Introduction 175
History and Evolution of Computer Crimes 176
Computer Crime Theories and Categorizations 179
Characteristics of the Computer Environment 182
Information Security (INFOSEC) 185
Profiling Internet Fraudsters 186
Summary 192
Notes 193

Chapter 10: Fraud and the Accounting Information System 195

Introduction 195
Accounting Concepts 196
Segregation of Duties 202
Accounting Information Systems 203
Key Personnel 204
Computer Hardware 208
Computer Software 210
New Forms of Media 211
Audit Trail Concept 211
Summary 212

Chapter 11: Gathering Evidence 213

Introduction 213
Rules of Evidence 213
Hearsay Exceptions 217
Other Rules of Evidence 218
Summary 223
Notes 223

Chapter 12: Cyber Forensics 225

Introduction 225
Expectation of Privacy 226
Types of Investigations 227
Sources of Digital Data 230
Types of Cyber Data 231
Cyber Forensics Investigation Process 234
Variety of Specialists in Cyber Forensics 236
Summary 237
Notes 237

Chapter 13: Obtaining and Evaluating Nonfinancial Evidence in a Fraud Examination 239

Introduction 239
Interviews 240
Body Language 242
Deception Cues 243
Eye Language 244
Statement Analysis 245
SCAN 246
Summary 247
Notes 247

Chapter 14: General Criteria and Standards for Establishing an Expert Witness's Qualifications 249

Introduction 249
Credentials 250
Personal Qualities of the Expert 255
Sources for Locating Expert Witnesses 259
Distinguishing the Actual Area of Competence 261
Summary 261
Notes 262

Chapter 15: The Legal Role and Qualifications of an Expert Witness **263**

Introduction 263
Role of a Forensic Accountant as a Witness in Court 264
Legal Qualifications for a Forensic Accountant as an Expert Witness 269
Qualification and Admissibility of Accounting Evidence 270
Expert's Role in the Litigation Team 272
Pretestimony Activities 272
Summary 273
Notes 274
Appendix 15A: Transcript of Typical Court Testimony of Expert Witness 275

Chapter 16: Effective Tactics and Procedures for the Expert Witness in Court **277**

Introduction 277
Effective Profile 278
Being a Credible Expert Witness 278
Expert's Role in the Litigation Team 279
Pretestimony Activities 280
Trial and Testimony 281
Survival Techniques 288
Summary 290
Notes 290

Chapter 17: Fraud and the Public Accounting Profession **291**

Introduction 291
History of Fraud and the Auditor: A Summary 291
Fraud and the Auditor's Liability 302
Fraud and the Auditor's Responsibility 303
Fraud and the Auditor's Role 306
Summary 308
Note 308

About the Authors **311**

Index **313**

Preface

When times are good, people steal. When times are bad, people steal more!

THIS QUOTE WAS MADE casually in a conversation by Tommie to an academic colleague, but does represent the raison d'être for the new edition of this book. Since time immortal, there have always been a number of humans who are bent in their ethics, morals, sociological makeup, psychological makeup, or sense of justice, and are ready, willing, and able to commit crimes of all types, including white-collar crimes. But hard economic times seem to cause a few more than normal to crumble under the economic pressure and give in to the temptation to commit a fraud.

The Association of Certified Fraud Examiners (ACFE) did an empirical study in 2009 on the effect of the weak economy on the number of frauds being detected by CFEs, entitled "Occupational Fraud: A Study of the Impact of an Economic Recession." Based on the results of the responses of 507 CFEs, more than half indicated that the number of frauds had increased since the recession began (37.3 percent slight increase, 18.1 percent significant increase). About 49 percent also saw an increase in the dollar amount of the losses due to fraud. Obviously, and empirically evident in the ACFE study, pressure has increased on an increasing number of people due to the recession. And as all antifraud professionals know, pressure is a key to the occurrence of frauds. Therefore, there is a greater need than ever for corporations, companies, and government agencies to be vigilant to protect assets that are more precious than ever.

We are proud to be a part of the fourth edition of this book. The book begins with a general background about fraud auditing and forensic accounting in

Chapter 1. Chapters 2 through 5 provide the basics of fraud such as fraud schemes, how they are perpetrated, what red flags (similar to fingerprints) exist for certain types of schemes, understanding the fraudster, and a fraud risk assessment to identify weak areas. Chapters 6 through 8 follow the "PDC" model for the antifraud profession: prevent, detect, and correct (respond). Chapters 9 though 12 cover the information technology (IT) aspects of fraud including the computer as an instrument of fraud, the target of fraud, and the fact systems are "data warehouses" that contain evidence of fraud. Chapter 13 focuses on the nonfinancial aspects of fraud investigation. Chapters 14 through 16 focus on the legal disposition of a fraud investigation and the major legal concepts, principles, and help for fraud auditors and forensic accountants, especially related to evidence and expert testimony. Chapter 17 is written specifically for public accounting and CPAs.

The material has been slightly reorganized from the third edition to make reading and assimilation of the content easier. New material includes updates in fraud response (a new Chapter 8), computer-related fraud (Chapter 9), cyber forensics (Chapter 12), physiological aspects of the fraudster (a new Chapter 13), and fraud and the CPA (Chapter 17).

We hope this book enables and empowers auditors, CPAs, law enforcement, risk and loss prevention professionals, and all others who have a responsibility related to fraud to better prevent, detect, and respond to fraud.

Tommie W. Singleton
Aaron J. Singleton
August 2010

Acknowledgments

IT IS TRUE THAT anything or anyone visible to the public eye is actually standing on the shoulders of others who made that moment possible. So we would like to acknowledge a few "shoulders."

First, we want to thank Jack Bologna and Robert Lindquist, authors of the first two editions of this book. In 1992, Dr. Tommie Singleton interviewed Jack Bologna as part of his dissertation at the University of Mississippi on the topic of pioneers in electronic data processing (EDP) audit. Mr. Bologna was indeed a pioneer not only in EDP audit, but also in forensic accounting. Jack was involved with the Association of Certified Fraud Examiners (ACFE) in its early days, was editor for what may have been the first forensic accounting journal in the 1980s, and was an academic who taught forensic accounting. His contributions are a monument and testimony to his knowledge and abilities regarding fraud. Robert Lindquist has a strong reputation of being a fraud expert and is sought after as an expert witness in fraud cases. His work and efforts are stellar, and he is a well-respected professional in Canada and the United States.

Second, we would like to thank some individuals who have helped us in our professional growth. Former FBI agent Alton Sizemore became a supporter and friend to Dr. Singleton about 14 years ago. He is a frequent guest lecturer in Tommie's classes, even when he was over 100 miles from the university where Dr. Singleton taught for many of those years. He has taught us much regarding the legal elements of fraud, digital evidence, and the law enforcement perspective of fraud. He also has taught us to have fun when circumstances allow it. Indeed, Alton is a favorite of former students for these reasons.

Kevin Andrews has been a supporter, continually involving us in the local chapter of the ACFE. Like Alton, Kevin is a staple in Dr. Singleton's classes speaking to students about the antifraud profession and how to develop a career as a forensic accountant. He also had a vision of a local, high quality, fraud seminar for Birmingham which he made happen two years ago, and of which we are pleased to be a part.

Another great friend is Ralph Summerford of Forensic/Strategic Solutions in Birmingham, Alabama. He became a supporter of Dr. Singleton instantly at their first meeting, and has been a faithful, instrumental supporter over the last eight years. No one has been more inspiring or financially supportive of Dr. Singleton's academic programs than Mr. Summerford.

Another person who has been instrumental in teaching, supporting, and modeling the antifraud profession to us is retired U.S. Treasury investigator Lynn Shobe. Lynn is a key leader in our area, especially for the local ACFE chapter. But he also is an adjunct professor for the forensic accounting program at UAB where Dr. Singleton is the director of that program and an associate professor.

Third, we want to extend a special thank you to Sheck Cho, Wiley editor. He has been a wonderful supporter of our efforts not only on two editions of this book, but on another book as well. Stacey Rivera, our development editor on this edition, was professional throughout, patient and kind, and a joy to work with.

CHAPTER ONE

Background of Fraud Auditing and Forensic Accounting

There's a sucker born every minute.

—*P. T. Barnum*

Trust everyone, but cut the deck.

—*P. T. Barnum*

INTRODUCTION

In the first decade of the twenty-first century, the news has been filled with reports on frauds and indicators that it is increasing in its scope and costs to the U.S. economy. Almost everyone has read about corporate financial statement frauds such as Enron and WorldCom, or frauds against the government such as false claims following Katrina, or huge Ponzi schemes such as the Madoff scam that set a new record for losses associated with a fraud.

Many people have been directly affected by identity theft. The economic downturn that began in 2008 has made it hard to rebound from such losses. To make matters worse, reports on activities related to fraud bear bad news.

A 2007 report from the Federal Bureau of Investigation (FBI) estimates that fraud in non-health insurance costs more than $40 billion per year, or put another way, costs the average U.S. family between $400 and $700 per year in increased premiums![1] In the same report, the FBI estimates that costs associated with fraudulent claims following the Katrina hurricane disaster accounted for as much as $6 billion. The FBI also reports that suspicious activity reports (SAR) filed by banks increased 36 percent for 2008 over 2007. Of the SARs filed in 2007, 7 percent indicated a specific dollar loss, which totaled more than $813 million.[2] The FBI was investigating over $1 billion in mortgage frauds in 2008.[3] All these facts existed *before* the economic meltdown and scrutiny brought to the subprime mortgage industry.

The Internet Crime Complaint Center (IC3) is a federal watchdog agency formed as a partnership of the National White Collar Crime Center (NW3C) and the FBI that serves as a center to receive, process, and refer criminal complaints regarding the rapidly expanding area of cybercrime. Its *2008 Annual Report* shows a 33 percent increase in complaint submissions over 2007, which is the trend over this decade. The total losses from 2008 complaints were $265 million with a median loss of $931,000 per complaint.[4]

The National Insurance Crime Bureau (NICB) says that 10 percent of all property or casualty insurance claims, 15 percent of auto theft claims, and 20 percent of workers' compensation claims involve some form of fraud. According to the NICB, auto insurance theft costs $20 to 30 billion a year. The NICB reports that questionable claims reports in the first half of 2009 has increased 13 percent over first half of 2008 and the numbers in nearly all referral categories are rising as well.

The Association of Certified Fraud Examiners (ACFE) provides periodic surveys of fraud and reports the results to the public in its *Report to the Nation* (RTTN). Results were published in 1996, 2002, 2004, 2006, and 2008. The 1996 RTTN reported an estimate of over $400 billion in losses due to fraud, which increased over the years to an estimated $994 billion in 2008. Fraud clearly continues to cost organizations and society huge sums of money, both recently and throughout the history of commercial business.

BRIEF HISTORY OF FRAUD AND THE ANTIFRAUD PROFESSION[5]

According to some, forensic accounting is one of the oldest professions and dates back to the Egyptians. The "eyes and ears" of the king was a person who basically served as a forensic accountant for Pharaoh, watchful over inventories of grain, gold, and other assets. The person had to be trustworthy, responsible, and able to handle a position of influence.

In the United States, fraud began at least as early as the Pilgrims and early settlers. Since early America was largely agricultural, many frauds centered around land schemes. Perhaps the most infamous colonial era land scheme was the purchase of Manhattan Island (what is now Brooklyn), bought from the Canarsie Indians. The land was bought for trinkets worth about $24. In this case, the Native Americans tricked the white man, as the Canarsie Indians sold land not even connected to Manhattan Island, and Manhattan Island was inhabited by Manhattan Indians, to whom the Dutch had to pay a second time for the land. Land swindles grew as America expanded west.

The advent of business organizations created new opportunities for fraud. The earliest corporations were formed in seventeenth-century Europe. Nations chartered new corporations and gave them public missions in exchange for a legal right to exist, separation of ownership from management, and limited liability that protected shareholders from losses of the business entity. One such corporation, the Massachusetts Bay Company, was chartered by Charles I in 1628 and had a mission of colonizing the New World.

The first major corporate fraud is probably the fraud known as the South Sea Bubble. The South Sea Company was formed in 1711 with exclusive trading rights to Spanish South America. The company made its first trading voyage in 1717 and made little actual profit to offset the £10 million of government bonds it had assumed. South Sea then had to borrow £2 million more. Tension between England and Spain led to the capture of South Sea ships by Spain in 1718. In 1719, the company proposed a scheme by which it would take on the entire remaining national debt in Britain, over £30 million, using its own stock at 5 percent in exchange for government bonds lasting until 1727. Although the Bank of England offered also to assume the debt, Parliament approved the assumption of the debt by the South Sea Company. Its stock rose from £128 in January 1720 to £550 by the end of May that year, in a speculation frenzy.

The company drove the price of the stock up through artificial means; largely taking the form of new subscriptions combined with the circulation of pro-trade-with-Spain stories designed to give the impression that the stock could only go higher. Not only did capital stay in England, but many Dutch investors bought South Sea stock, thus increasing the inflationary pressure.[6]

Other joint-stock companies then joined the market, usually making fraudulent claims about foreign ventures, and were nicknamed "bubbles." In June 1720, the Bubble Act was passed, which required all joint-stock companies to have a royal charter. Partly because it had a royal charter, the South Sea Company shares rocketed to £890 in early June 1720. The price finally reached £1,000 in early August, and a sell-off that began in June began to accelerate. The sell-off was begun largely by directors themselves cashing in on huge stock profits. As the stock price began to decline, the company directors attempted to talk up and prop up the stock (e.g., having agents buy stock) but to no avail—the stockholders had lost confidence and a run started in September. By the end of the month, the stock price dropped to a low of £150.

With investors outraged, and as many of them were aristocrats, Parliament was recalled in December and an investigation began. As part of that investigation, an external auditor, Charles Snell, was hired to examine the books of the South Sea Company. This hiring was the first time in the history of accounting that an outside auditor was brought in to audit books, and marks the beginning of Chartered Accountants in England and thus the beginning of Certified Public Accountants (CPAs) and financial audits as we know them today. Thus CPAs owe their profession, at least to a large extent, *to a fraud.*

In 1721, Snell submitted his report. He uncovered widespread corruption and fraud among the directors in particular and among company officials and their friends at Westminster. Unfortunately, some of the key players had already fled the country with the incriminating records in their possession. Those who remained were examined and some estates were confiscated.

At about the same time, France was experiencing an almost identical fraud from a corporation originally known as the Mississippi Company that had exclusive trading rights to North America in the French-owned Mississippi River area. Using similar tactics of exaggerating the potential profits, the company owner, famous economist John Law, was able to cause a frenzied upward spiral of its stock prices, only to see it collapse after the Regent of Orleans dismissed him in 1720. The company sought bankruptcy protection in 1721. Like South Sea, it was a fraud perpetrated by the exaggerations of executive management.

In 1817, the *Meyer v. Sefton* case involved a bankrupt estate. Since the nature of the evidence was such it could not be examined in court, the judge allowed the expert witness who had examined the bankrupt's accounts to testify to his examination. Forensic accounting professor and author Dr. Larry Crumbley considers this accountant to be the first forensic accountant in history and the beginning of forensic accounting as a profession.

In 1920, Charles Ponzi planned to arbitrage postal coupons, buying them from Spain and selling them to the U.S. Postal Service, using foreign exchange rates as leverage to make a profit. In order to raise capital for the scheme, he promised outlandish returns to investors—50 percent in 90 days. Ponzi paid the first returns with the cash proceeds from those coming in later, then he personally took the proceeds from later entrants to the scheme. He was imprisoned for defrauding 40,000 people of $15 million. To this day, that type of scheme is referred to as a Ponzi scheme.

In the 1920s, Samuel Insull was involved in a fraud scheme similar to the railroad and South Sea Bubble schemes, but it occurred in the electric utility business. Insull sold millions of dollars of common stock in electric utility companies to unwary investors. The stock was greatly overpriced in terms of the utilities' real assets. When the stock market collapsed in 1929, it was apparent that Insull's holding company was insolvent and had been for some time.

Some researchers, such as Dr. Dale Flesher and Dr. Tonya Flesher, have presented sound arguments that the Securities Act of 1933 and the Securities Exchange Act of 1934 are a direct result of the Ivar Kreuger ("Match king") fraud rather than the stock market crash of 1929. Kreuger & Toll, a multibillion-dollar conglomerate, was a huge fraud built on shell companies and *unaudited financial statements*. Kreuger & Toll securities were among the most widely held in the United States. When the company went under in 1932, after Kreuger had committed suicide, investors lost millions in the largest bankruptcy of its time. Therefore, the argument goes, the existence of these legislative acts requiring financial audits of all companies with listed securities and the Securities and Exchange Commission (SEC) is the result of a major financial fraud, and can be seen by comparing the tenets of the acts against the financial fraud perpetrated by Kreuger versus the stock market crash itself. The acts of 1933 and 1934 essentially created the demand for financial auditors and the CPA profession that exists to this day.

A major savings and loan scandal hit hard in the early 1980s, preceding the energy and telecommunication companies' frauds in the 1990s. The latter led the seeming explosion of fraud around the last half of the 1990s and the early 2000s. During this period, high-dollar frauds reached all types of industries. For example, Waste Management in trash services, Phar-mor in pharmacy, Sunbeam in manufacturing, Enron in energy, WorldCom in telecommunications, Adelphia in media, Fannie Mae in government, and HealthSouth in health services all occurred during this time. Several of these frauds were among the *largest ever*, and they occurred during a short period of time.

Although the cost of the WorldCom fraud was far greater, the most notable fraud, as far as impact on the business community, is probably Enron. In 2001, Enron filed bankruptcy after disclosing major discrepancies in revenues and liabilities in its financial reports. The audit firm Arthur Andersen came to an end as a result of the ramifications of the Enron scandal by 2002. In 2002, the U.S. Congress passed the Sarbanes-Oxley Act (SOX) due to that fraud and others, such as WorldCom. Perhaps nothing has brought more attention to fraud audits and forensic accounting than the Enron scandal and SOX.

More recently, the housing and real estate boom of the 2000s has led to increased fraud particularly in the area of mortgage fraud. While the impact of these frauds is not yet entirely clear, mortgage fraud losses for 2007 alone have been estimated to be at least $800 million. SARs from financial institutions indicated an increase in mortgage fraud reporting. SARs increased 31 percent to 46,717 during fiscal year (FY) 2007. The total dollar loss attributed to mortgage fraud is unknown. However, 7 percent of SARs filed during FY 2007 indicated a specific dollar loss, which totaled more than $813 million.[7] Various pieces of legislation have been passed in response, continuing the cycle of evolving frauds and attempts to control them.

Are all of these events merely historical flukes? Did media attention create them? Perhaps. Media attention may have created the original public awareness, but the frauds and corruption were there all the time, and there exists no real way of measuring or comparing them. Part of the problem during the period of time when such large frauds occurred was the mind-set of the regulators and auditors, which has since turned around completely. Claims by management and others are less likely to be accepted at face value, and the financial well-being of the general public is more of a concern to antifraud and audit professions. Suspicion fell on industries, professions, and various areas of government. The undivided attention of auditors, regulators, management, and employees then led to wholesale charges of fraud, theft, and corruption.

The fraud environment can be and often is viewed as a pendulum, swinging from one extreme to the other with little time in between at the proper balancing point. After 2002, the pendulum was close to an extreme end, one that entailed ultraconservatism on the part of companies, and auditors as well, and the stiffest requirements and enforcement by regulators and legislators. After swinging toward a more balanced position, the recent economic crisis has moved the pendulum back toward the extreme of 2002. This cycle (pendulum swing) is a natural result of human nature, business cycles, and the nature of legislation and regulation. The cycle can certainly be influenced and controlled to some extent, but it will probably never cease.

Fraud auditing literature discloses a common theme: Fraud is endemic and pervasive in certain industries, locales, companies, and occupations at particular points in history. For example, railroad promoters in the 1870s raised more capital from less informed investors than ever before and the railroad industry had numerous frauds exposed. During the 1950s, more doctors were involved in more income tax frauds than ever before or since. Food franchisers, in the late 1960s, are another example of the fraud phenomenon. Some fast-food franchisers sold unwary small investors on untested restaurant concepts at overvalued prices. These half-baked concepts led to the bankruptcy of many of the franchisees. During the Watergate era of the early 1970s, politicians were involved in corruption and fraud against taxpayers, and corporations were involved in political and commercial bribery, leading to the Foreign Corrupt Practices Acts of 1977.

THE FRAUD CYCLE

The fraud cycle essentially begins with the plans of the fraudster leading up to the committing of the fraud act. Once committed, the fraudster converts the asset to cash, if necessary, and conceals the fraud.

The existence of a fraud usually comes to light through (1) an allegation, complaint, or a rumor of fraud brought by a third party (a disgruntled supplier or a fellow employee); (2) an investigator's intuition or general suspicion that something is awry; (3) an exception from an expectation of a person senior to the suspect (an unacceptable condition, profits, sales, costs, assets, or liabilities are too low or too high); (4) the accidental discovery that something is missing—cash, property, reports, files, documents, or data; (5) results from an audit; or (6) results of controls, especially antifraud controls. Based on the statistics from the ACFE's RTTNs, an average of about 60 percent of all frauds reported were discovered either by a tip or accident, indicating the need for more effective proactive detection methods such as internal controls and internal audits.

A fraud investigation is of necessity based on legal factors, because any fraud may end up in a court of law. The immediate facts to determine are whether a fraud has occurred and whether there is: (1) a criminal law, (2) an apparent breach of that law, (3) a perpetrator, and (4) a victim. The six basic steps in the fraud investigation are:

1. Acquire all available details and documents relating to the allegation.
2. Assess the allegation against the available documentation.
3. Assess the corporate environment relative to the person in question.
4. Ask whether a theory of fraud can be developed at this stage. Is there motive and opportunity?
5. Determine whether the available evidence makes sense. Does it meet the test of business reality?
6. Communicate with appropriate parties on the details and status of the fraud.

After performing these steps, two possibilities exist. Either one has identified the fraudster and knows who she is, or one has not. If not, more investigation is necessary. But if one does identify the fraudster, the process becomes critical to what is no longer an investigation, rather a pursuit of legal action.

Evidence gathered may consist of the testimony of witnesses, documents, items (means and instruments, or fruits of the crime), and possibly the confession of the perpetrator. Experienced fraud investigators know what evidence is needed to prove the crime and how to attain that evidence. Typically, interviewing the alleged, or known, fraudster is done only after competent and sufficient data have been gathered, assessed, and reasoned. If prosecution of a civil or criminal charge is sought, evidence must be presented in court—which is where the expert witness skill of a forensic accountant or fraud auditor is valuable. The court, trier of fact, then resolves the charge of fraud ending the fraud cycle. A successful prosecution needs someone who can explain, in layperson's terms, the records, data, documents, financial information, and files supporting the prosecutor's position.

This book provides readers with insight into each of these phases of the fraud life cycle. It also delves into the mind and behavior patterns of fraud perpetrators, their schemes, and the evidence they leave behind—from which their crimes can be reconstructed. Every fraud has its own unique wrinkles. All thieves do not think alike. They tend to be opportunists. Given a set of circumstances that allow them to steal, they take the easiest way, usually weighing risks and rewards carefully. Culprits usually leave trails and sometimes make mistakes. Auditors must learn to look for these signs, or red flags, as they will be referred to in this book. While each fraud is different in some ways, they all have some similarities.

REVIEW OF TECHNICAL LITERATURE

The technical literature begins with criminal and regulatory statutes involving business. For example, such literature includes the Sherman Antitrust Act (1890), the Internal Revenue Act (1913), the Securities Act of 1933 and Securities Exchange Act of 1934, Foreign Corrupt Practices Act (1977), Financial Fraud Detection and Disclosure Act (1986), Health Insurance Portability and Accountability Act of 1996 (HIPAA), Gramm-Leach-Bliley Act of 1999 (GLBA), and of course the Sarbanes-Oxley Act (SOX) (2002). Other applicable laws are related to mail fraud, fraud by wire, and the Federal Trade Commission (FTC). Federal laws that have contributed to the growth of fraud auditing include the Labor-Management Reporting and Disclosure Act, the Welfare-Pension Fund Act, and Employee Retirement Income Security Act (ERISA).

The savings and loans scandals of the early 1980s led to the National Commission on Fraudulent Financial Reporting (commonly known as the Treadway Commission, named after the chair of the Commission), which carried on its work as the Committee of Sponsoring Organizations (COSO), which is still functioning today. According to Treadway Commission findings, the most effective way to prevent financial scandals, such as the savings and loan ones, is for companies to have a strong set of internal controls. The model developed by the group has come to be known as the COSO Model of Internal Controls. It focuses on five key areas of internal controls:

1. Risk assessment
2. Control environment
3. Information and communication
4. Monitoring
5. Control activities

In 1992, the American Institute of Certified Public Accountants (AICPA) adopted the COSO Model as Statement on Auditing Standards (SAS) No. 78,

Consideration of Internal Control in a Financial Statement Audit. The COSO Report was becoming a widely accepted framework for evaluating internal controls, and its acceptance and use was expected to grow. As a result, SAS No. 55 was amended to incorporate the COSO Report framework to provide useful guidance to financial auditors.[8]

In the late 1990s and early 2000s, a strong global economy met an increase in fraud in public companies and a lack of effective oversight. The result was a serious shock to the economy and to society as a whole. Public concern over fraud, in general, erupted to new and seemingly endless heights. Although concern over fraud has decreased some (a natural pendulum effect), the mentality toward fraud has clearly changed and for the better. Another positive result is that these large scandalous frauds have created a greater awareness of the need to further develop the discipline of fraud auditing. However, billions of dollars were lost, creating a serious "black eye" for the financial audit profession, and a wave of legislation resulted.

The latest round of legislation passed in the fight against fraud includes SOX, GLBA, and HIPAA. In the current environment, there is an extremely heightened expectation for businesses, auditors, investigators, and regulators to stop fraud. In order to control fraud, the response spurred by legislation must equal or exceed the energy exerted by fraudsters, which appears to have pervasively infiltrated society.

SOX in particular has greatly affected the awareness of and attention to fraud. The AICPA's SAS No. 99, *Consideration of Fraud in a Financial Statement Audit*, codified and complemented many of the tenets of SOX, or best practices in antifraud. The Public Company Accounting Oversight Board (PCAOB), created by SOX and responsible for overseeing standards and enforcement, is setting its own standards affecting internal controls and fraud audits. The bottom line is, management of public companies has to accept responsibility for fraud per SOX and financial auditors have to be active in detecting fraud to comply with SAS No. 99.

SAS No. 99 has two basic requirements for financial statement audits. One is for auditors to exercise *professional skepticism*; that is, auditors are to be constantly mindful of the potential for fraud. The other is that fraud assessment must be included in audit steps from planning to reporting findings. SAS No. 99 emphasizes that evaluating audit evidence and adjusting the audit is a continual process. The audit team must identify, assess, and respond to fraud risks. Subsequently, the audit team must evaluate the findings of the audit tests and report to an appropriate level of management (usually the audit committee). Documentation must exist for all of these audit steps.

Section 404 of SOX requires management to evaluate the effectiveness of internal controls over financial reporting and to report on their evaluation in the annual report. This section also forces management to state their responsibility for internal controls. The internal control evaluation report and certain financial reports have to be signed by the chief executive officer (CEO) and chief financial officer (CFO), providing a legally enforceable claim. Management's internal controls must be evaluated by the financial (external) auditors who opine on that evaluation.

SOX also brought about these changes:

- More independent boards of directors (especially the audit committee)
- Increased involvement of the audit committee (especially oversight of management and antifraud programs)
- More financial expertise on the audit committee
- More independent reporting lines (external and internal auditors often report directly to the audit committee)

PCAOB Audit Standards No. 5 (AS 5) and No. 3 (AS 3) both address fraud. PCAOB guidance is applicable to issuers, or public companies, and AICPA guidance (SAS) is applicable to nonissuers, or private companies and issuers. AS 5 adopts many SAS 99 requirements. As part of that adoption, AS 5 (via SAS 99) notes the audit of internal control and the financial statement audit are connected, should be risk-based, and requires the nature, timing, and extent of financial statement audit procedures to be adjusted according to the results of the internal control audit. Results here certainly include any findings regarding fraud. AS 5 references the COSO Internal Control model with regard to managing fraud risk.

SOX, SAS No. 99, and AS 5 contain more details than can be summarized here, but these regulations and technical standards have stimulated similar legislation and standards abroad. Yet the need for fraud-auditing talents is not related solely to compliance with new governmental regulations.

FORENSIC ACCOUNTANT AND AUDITS

It is important to define the term *forensic accountant* to ensure readers understand concepts and narratives throughout the book. One of the key points to understand about forensic accountants is the difference and roles of financial audits versus fraud audits. This section will discuss some of the issues and differences.

Forensic Accounting Defined

In this book, the term *forensic accounting* refers to the comprehensive view of fraud investigation. It includes preventing frauds and analyzing antifraud controls. Forensic accounting would include the audit of accounting records in search for evidence of fraud; a fraud audit. A fraud investigation to prove or disprove a fraud would be part of forensic accounting. It also includes the gathering of nonfinancial information, such as interviews of all related parties to a fraud, when applicable. Forensic accounting includes writing a report to management or court. Serving as an expert witness and litgation support are part of forensic accounting.

Although relatively new to the accounting profession, the role of a forensic expert in other professions has been in place for some time. *Webster's Dictionary* defines the word *forensic* as "belonging to, used in, or suitable to courts of judicature or to public discussions and debate."[1] Accordingly, the term *forensic* in the accounting profession deals with the relation and application of financial facts to legal problems. Forensic accounting evidence, therefore, is oriented to a court of law.

Financial Auditors, Fraud Auditors, and Forensic Accountants

In the lexicon of accounting, terms such as *fraud auditing, forensic accounting, fraud examination, fraud investigation, investigative accounting, litigation support,* and *valuation analysis* are not clearly defined. Some distinctions apply between fraud auditing and forensic accounting. Fraud auditing involves a specialized approach and methodology to discern fraud; that is, the auditor is looking for evidence of fraud. The purpose is to prove or disprove a fraud exists. Historically, forensic accountants, however, have been called in after evidence or suspicion of fraud has surfaced through an allegation, complaint, or discovery.

Forensic accountants are experienced, trained, and knowledgeable in all the different processes of fraud investigation including: how to interview people (especially the suspect) effectively, how to write effective reports for clients and courts, how to provide expert testimony in court, and rules of evidence. The ACFE refers to this definition of forensic accounting as *fraud examination.* In recent years, the broadest of these terms in the antifraud profession is *forensic accounting,* which typically refers to the incorporation of all the terms involved with investigation, including fraud auditing; that is, fraud auditing is a subset of forensic accounting.

Fraud investigation usually encompasses about the same thing as a fraud audit except investigation typically involves a lot more nonfinancial evidence, such as testimony from interviews, than a fraud audit. So fraud investigation includes fraud audit but goes beyond it in gathering nonfinancial forensic evidence.

Litigation support refers to a forensic accountant assisting attorneys in prosecuting or defending a case in the legal system. That support can take on a variety of skills but ultimately is intended to conclude with the forensic accountant offering an opinion in a court of law as an expert witness on whether a fraud occurred.

Valuation is a cottage industry of its own that overlaps with fraud. Especially in cases of litigation or insurance investigations, a forensic accountant or equivalent (Accredited in Business Valuation [ABV], Certified Valuation Analyst [CVA]) has to establish a value on the loss associated with a fraudulent event, whether it is a spouse trying to hide assets in a divorce case, or a customer claiming exorbitant losses in an insurance claim, or a victim entity suffering from a bad merger/acquisition that ended in a bankruptcy of the subsidiary.

Financial auditing is a wholly different term that needs to be distinguished from forensic accounting and fraud auditing. Financial auditing typically refers to the process of evaluating compliance of financial information with regulatory standards, usually for public companies, by an external, independent entity. The well-publicized SOX incorporates concepts and procedures to deter and to catch fraud in audits of internal controls over financial reporting. However, the focus of financial audits and financial reporting ultimately is concerned with providing *reasonable* assurance that a *material* misstatement to financial statements has not occurred, regardless of the reason.

Financial Auditors

The term *financial auditor* broadly applies to any auditor of financial information or the financial reporting process. The largest classification of financial auditors is those who work for public accounting firms and perform audits of financial statements for public companies. This classification is the most commonly used in this book when referring to financial auditors.

Financial auditors have expertise in their knowledge of accounting and financial reporting (such as in generally accepted accounting principles [GAAP], PCAOB standards, or International Financial Reporting Standards [IFRS]), auditing (generally accepted audit standards [GAAS]), and how those standards apply to business transactions. As expressed in the GAAS literature, the most important financial auditing attributes are independence, objectivity, and professional skepticism.

Financial auditors traditionally have been seen as, and to an extent have been, numbers oriented, and their processes have been driven by the audit trail. The financial audit procedures are designed to detect material misstatements, and thus financial auditors focus on misstatements that singularly or in the aggregate are large enough to be material. Fraud auditors and forensic accountants are not constrained by materiality. The discipline of financial auditing has been thought to be almost a checklist of items to complete. In reality, judgment is crucial in financial auditing and has progressively increased in the direction of more dependence on auditor judgment. SOX requirements involve auditor judgment to a large degree; auditors are to understand processes significant to financial reporting and to evaluate management's controls over those processes. Additionally, auditors are to consider environmental, including soft, intangible, factors in that evaluation.

Fraud Auditors

Fraud auditors are generally accountants or auditors who, by virtue of their attitudes, attributes, skills, knowledge, and experience, are experts at detecting and documenting frauds in books of records of accounting and financial transactions and events. Their particular attitudes include these beliefs:

- Fraud is possible even in accounting systems that have tight controls.
- The visible part of a transaction fraud may involve a small amount of money, but the invisible portion can be substantial.
- Red flags of fraud are discernible if one looks long enough and deep enough.
- Fraud perpetrators can come from any level of management or society.

The skills fraud auditors require include all of those that are required of financial auditors, plus the knowledge of how to gather evidence of and document fraud losses for criminal, civil, contractual, and insurance purposes; how to interview third-party witnesses; and how to testify as an expert witness.

Fraud auditors must know what a fraud is from a legal and audit perspective, an environmental perspective, a perpetrator's perspective, and a cultural perspective. They also need both general and specific kinds of experience. They should have a fair amount of experience in general auditing and fraud auditing, but should have industry-specific experience as well (e.g., banking; insurance; construction; and manufacturing, distribution, and retailing).

Fraud auditing is creating an environment that encourages the detection and prevention of frauds in commercial transactions. In the broadest sense, it is an awareness of many components of fraud, such as the human element, organizational behavior, knowledge of fraud, evidence and standards of proof, an awareness of the potentiality for fraud, and an appreciation of the red flags. Some of the functions of a fraud auditor follow.

In short, fraud auditing is the process of detecting, preventing, and correcting fraudulent activities. While completely eliminating fraud is the goal, it is simply not feasible. The concept of reasonableness is applicable here, and this concept is often associated with the fraud-related fields of financial accounting and auditing. Fraud auditors should be able to thwart a reasonably preventable fraud.

Accounting-type frauds are usually accompanied by the modification, alteration, destruction, or counterfeiting of accounting evidence. But accounting records can be either intentionally or accidentally modified, altered, or destroyed, by human error or omission. The first objective for the fraud auditor, then, is to determine whether a discrepancy in accounting records is attributable to human error. If it is, there may be no actual fraud. If the discrepancy (missing records, destroyed records, modified records, counterfeit records, errors, omissions) cannot be attributed to accidental or human error, further investigation should follow at an appropriate level.

Forensic Accountants

Forensic accountants may appear on the crime scene a little later than fraud auditors, but their major contribution is in translating complex financial transactions and numerical data into terms that ordinary laypersons can understand. That is necessary because if the fraud comes to trial, the jury will be made up of ordinary laypersons. Areas of expertise of forensic accountants are not only in accounting and auditing but in criminal investigation, interviewing, report writing, and testifying as expert witnesses. They must be excellent communicators and professional in demeanor.

The involvement of the forensic accountant is almost always reactive; this distinguishes forensic accountants from fraud auditors, who tend to be actively involved in prevention and detection in a corporate or regulatory environment. Forensic accountants are trained to react to complaints arising in criminal matters, statements of claim arising in civil litigation, and rumors and inquiries arising in corporate investigations. The investigative findings of the forensic accountant will impact an individual and/or a company in terms of their freedom or a financial award or loss. The ACFE refers to this person as a fraud examiner.

The forensic accountant draws on various resources to obtain relevant financial evidence and to interpret and present this evidence in a manner that will assist both parties. Ideally, forensic accounting should allow two parties to more quickly and efficiently resolve the complaint, statement of claim, rumor, or inquiry, or at least reduce the financial element as an area of on-going debate. Objectivity and independence of the forensic auditor are paramount for these purposes.

Differences among the Three

Forensic accountants, fraud auditors, and investigative auditors measure financial transactions in relation to various other authorities, such as the Criminal Code, an insurance contract, institutional policies, or other guidelines for conduct or reporting. The accountant/auditor prepares the report rather than the client or subject and does not include an opinion on the findings. In the investigation, one does not reject evidence as being immaterial; indeed, the smallest item can be the largest clue to the truth.

Fraud auditors, forensic accountants, and/or fraud investigators (i.e., all professionals involved with forensic accounting) put things together rather than taking them apart, as is the case in classic financial auditing or the modern method of systems analysis. The process of forensic accounting is also sometimes more intuitive than deductive, although both intuition and deduction play important parts. Financial auditing is more procedural in many regards and is not intended to work as effectively in detecting frauds as the tenets of fraud auditing and forensic accounting.

When a questionnaire was circulated among the staff members of Peat Marwick Lindquist Holmes, a Toronto-based firm of chartered accountants responsible for the forensic and investigative accounting practice, responses were insightful and should be of interest to the reader.

Q1: *How would you distinguish forensic accounting, fraud auditing, and investigative auditing from financial auditing?*

A. The distinction is related to one's goals. Financial auditing attempts to enable the auditor to render an opinion as to whether a set of transactions is presented fairly in accordance with GAAP. The financial statements upon which the opinion is rendered are always the representations of management. The auditor is primarily concerned with qualitative values (hence the concept of materiality comes into play) and generally is not concerned about whether the financial statements communicate the policies, intentions, or goals of management.

B. *Forensic accounting* is a general term used to describe any financial investigation that can result in a legal consequence. Fraud auditing is a specialized discipline within forensic accounting, which investigates a particular criminal activity, namely fraud. Investigative auditing involves reviewing financial documentation for a specific purpose, which could relate to litigation support and insurance claims as well as criminal matters.

C. The objective of financial auditing is to provide the auditor with a degree of assurance in giving an opinion with respect to a company's financial statements. The materiality level of an investigative auditing engagement is much lower and more focused than that of the normal financial auditing engagement.

Q2: *How would you define what you do as a forensic accountant?*

A. I think of myself as one who seeks out the truth.

B. I would define my forensic accounting responsibilities as follows: (1) Investigation and analysis of financial documentation; (2) communication of the findings from my investigation in the form of a report, accounting schedule, and document briefs; and (3) coordination of and assistance in further investigation, including the possibility of appearing in court as an expert witness.

C. My role is that of an objective observer or expert. The final report that is issued as a result of my work will be used to negotiate some sort of settlement, be it financial or be it imprisonment. My role as a forensic accountant extends beyond the particular financial circumstances and seems to be one of an objective individual who provides the buffer between, in civil instances, the client and counsel, and, in criminal instances, the investigator and the prosecutor. Therefore, I am considered an integral member of the team of professionals assigned to any given case. Related to the specific work that I do, it has been described to me, and I agree, that the makeup of a given forensic accountant is one-third business person, one-third investigator, and one-third accountant.

Q3: *What qualities of mind and/or body should a forensic accountant possess?*

A. Creativity: the ability to step out of what would otherwise be a normal business situation and consider alternative interpretations that might not necessarily make business sense; curiosity: the desire to find out what has taken place in a given set of circumstances; perseverance: the ability to push forward even when the circumstances don't appear to substantiate the particular instance being investigated or when the documentation is very onerous and presents a needle-in-a-haystack scenario; common sense: the ability to maintain a "real-world" perspective; business sense: the ability to understand how businesses actually operate, not how business transactions are recorded; confidence: the ability to believe both in yourself and in your findings so that you can persevere when faced with cross-examination.

B. As with any other pursuit, a healthy mind in a healthy body is a solid foundation. Beyond that, one should have generous proportions of common sense, inquisitiveness, skepticism, and an ability to avoid the natural tendency to prejudice—that is, to be fair and independent. In addition, because forensic work ultimately can lead to court appearances, good posture, grooming, vocal projection, and stamina can all be valuable attributes.

C. The foremost quality a forensic accountant requires is independence, because a forensic accountant is often forced to balance conflicting opinions about the same piece of documentation. The second major quality is an intense sense of curiosity coupled with a sense of order—a desire to put the puzzle back together.

D. Common sense/street smarts; sensitivity/understanding of human behavior; analytical; logical/clear; ability to simplify complexities and delete jargon; not be prone to lose the forest for the trees; ability to identify and assess alternative explanations and interpretations; ability to quickly assess cost-benefit of pursuing alternative avenues of investigation and reporting contents/formats.

E. The forensic accountant needs to be calm, cool, and collected; have good business judgment; and have a mind that can deal logically with esoteric issues and precise matters. A forensic accountant involved in litigation must be physically fit to withstand the long days and long nights of investigation and preparation for trial and the trial itself. Forensic accountants need to have a pleasant appearance and demeanor so that they will not be offensive when in the witness box.

Q4: *What skills are most important to the successful practice of forensic accounting?*

A. Solid technical accounting and financial skills—the basis of your "expertise"; ability to quickly prioritize issues and map out a "game plan"—good judgment; ability to communicate well—both verbally and in writing—is necessary to obtaining information, directing your staff, presenting your findings, and achieving your desired results. Even the best-planned and executed assignment can fail if you are unable to clearly and concisely present your findings.

B. A forensic accountant needs to be precise, pay attention to detail, and be a broad thinker; that is, not suffer from tunnel vision.

C. When looking at a given forensic accounting engagement, there are two major areas that come to mind in the completion of a given case. First, there is the investigative aspect, and second, the communication aspect. I feel that investigative skills would include areas such as the ability to assimilate large volumes of information, general organization and administrative skills, use the microcomputer or understand the abilities of the microcomputer, and interpersonal skills. Communication skills would include the ability to write a comprehensive report understandably.

D. Communications skills: oral/written; interpersonal skills; listening skills; ability to synthesize/integrate; ability to identify/prioritize objectives/issues.

Financial Audit versus Fraud Audit

Many in the public, and some in the U.S. Congress, have questioned why financial auditors do not detect more fraud. The general public believes that a financial auditor would detect a fraud if one were being perpetrated during the financial auditor's audit. The truth, however, is that the procedures for financial audits are designed to detect material misstatements, not immaterial frauds. While it is true that many of the financial statements and frauds could have, perhaps should have, been detected by financial auditors, the vast majority of frauds could not be detected with the GAAS of financial audits. Reasons include the dependence of financial auditors on a sample and the auditors' reliance on examining the audit trail versus examining the events and activities behind the documents. The latter is simply resource prohibitive in terms of costs and time.

There are some basic differences today between the procedures of fraud auditors and those of financial auditors. Fraud auditors look behind and beyond the transactions and audit trail to focus on the substance of the transactions instead. The fraud auditor doesn't question how the accounting system and internal controls stack up against applicable standards but rather:

- Where are the weakest links in this system's chain of controls?
- What deviations from conventional good accounting practices are possible in this system?
- How are off-line transactions handled, and who can authorize such transactions?
- What would be the simplest way to compromise this system?
- What control features in this system can be bypassed by higher authorities?
- What is the nature of the work environment?

Another difference is the current status of technical guidance combined with research on frauds. Frauds can be divided into three main categories: (1) financial frauds, (2) asset misappropriations, and (3) corruption (ACFE fraud tree, discussed in Chapters 2 and 3). Financial frauds are typically perpetrated by executive management and average millions of dollars in losses. According to a recent KPMG *Fraud Survey*, that average is about $258 million. Generally speaking, therefore, financial frauds are likely to be material, and thus financial audit procedures have the potential to detect them—because they would be a material misstatement, due to a material fraud. However, those who might be responsible for fraud audits internal to the firm could be constrained or thwarted in detecting the fraud because executives are in a position to hide the fraud or misdirect fraud auditors' efforts. Cynthia Cooper argues that at WorldCom she was thwarted from doing her job as internal auditor, but she eventually did uncover the financial fraud being perpetrated there.

FORENSIC ACCOUNTANTS

The forensic accountant has skills, abilities, and knowledge related to the fraud cycle, including legal resolution. Because of the scope of fraud, the fact that fraud occurs in a lot of different arenas, there are a lot of different groups who could benefit from the services of a forensic accountant.

Who Needs Forensic Accountants?

The increased business complexities in a litigious environment have enhanced the need for the forensic accounting discipline. It is possible to summarize the range of application into the following general areas:

- *Corporate investigations.* Companies react to concerns that arise through a number of sources that might suggest possible wrongdoing initiated from within and without the corporate environment. From the anonymous phone call or e-mail from disgruntled employees and third parties, these problems must be addressed quickly and effectively to permit the company to continue to pursue its objectives. More specifically, the forensic accountant assists in addressing allegations ranging from kickbacks and wrongful dismissals to internal situations involving allegations of management or employee wrongdoing. At times, a forensic accountant can meet with those persons affected by the allegations, rumors, or inquiries; they may view the accountant as an independent and objective party, and thus be more willing to engage in discussion.
- *Litigation support.* Litigation support includes assisting counsel in investigating and assessing the integrity and amount relating to such areas as loss of profits, construction claims, product liability, shareholder disputes, bankruptcies, and breach of contract. Obviously, litigation support is initiated by an attorney responding to some kind of legal action, whether criminal or civil.
- *Criminal matters.* Efforts to prevent white-collar crime have consistently used accountants and auditors in attempts to sort out, assess, and report on financial transactions related to allegations against individuals and companies in a variety of situations such as arson, scams, fraud (e.g., kickbacks or embezzlement), vendor frauds, customer frauds, investment scams, and stock market manipulations. In criminal matters, accountants and auditors as expert witnesses are increasingly important in court cases.
- *Insurance claims.* The preparation and assessment of insurance claims on behalf of the insured and insurers may require the assistance of a forensic accountant to assess both the integrity and the quantum of a claim. The more significant areas relate to the calculation of loss arising from business interruption, fidelity bond, and personal injury matters. Whereas certain of these cases require financial projections, many need historical analysis and other accounting and auditing-oriented services.

- *Government/Regulation/Compliance.* Forensic accountants can assist entities to achieve regulatory and contractual compliance by ensuring that companies follow the appropriate legislation, law, or contract terms. Grant and subsidy investigations and public inquiries form a part of this service to government.

Forensic Accountant: Required Knowledge, Skills, and Abilities

Many of the aspects of forensic accounting fall outside the traditional education, training, and experience of auditors and accountants. The following skills, abilities, and/or knowledge are necessary to serve as an effective forensic accountant:

- *Ability to identify frauds with minimal initial information.* Many times, the fraud investigation begins with minimal knowledge of the specifics of a potential fraud. The forensic accountant needs to be able to identify the possible scheme (i.e., fraud theory approach), the possible manner it was perpetrated, and potentially effective procedures to prove or disprove the potential fraud (i.e., the "theory").
- *Interviewing.* Throughout the course of seeking evidence and information, the forensic accountant becomes involved in interviewing. For the forensic accountant, this function is another art to master. There are many things about interviewing, including what is the best order in which to interview parties of interest, that the forensic accountant must know. Most important, the forensic accountant must be prepared to handle a confession in such a way that the process ensures the evidence is admissible in a court of law.
- *Mind-set.* One of the critical success factors of forensic accountants, and one of the hardest to define or measure, is mind-set. A successful forensic accountant has a certain mind-set that includes several abilities. He or she is able to think like a crook. This attribute is basically counter to the average auditor who has lived a life with integrity and believes strongly in honesty. The successful forensic accountant knows almost instinctively that something "does not pass the smell test." He or she is able to sense the anomaly sometimes before actually knowing the nature of the anomaly. This person has a healthy skepticism at all times, neither fully trusting people nor fully distrusting them. They have a natural tendency to question the substance behind transactions, documents, and testimony

(written or oral) that others do not have. They also know, and have, the following mind-set factors:

- Fraud can be detected as well as discovered by accident or tip.[9]
- Financial audit methodologies and techniques are not really designed to detect fraud but rather designed to detect material financial misstatements.
- Fraud detection is more of an art than a science. It requires innovative and creative thinking as well as the rigors of science.
- Determination, persistence, and self-confidence are more important attributes for a fraud auditor than intelligence.
- Logic and problem-solving and detective skills are critical success factors for fraud auditors and forensic accountants.

- *Knowledge of evidence.* The forensic accountant must understand what constitutes evidence, the meaning of "best" and "primary" evidence, and the form that various accounting summaries can take to consolidate the financial evidence in a way that is acceptable to the courts. It is imperative that a forensic accountant understand the rules of evidence in court and how to conduct the investigation from the beginning as if all evidence will make it to a court of law. If these rules are ignored, evidence could be compromised and found inadmissible if it does get to court.
- *Presentation of findings.* The forensic accountant must have the ability to clearly communicate the findings resulting from the investigation in a fashion understandable to the layperson. The presentation can be oral or written and can include the appropriate demonstrative aids. The role of forensic accountants in the witness box is the final test of the findings in a public forum. By its nature, however, accounting and financial information is difficult for the average person to comprehend. Therefore, the forensic accountant as an expert witness must have above-average communication skills in distilling financial information in a manner that the average citizen can understand, comprehend, and assess to reach a sound conclusion.
- *Knowledge of investigative techniques.* When the issues have been identified, it is imperative that further information and documentation be acquired to obtain further evidence to assist in either supporting or refuting the allegation or claim. It is a question of knowing not only where the relevant financial documentation exists but also the intricacies of GAAP, financial statement disclosure, and systems of internal control, and being aware of the human element involved in frauds.

- *Investigative skills.* Forensic accountants usually apply investigative skills at the appropriate time during the course of their investigations. For example, in dealing with criminal matters, the primary concern is to develop evidence around motive, opportunity, and benefit. Of equal concern is that the benefit of doubt is given to the other side to ensure that proper interpretations are given to the transactions. Other concerns, such as the question of method of operation and the issue of economic risk, must also be addressed.

  Similarly, investigative skills are needed in litigation support. The forensic accountant must ensure that: a proper foundation exists for the calculation of future lost profits; all assumptions incorporated into the work product are recognized and identified; he understands his limitations as an expert; and the issue of mitigation of damages is considered.
- *Investigative mentality.* Along with their accounting knowledge, forensic accountants develop an investigative mentality that allows them to go beyond the bounds set out in either GAAP or GAAS. The following three tenets in forensic accounting are driven by the necessity to prove intent in court in order to prove there was a fraud. The investigative mentality develops in the search for best evidence, for competent and sufficient evidence, for forensic evidence. For example:
  - *Scope is not restricted as a result of materiality.* Often, especially in the early stages of a management/employee fraud, the transactions are small and accordingly are more easily conveyed to the court to show a pattern of conduct that is deceitful. As the dollar value of the transactions and their complexity increase, the ability to convey the essence of the transaction is hampered, and the forensic accountant's task is made more difficult.
  - For the most part, the *use of sampling* is not acceptable in establishing evidence.
  - A critical element of corporate investigations in particular is the assumption of integrity by management, both personal statements and its documentation of financial transactions and events.

  The investigative mentality is best developed by continued experience as a forensic witness. It is through this process that the forensic accountant's eyes are opened, because counsel for the opposing side raises issues and possibilities the accountant may not have considered up to that point. Repeated experience as a forensic witness creates a greater awareness of what is relevant and must be considered, so the expert witness can present financial evidence independently and objectively to reflect the reality of the situation.

- *Identification of financial issues.* When forensic accountants are presented with a situation generated by a complaint, allegation, rumor, inquiry, or statement of claim, it is important that they clearly identify the financial issues significant to the matter quickly. They base their decisions on experience and knowledge, and any resulting recommendations must reflect both common sense and business reality. For example, if documents are needed from a foreign jurisdiction, although the most obvious recommendation would be to obtain these records, it is usually not practical to do so. Other alternatives must be considered.
- *Interpretation of financial information.* It is unusual for a transaction or a series of events to have only one interpretation. The forensic accountant must be extremely conscious of a natural bias that can exist in the interpretation process. It is important that transactions be viewed from all aspects to ensure that the ultimate interpretation of the available information fits with common sense and the test of business reality. A proper interpretation of information can be assured only when one has looked behind and beyond the transaction in question without any scope limitations. In particular, a forensic accountant who is called as an expert witness must be aware of alternative accounting or financial formulas, rules, and interpretations.

FRAUD AUDITORS

Just as forensic accountant services are needed by a variety of groups, fraud audits also have a number of groups who could potentially benefit from their services, although it is somewhat less in scope than forensic accountants. The scope is less because fraud audits involve only a limited phase of the fraud cycle.

Who Needs Fraud Auditors?

The need for fraud-auditing talent is not related solely to compliance with new governmental regulations. In the private sector, fraud-auditing skills are also useful in most cases of financial crime, such as embezzlement; misrepresentations of financial facts; arson for profit; bankruptcy fraud; investment frauds of all manner and description; bank fraud; kickbacks and commercial bribery; computer frauds; electronic funds transfer (EFT) systems frauds; credit card frauds; and scams and shams by vendors, suppliers, contractors, and customers.

In the United States, the largest body of trained and experienced fraud auditors comes from government audit and investigative agencies like the Internal Revenue Service (IRS), FBI, Government Accounting Office (GAO), and the SEC. Police authorities on the state and local levels have few audit resources at their disposal; as a consequence, their ability to investigate certain white-collar crimes is limited. There is a need for fraud auditing in both public and private sectors of the economy.

Public accounting firms and other organizations in the private sector are developing fraud audit expertise. Although relatively few public accountants and internal auditors are specifically trained and experienced in this discipline, their numbers are rapidly increasing.

Fraud Auditor: Required Knowledge, Skills, and Abilities

More broadly, fraud auditing focuses on creating an environment that encourages the detection, prevention, and correction of intended or executed fraud. The main thrust of this book is to provide auditors, investigators, and other persons in the fraud environment with the ability to establish and influence forces that effectively counter attempts at fraud. Ability comes from insight, knowledge, and experience in viewing fraud as an economic, social, and organizational phenomenon.

Fraud auditors should know the aspects of the common body of knowledge regarding fraud. That knowledge includes: fraud schemes, red flags and the ones associated with specific frauds, the fraud triangle, fraud research, emerging fraud issues, steps in a fraud investigation, legal aspects of fraud (especially evidence), fraud professional organizations, fraud certifications, behavioral characteristics of white-collar criminals, and so on. The fraud auditor, of course, needs to be able to apply that knowledge in the fraud environment.

The personal attributes of fraud auditors include self-confidence, persistence, commitment to honesty and fair play, creativity, curiosity, an instinct for what is out of place or what is out of balance, independence, objectivity, good posture and grooming (for courtroom testimony), clear communication, sensitivity to human behavior, common sense, and an ability to fit pieces of a puzzle together without force or contrivance.

Inevitably, accounting and investigative (legal) skills cross over and are inextricably tied together in the context of a forensic audit. Although auditors and investigators exhibit similar skills in some ways, when separated they demonstrate different abilities. As for accounting skills, an effective fraud auditor should be able to do the following competently:

- Establish accounting, audit, and internal control (when, where, and how fraud is most likely to occur in books of account and in financial statements).
- Conduct a review of internal controls.
- Assess the strengths and weaknesses of those controls.
- Design scenarios of potential fraud losses based on identified weaknesses in internal controls.
- Know how to identify questionable and exceptional transactions (too high, too low, too often, too rare, too much, too little, odd times, odd places, odd people).
- Identify questionable and exceptional account balances and variations.
- Distinguish between simple human errors and omissions in entries and fraudulent entries (intentional error, such as recurring small errors versus unintentional random error and ignorance).
- Know how to follow the flow of documents that support transactions.
- Follow the flow of funds in and out of an organization's account.
- Search for underlying support documents for questionable transactions.
- Review such documents for peculiarities like fake billings, destruction of data, improper account classification, irregularities in financial data, and substitution of copies for original documents.

A couple of notes with regard to these skills should be made. One of these is the "toos" and the "odds" method for identifying possibly fraudulent transactions. Transactions are suspect if they are too high, too low, too often, too rare, too close, at odd times, in odd places, and so forth. A good example of the "too close" idea is the common check fraud perpetrated at a high dollar amount that bypasses the usually necessary high-level approval by paying the amount with multiple checks just under the threshold for (extra) approval. A mid-level accounts payable manager may be able to solely sign checks only for $1,000 and under, but can get $1,998 without additional approval with just two checks of $999 each, just below the approval threshold.

Beyond these skills that also relate to investigation, fraud auditors should be reasonably able to:

- Verify compliance with regulatory, legal, and evidential matters (how to discern, detect, and document such frauds).

- Gather and preserve evidence to corroborate asset losses, fraudulent transactions, and financial statements.
- Document and report a fraud loss for criminal, civil, or insurance claims.
- Be aware of management, administrative, and organizational policies, procedures, and practices.
- Review documents related to legal and general business functions.
- Test the organization's motivational and ethical climate.

The skills of a criminal investigator are in some respects similar to those of an auditor. An auditor and a detective both seek the truth: the auditor with respect to the proper accounting of business transactions and the detective/investigator with respect to the proper, legal behavior of citizens. Both should have inquisitive minds and challenge things that appear to be wrong, knowing that many times, the opposite of what one would logically expect is the logical place to start.

Auditing for fraud is as much of an intuitive process as it is a formal, analytic methodology. It is as much of an art as it is a science. As a consequence, it is difficult to teach and more difficult to learn. Skill depends on the right mind-set (thinking like a thief, probing for weaknesses) and practice. But it is not technique that one should master; rather, it is mental disposition: doggedness and persistence. One seeks relevant information without assumption, organizes it in some meaningful way, and then sees the pattern it creates. One goes behind and beyond those transactions to reconstruct what may have led to them and what has followed from them.

Investigative Intuition

Laypersons call this gift investigative intuition. Investigators call it professional judgment—judgment derived from knowledge, education, training, acquired skills, and experience. No one is wholly born with it, although certainly some are born more capable and some learn better. Intuition is learned mainly by trial and error. It is not a formula, and it cannot actually be taught.

The hunch of an amateur may not be worth much, based as it is on naiveté. The hunch of a trained investigator is worth much more, because it is based on experience, knowledge, and training. Even when auditors or investigators say they have discovered a fraud in accounting records by accident, it may be no accident; their trained eyes and ears can discern the truth. Police detectives also attribute some of their investigative insights to accident, chance, or good luck. But there again, their breakthroughs are not simply random events; they are brought about by their concentration and focus on the issue at hand. It is not black magic or fortuitous circumstances.

The authors would like to counter the feigned humility of some investigators and auditors by proposing that "accidental" discoveries of crimes by investigators and frauds by auditors usually are attributable not to pure chance but to know-how. Unfortunately, not all investigators or auditors have such know-how. The investigative mentality comes with age, training, self-discipline, experience, and a mind-set that understands that crime and fraud are possible in any environment, at any time, by anyone, *if the circumstances are ripe.*

Applicable Laws and Regulations

Fraud auditors should be familiar with applicable legislation, standards, and other requirements. That includes criminal and regulatory statutes involving business (see the "Review of Technical Literature" section in this chapter for details). These laws, together with the increase in fraud in public companies, waste and abuse in government contracting, and the current public concern over white-collar crime, create a greater need for further development of the discipline of fraud auditing.

Thinking Like a Fraud Auditor: Mind-Set

Investigating fraud requires the combined skills of a well-trained auditor and a criminal investigator. However, finding these skill sets in one person is rare. Part of the mission of this book is to better acquaint auditors with criminal-investigative rules, principles, techniques, and methods and to provide criminal investigators with some knowledge of accounting and auditing rules, principles, techniques, and methods. The result is, it is hoped, an ability to think more like a fraud auditor.

Financial auditors tend to use the inductive approach, whereas investigators tend to use the deductive approach. Fraud auditors may have to use both approaches in developing their investigative mentality.

Fraud involves so many variables in terms of fraud types, defrauder types, victim types, crime methods, techniques, tools, means, and instruments that any effort to unify them into a comprehensive theory of causation or solution seems impossible. This fact is why intuition, experience, and training are so vital to fraud auditing. Thinking like a fraud auditor means being perceptive, using inductive logic based on perception, and knowing how fraud plays into audits and criminal investigations.

Setting the Tone

Fraud auditors should set the tone and the standard, including demonstrating the highest standards of ethical conduct. This goal means that the fraud auditor within a company should have in place, and communicated to all employees, an effective corporate code of conduct, which should also include conflict-of-interest policy guidelines signed by employees to provide a clear understanding of the intent of management and the level of expectations.

Effective Corporate Governance

In many ways, SOX is an attempt to mandate good corporate governance tenets, or best practices, for publicly-traded companies. Fraud auditors need to be familiar with best practices of corporate governance as they relate to fraud. Closely aligned to "tone at the top" is the need for fraud auditors to assist the board in ensuring the entity is reasonably vigilant regarding fraud detection and prevention. Of particular importance would be the audit committee of the board of directors having oversight of a strong antifraud program or set of programs. Therefore, fraud auditors should be able to contribute to an effective antifraud program as a part of overall corporate governance.

Principles of Fraud Audits

Many principles of fraud audits should be understood by all auditors. They are:

- Fraud auditing is different from financial auditing. It is more a mind-set than a methodology.
- Fraud auditors have different approaches from financial auditors. Fraud auditors mostly focus on exceptions, oddities, accounting irregularities, and patterns of conduct. Financial auditors mostly focus on the audit trail and material misstatements.
- Fraud auditing is learned primarily from experience, not from audit textbooks or last year's work papers. Learning to be a fraud auditor means learning to think like a thief: "Where are the weakest links in this chain of internal controls?" "How can I steal on my job and get away with it?"
- From an audit perspective, fraud is intentionally misrepresenting financial facts of a material nature. From a fraud-audit perspective, fraud is an intentional misrepresentation of material financial facts.
- Frauds are committed for economic, egocentric, ideological, emotional, and psychotic reasons. Of the five, the economic motive is the most common.

- Fraud tends to encompass a theory structured around motive, opportunity, and rationalization (the "fraud triangle").
- Fraud in a computerized accounting environment can be committed at any state of processing—input, throughput, or output. Input frauds (entering false and fraudulent data) are the most common.
- The most common fraudulent schemes by lower-level employees involve disbursements (payables, payroll, and benefit and expense claims).
- Accounting-type frauds are caused more often by absence of controls than by loose controls.
- Fraud incidents may not be growing exponentially, but fraud losses are growing fairly rapidly ($400 billion in 1996 to $994 billion in 2008).[10]
- Accounting frauds are discovered more often by reactive measures than by proactive ones. (Tips and accidents make up over 65 percent of frauds detected.) Only about 10 percent of frauds are detected by financial auditors, and only about 23 percent of frauds are detected by internal controls, which is the highest of any proactive measures.
- Fraud prevention is a matter of adequate controls and a work environment that places a high value on personal honesty and fair dealing.

KEYS TO EFFECTIVE FRAUD INVESTIGATION

Perhaps a brief overview of a fraud investigation is the best way to convey the principles of forensic accounting. In terms of organizational fraud, the objective is to determine whether a fraud has occurred or is occurring and to determine who the fraudster is. In litigation support, the objective is determined by the client.

Predication is necessary to initiate the fraud investigation. Predication is the set of circumstances that would lead the prudent, reasonable, and professionally trained individual to believe that a fraud has occurred, is occurring, or will occur. In litigation support, however, predication is a call from a lawyer.

If the specific fraud is not known, or if there is limited information on the fraud, then the next step would be the *fraud theory approach*. In this approach, the forensic accountant, probably in a brainstorming setting, would propose the most likely fraud scheme (if not previously known), and the manner in which that fraud scheme could have been perpetrated on the victim organization. This latter substep is often necessary even in litigation support. Obviously, the forensic accountant needs to be familiar with fraud schemes and red flags associated with each (see Chapters 3 and 4). The theory then serves as the basis for developing a fraud investigation plan.

Using the theory, the forensic accountant develops a plan to gather sufficient and competent evidence (i.e., forensic evidence). This step is where the fraud auditor is particularly applicable (see Chapters 4 through 13 for various concepts in gathering evidence). In this step, an examination is made of accounting records, transactions, documents, and data (if applicable) to obtain sufficient evidence to prove or disprove that the fraud identified earlier has occurred. Issues of importance include custody of evidence and other legal matters (see Chapter 11).

It is important to note that the *last step* in the process of the investigation is to *approach the suspect*. That can happen intentionally and accidentally. The intentional approach should be easy enough to avoid, but the accidental requires some extra effort. When an auditor comes across an anomaly (document, accounting transaction, or other evidence of something that "should not be" or a red flag associated with known frauds, or a violation of internal controls), before approaching someone for an explanation, *first* he should ascertain the probability that the reason for the anomaly is *not fraud*. The reason for this caution is often when an auditor unwittingly has evidence of a fraud in hand, she goes to a party responsible for the fraud and asks for an explanation for the anomaly. At this point, the investigation at best has been severely hampered and at worst has been compromised for obtaining a confession or conviction in court.

For example, an internal auditor notices on performance reports that actual expenses are exactly twice the budget. That is classified, in our terminology, as an anomaly ("should not be"). The natural inclination is to go to the person responsible for authorizing checks in that business unit and ask for an explanation. However, if that person is using an authorized maker fraud scheme combined with forged endorsement, he could be cutting two checks for a single invoice—one for the vendor and one for the fraudster to forge an endorsement and convert to cash. If the auditor does approach that person, either he will come up with a viable excuse, or the auditor could unknowingly offer one. In a real case, the fraudster remained silent, and the auditor said, "You must have paid the vendor twice," to which she replied, "Yes. That is what I did." The fraudster then had the opportunity to replace the stolen funds without getting caught. Had the auditor assumed it could be fraud, then he would have had the opportunity to gather evidence to determine whether it was error or fraud, and possibly would have found the fraud. But by going to the fraudster, he gave her an undetectable exit strategy to the fraud. In other cases, fraudsters confronted by accident have suddenly retired, burned the business building (destroyed accounting records), or done other things that frustrated any appropriate conclusion to the fraud.

After gathering accounting evidence, the forensic accountant will attempt to gather evidence from eyewitnesses, using interviews. This process goes from people the greatest distance from the fraud (not involved but possibly knowledgeable), to an ever-narrowing circle of people close to the fraud (firsthand knowledge), and, as said before, interview the suspect last. Care should be taken to make sure the suspect does not know a fraud investigation is under way until the forensic accountant is sure he/she has forensic evidence of a crime.

Finally, the forensic accountant writes up the findings in a report to the party who hired him. If the case goes to court, this report, or a similar one, may be necessary during the trial. But regardless, if the case goes to trial, the forensic accountant's work will have to be presented in an effective manner to the judge or jury (see Chapters 14–16 for more detailed steps). It is part of the forensic accountant's ethics to *never* make a claim of innocence or guilt on the part of a suspect. Much like Sergeant Joe Friday of the Dragnet series, "Just the facts ma'am" is key to any report or testimony by the forensic accountant.

THE ANTIFRAUD PROFESSIONAL'S CAREER

There are several professional organizations that either focus on fraud and forensic accounting, or are key players in education, training, and identifying forensic accountants through certification. As in other areas of accounting and audit, certification is a key differentiator.

Certification

The Association of Certified Fraud Examiners (ACFE) was founded in 1988 by Joe Wells and others. It was the dream of Donald Cressey and Edwin Sutherland, two pioneers in white-collar crime, which was made a reality by Wells. The ACFE is a global, professional organization dedicated to fighting fraud and white-collar crime, with over 30,000 members in over 100 countries. Since its inception, the ACFE has been a major resource for fraud information and training. The Certified Fraud Examiner (CFE) program is an internationally recognized accrediting process for individuals who possess the specialized skills required to detect, investigate, and deter fraud. The domains of the CFE exam include: criminology and ethics, financial transactions, fraud investigation, and legal elements of fraud. Some have said that the ACFE is the premier financial sleuthing organization in the world today.

The AICPA introduced the Certified in Financial Forensics (CFF) program in the fall of 2008. Like all other AICPA certifications, a person has to be a CPA in order to attain the CFF. While the CFF began as an experienced-based certification, the AICPA plans to go to an exam-based certification in the summer of 2010. The domains of the CFF body of knowledge (BOK) include: bankruptcy and insolvency, computer forensics, economic damages, family law, fraud investigation, litigation support, stakeholder disputes, and valuations. Obviously, the CPA designation is deemed a qualification in order to serve as an expert witness on fraud. The CFF adds to that value, and expands the CPA's knowledge to specific fraud-related knowledge.

Business valuation is a profession of its own, and plays a common role in the fraud profession. That service is needed in lawsuits for failed mergers and aquisitions (M&A) (where the acquired company goes bankrupt soon after the merger or acquisition), failed marriages (where one spouse suspects the other is hiding assets), and other fraud-related resolutions. The AICPA offers the ABV certification. The domains of the exam include: the engagement, professional and regulatory standards, qualitative and quantitative analysis, valuation analysis, and related topics. The National Association of Certified Valuation Analysts (NACVA) offers a similar certification, the CVA. The domains for the exam include: fundamentals-techniques-theory, applications and calculations of the income and asset approaches, case analysis, and special purpose valuations.

The Association of Certified Forensic Specialists (ACFS) offers the Certified Forensic Specialist (CFS) certification. This certification is experienced based.

Another antifraud organization is the American College of Forensic Examiners Institute (ACFEI). The ACFEI is an independent, scientific, and professional society that is multidisciplinary in its scope, covering a large number of forensic-related disciplines or areas including forensic accounting. The ACFEI's purpose is the continued advancement of forensic examination and consultation across the many professional fields of its membership. The ACFEI has elevated standards through education and training.

One of the ACFEI certifications is the Certified Forensic Accounting (Cr.FA). The role of the forensic accountant necessitates specialized training and skills that are not typically part of an accountant's formal education. Forensic accountants are professionals who use a unique blend of education and experience to apply accounting, auditing, and investigative skills to uncover truth, form legal opinions, and assist in investigations. Forensic accountants may be involved in both litigation support (providing assistance on a given case, primarily related to the calculation or estimation of economic damages and related issues) and investigative accounting (looking into illegal activities). Thus the Cr.FA program provides advanced education and training to cover the wide range of skills, abilities, and knowledge necessary in forensic engagements. As of January 1, 2006, a person must be a CPA to acquire the Cr.FA certification.

Training/Education

Until the Enron scandal, there were few young accountants in the field of fraud. Those in this specialized field tended to be experienced in financial auditing, either in public accounting or fraud auditing in government agencies, before they ventured into private practice. But beginning with 2000, training for fraud auditors and forensic accountants has changed. For instance, prior to 2000, there were very few courses in fraud, and no degree with 18 hours or more of fraud education. Now there are a few college degree programs in fraud auditing or forensic accounting, and the number of these courses or degrees is growing rapidly.

Also, many professional associations now provide fraud training. The ACFE offers many seminars and training, featuring its weeklong course known as fraud boot camp. The ACFEI provides continuing education and seminars specifically on fraud. The Institute of Internal Auditors (IIA) provides periodic specialized training and conferences on fraud auditing, as does the Information Systems Audit and Control Association (ISACA) and the AICPA. In fact, it is hard to find an accounting or auditing professional organization that does not offer training for fraud today.

Subjects that could be or should be covered by training for fraud auditors include:

- Legal process, criminology, rules of evidence
- Financial accounting
- Fraud schemes, including red flags and countermeasures
- Fraud principles, such as the fraud triangle and fraud tree (see Chapters 2 and 3)
- Profile, sociology, and psychology of the white-collar criminal
- Interviewing skills
- Roles of various auditors

- Fraud in manual versus computerized accounting systems
- Preventing fraud, detecting fraud, and response to fraud
- Fraud risk assessment
- Internal controls, especially antifraud controls
- Tools and techniques for detecting fraud
- Testifying as an expert witness in accounting matters
- Deterring fraud in books of account—creating awareness of the risk of fraud, establishing personnel policies, ethical codes, and loss prevention programs, conducting audits

SUMMARY

What can be learned from fraud statistics and news reports? First, fraud can happen anywhere. Second, fraud is pervasive and continues to grow in terms of losses and perhaps in frequency—no one knows how much fraud has gone undetected.

What can be learned from reviewing the history of fraud? First, that a certain percentage of humanity will always be drawn to white-collar crimes and fraud, just as a certain faction of humanity is drawn to crime in general. There will always be fraudsters willing to take the risk in order to gain the ill-gotten gains of fraud. Second, financial statement frauds across history have been associated with stock prices throughout history. Last, fraudsters are sometimes quite intelligent, sometimes charming personalities, and sometimes just plain stupid.

The fraud cycle describes the necessary phases of resolving fraud, and the need to understand and incorporate legal factors in all aspects, all steps, in the fraud life cycle.

The technical literature related to forensic accounting describes the role of accountants and auditors, and their responsibilities related to fraud.

The forensic accountant has a relatively large scope of the fraud cycle in terms of role and responsibility. For example, it is the forensic accountant, generally speaking, who becomes the expert witness in the resolution stage of fraud. However, the fraud auditor's role is, generally speaking, limited to gathering evidence of a fraud, and primarily financial evidence. That being said, a fraud auditor may be required to serve as a fact witness or possibly an expert witness. But both of these roles require skills, knowledge, and abilities beyond the traditional financial auditor.

There are some keys to fraud investigation, many of which will be revealed in subsequent chapters. There is the requirement of predication before beginning an investigation, and the need to make sure no accusation is made during the investigation, written or oral. The fraud theory approach is an effective way to provide strategic direction to a fraud investigation. But perhaps the most important key to a successful investigation is to approach the suspect later in the investigation.

The antifraud profession has grown significantly over the last decade and there are a number of organizations that will support one's career in antifraud, a number of certifications available, and lots of training and education compared to decades past.

The following chapters will expand on many of these ideas hopefully to provide valuable information to those with responsibilities to prevent or detect fraud.

NOTES

1. FBI Insurance Fraud Report, www.fbi.gov/publications/fraud/insurance_-fraud.htm, last accessed September 11, 2009.
2. www.fbi.gov/publications/fraud/mortgage_fraud07.htm, last accessed August 31, 2009.
3. FBI Mortgage Fraud Report "Year in Review," www.fbi.gov/publications/fraud/mortgage_fraud08.htm#1, last accessed September 11, 2009.
4. www.nicb.org, last accessed September 11, 2009.
5. Some of the information in this section comes from Dr. Robert E. Jensen's web site at Trinity University, www.trinity.edu/rjensen/415wp/AmericanHistoryOfFraud.htm, last accessed January 13, 2006.
6. http://myweb.dal.ca/dmcneil/bubble/bubble.html, last accessed April 26, 2010.
7. www.fbi.gov/publications/fraud/mortgage_fraud07.htm.
8. David R. Frazier and L. Scott Spradling, "The New SAS No. 78," *The CPA Journal*, May 1996.
9. According to the ACFE 2004 Report to the Nation, the number one method of detection is tip and the number three method is accident.
10. ACFE, RTTN, 1996, 2002, 2004, 2006, and 2008.

CHAPTER TWO

Fraud Principles

INTRODUCTION

Fraud has several potentially ambiguous definitions, and is categorized in various ways. A proper understanding of these definitions and models is fundamental to preventing and detecting fraud. The fraud principles are the building blocks of an effective antifraud program, or of effective prevention and early detection of fraud.

First, it is important to establish a definition for fraud both for the profession and for an entity devising an antifraud program. It is good to be reminded of the possibility of fraud in order to avoid the "it-can't-happen-here" syndrome. Understanding effective models such as the fraud triangle is useful in understanding why fraud occurs. There are numerous classification models (taxonomies) for fraud schemes, but it is important to pick one that can be effectively applied in fraud prevention and early detection. Lastly, an understanding of the profile of the white-collar criminal is helpful as well.

DEFINITION: WHAT IS FRAUD?

Fraud means different things to different people under different circumstances. For instance, fraud can be perceived as deception. One might say that fraud in the form of intentional deception (including lying and cheating) is the opposite of truth, justice, fairness, and equity. Although deception can be intended to coerce people to act against their own self-interest, deception can also be used for one's own defense or survival. Despite that rationale for deception, deception by current standards of behavior is generally considered mean and culpable, but deception can be intended for a benevolent purpose, too. Benevolent deceivers in society are not looked on as harshly as are those whose intentions and motives are impure. Those who act out of greed, jealousy, spite, and revenge are not so quickly excused or forgiven.

Fraud can also be associated with injury. One person can injure another either by force or through fraud. The use of force to cause bodily injury is frowned on by most organized societies; using fraud to cause financial injury to another does not always carry the same degree of stigma or punishment.

Fraud is a word that has many definitions. Some of the more notable ones are:

- *Fraud as a crime. Fraud* is a generic term, and embraces all the multifarious means that human ingenuity can devise, which are resorted to by one individual, to get an advantage by false means or representations. No definite and invariable rule can be laid down as a general proposition in defining fraud, as it includes surprise, trick, cunning, and unfair ways by which another is cheated. The only boundaries defining it are those that limit human knavery.[1]
- *Corporate fraud.* Corporate fraud is any fraud perpetrated by, for, or against a business corporation.
- *Management fraud.* Management fraud is the intentional misrepresentation of corporate or unit performance levels perpetrated by employees serving in management roles who seek to benefit from such frauds in terms of promotions, bonuses or other economic incentives, and status symbols.
- *Layperson's definition of fraud. Fraud.* as it is commonly understood today, means dishonesty in the form of an intentional deception or a willful misrepresentation of a material fact. Lying, the willful telling of an untruth, and cheating, the gaining of an unfair or unjust advantage over another, could be used to further define the word *fraud* because these two words denote intention or willingness to deceive.

- *ACFE's definition of fraud.* The Association of Certified Fraud Examiners (ACFE) defines "occupational fraud and abuse" (employee frauds) as: "the use of one's occupation for personal gain through the deliberate misuse or theft of the employing organization's resources or assets." The ACFE defines financial statement fraud as: "the deliberate misrepresentation of the financial condition of an enterprise accomplished through the intentional misstatement or omission of amounts or disclosures in the financial statements in order to deceive financial statement users."[2]
- *Fraud as a tort.* The U.S. Supreme Court in 1887 provided a definition of fraud in the civil sense as:

> *First:* That the defendant has made a representation in regard to a *material fact;*
> *Second:* That such representation is *false;*
> *Third:* That such representation was *not actually believed by the defendant,* on reasonable grounds, to be true;
> *Fourth:* That it was made with *intent* that it should be acted on;
> *Fifth:* That it was acted on by complainant to his *damage*; and
> *Sixth:* That in so acting on it the complainant was ignorant of its falsity, and *reasonably believed it to be true.*
> The first of the foregoing requisites excludes such statements as consist merely in an expression of opinion of judgment, honestly entertained; and again excepting in peculiar cases, it excludes statements by the owner and vendor of property in respect of its value. [Emphasis added.][3]

Of the six elements of the tort definition, the fourth (*intent*) is usually the most difficult to establish in a court case.

Of all the definitions of fraud just listed, the legal one is preeminent in antifraud. The reason for that ranking is that any fraud has the potential to end up in court and the definition for fraud determined by the U.S. Supreme Court in 1887 will be the one a victim needs to prove in a court of law.

The legal definition of fraud also matters at the beginning of a fraud investigation. For instance, it was said that intent is the most difficult aspect of the legal definition to prove. Intent occurs in one's mind and thus proof is somewhat circumstantial. Basically, one has to establish a sufficient pattern of fraudulent transactions or activities in order to prove intent, or the courts often see shredding of documents as self-incriminating. For instance, if a victim company happens upon a single misuse of the corporate credit card and proceeds with a criminal case, the defendant can easily defend the claims with the "oops" theory;[4] that is, oops, I made a mistake—I meant to use my personal credit card and did not notice that I used the corporate one by mistake. Guilty parties can use the excuse of an accident or carelessness as the cause of the incident, rather than a deliberate intent to steal or commit the fraud, along with a plethora of other viable excuses.

But, if *at the beginning of the fraud investigation*, the victim entity's antifraud personnel take the time to establish a pattern, even if that means allowing the fraudster to continue to steal for awhile, then the victim can establish "forensic" evidence related to intent. The fraudster might try the "oops defense," but if the victim is able to produce dozen of instances, the judge or jury will probably not believe it.

Likewise, it is incumbent on entities to define fraud, make the definition part of its ethics or fraud policy, and have employees sign their acknowledgment of understanding and agreeing to abide by it. Without a signed policy statement on the definition, certain kinds of frauds would be difficult to prove to a jury of peers (e.g., using corporate cameras, computers, and time to manage an eBay account), leading to disagreements as to whether those events are fraud. Thus it is in the best interest of the entity to provide a definition for fraud, e.g., the ACFE definition for employee fraud, and have employees sign it.

SYNONYMS: FRAUD, THEFT, AND EMBEZZLEMENT

Fraud, theft, defalcation, irregularities, white-collar crime, and *embezzlement* are terms that are often used interchangeably. Although they have some common elements, they are not identical in the criminal law sense. For example, in English common law, theft is referred to as *larceny*—the taking and carrying away of the property of another with the intention of permanently depriving the owners of its possession. In larceny, the perpetrator comes into possession of the stolen item illegally. In *embezzlement*, the perpetrator comes into initial possession lawfully, but then converts it to his or her own use. Embezzlers have a fiduciary duty to care for and to protect the property. In converting it to their own use, they breach that fiduciary duty.

CLASSIC FRAUD RESEARCH

The cost of frauds to individual businesses and society is substantial. But it is still true that too few people have a sufficient understanding of fraud.

Reviewing the literature creates an appreciation for the scope and nature of fraud and builds a foundation for understanding fraud topics.

The current term *fraud* was traditionally referred to as *white-collar crime,* and the two are used synonymously here. The classic works on fraud are *White Collar Crime* by Edwin H. Sutherland; *Other People's Money* by Donald R. Cressey; *The Thief in the White Collar* by Norman Jaspan and Hillel Black; and *Crime, Law, and Society* by Frank E. Hartung.[5] These authorities essentially tell us:

> White-collar crime has its genesis in the same general process as other criminal behavior; namely, differential association. The hypothesis of differential association is that criminal behavior is learned in association with those who define such behavior favorably and in isolation from those who define it unfavorably, and that a person in an appropriate situation engages in such criminal behavior if, and only if, the weight of the favorable definitions exceeds the weight of the unfavorable definitions.[6]

In other words, birds of a feather flock together, or at least reinforce one another's rationalized views and values. But people make their own decisions and, even if subconsciously, in a cost-benefit manner. In order to commit fraud, a rationalization must exist for the individual to decide fraud is worth committing (i.e., the fraud will not be prevented, detected, and/or punished in accordance with the potential rewards).

> Trusted persons become trust violators when they conceive of themselves as having a financial problem which is nonshareable, are aware that this problem can be secretly resolved by violation of the position of financial trust, and are able to apply their own conduct in that situation, verbalizations which enable them to adjust their conceptions of themselves as users of the entrusted funds or property.[7]

Jaspan and Black tried to derive antifraud measures in their research. Their book, *The Thief in the White Collar,* is based on their many years of consulting experience on security-related matters, and contains a number of notable and often quoted generalizations. In a nutshell, Jaspan and Black exhort employers to: (1) pay their employees fairly, (2) treat their employees decently, and (3) listen to their employees' problems, if they want to avoid employee fraud, theft, and embezzlement. But to temper that bit of humanism with a little reality, they also suggest that employers should never place full trust in either their employees or the security personnel they hire to check on employees.[8]

Hartung disagrees with Jaspan's and Black's generalizations and focuses on the individual. He argues:

> It will be noticed that the criminal violator of financial trust and the career delinquent have one thing in common: Their criminality is learned in the process of symbolic communication, dependent upon cultural sources of patterns of thought and action, and for systems of values and vocabularies of motives.[9]

In reality, both Jaspan and Black, and Hartung appear to have been correct. Hartung noted that individuals are inevitably affected by their environment. Although Jaspan and Black might be considered too empathetic to the individual, their suggestions to deter fraud echo the same as modern efforts do: Create an environment with few reasons and with few opportunities to commit fraud.

FRAUD TRIANGLE

In order to properly prevent, detect, and respond to fraud, antifraud stakeholders need to understand why fraudsters commit a fraud. No model or framework has been more useful than Cressey's Triangle in providing that understanding.

"Fraud Triangle"

In the 1950s, Donald Cressey was encouraged by Edwin Sutherland, who was serving on his dissertation committee, to use a thesis of why a person in a position of trust would become a violator of that trust. Sutherland and Cressey decided to interview fraudsters who were convicted of embezzlement. Cressey interviewed about 200 embezzlers in prison. One of the major conclusions of his efforts was that every fraud had three things in common: (1) pressure (sometimes referred to as motivation, and usually a "nonshareable need"); (2) rationalization (of personal ethics); and (3) knowledge and opportunity to commit the crime. These three points are the corners of the fraud triangle (see Exhibit 2.1). His book *Other People's Money* is based on his dissertation work.

Pressure

Pressure (or incentive, or motivation) refers to something that has happened in the fraudster's personal life that creates a stressful need that motivates him to steal. Usually that motivation centers on some financial strain, but it could be

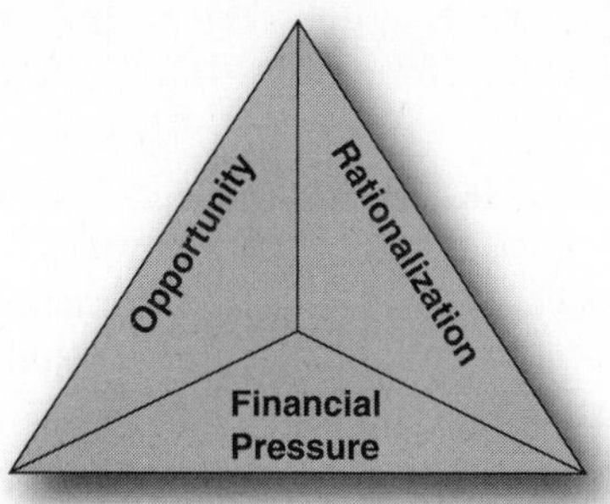

EXHIBIT 2.1 The Fraud Triangle

the symptom of other types of pressures. For example, a drug habit or gambling habit could create great financial need in order to sustain the habit and thus create the pressure associated with this aspect of the fraud triangle. Sometimes a fraudster finds motivation in some other incentive. For instance, almost all financial statement frauds were motivated by some incentive, usually related to stock prices or performance bonuses or both. Sometimes an insatiable greed causes relatively wealthy people to commit frauds.

Beyond the realm of competitive and economic survival, what other motives precipitate fraud? Social and political survival provide incentives, too, in the form of egocentric and ideological motives, especially in financial statement frauds. Sometimes people commit fraud to aggrandize their egos, put on airs, or assume false status. Sometimes they deceive to survive politically, or have a burning desire for power. They lie about their personal views or pretend to believe when they do not. Or they simply cheat or lie to their political opponents or intentionally misstate their opponents' positions on issues.

Motives to commit fraud in business usually are rationalized by the old saying that all is fair in love and war—and in business, which is amoral, anyway. There is one further category of motivation, however. It might be called psychotic, because it cannot be explained in terms of rational behavior. In this category are the pathological liar, the professional confidence man, and the kleptomaniac.

Rationalization

Most fraudsters do not have a criminal record. In the ACFE *Report to the Nation* (RTTN) 2008,[10] 93 percent of the reported fraudsters had no prior criminal convictions. In fact, white-collar criminals usually have a personal code of ethics. It is not uncommon for a fraudster to be religious. So how do fraudsters justify actions that are objectively criminal? They simply justify their crime under their circumstances. For instance, many will steal from employers but mentally convince themselves that they will repay it (i.e., "I am just borrowing the money"). Others believe it hurts no one so that makes the theft benign. Still others believe they are entitled to the benefits of the fraud and are simply taking matters into their own hands to administer fair treatment (e.g., they deserve a raise or better treatment). Many other excuses could serve as a rationalization, including some benevolent ones where the fraudster does not actually keep the stolen funds or assets but uses them for social purposes (e.g., to fund an animal clinic for stray animals).

Opportunity

According to Cressey's research (i.e., the Fraud Triangle), fraudsters always have the knowledge and opportunity to commit the fraud. The former is reflected in known frauds, and in research studies such as the ACFE's RTTNs that show employees and managers tend to have a long tenure with a company when they commit the fraud. A simple explanation is that employees and managers who have been around for years know quite well where the weaknesses are in the internal controls and have gained sufficient knowledge of how to commit the crime successfully.

A prerequisite to opportunity is that the perpetrator be in a position of trust. Remember Cressey's thesis was about trust violators. And it is difficult to commit a fraud without being in a trusted position over assets.

But the main factor in opportunity is internal controls. A weakness in or absence of internal controls provides the opportunity for fraudsters to commit their crimes. It is noteworthy that the Treadway Commission (later known as the Committee of Sponsoring Organizations, or COSO) was formed to respond to the savings and loan frauds and scandals of the early 1980s. The committee's conclusion was that the best prevention was strong internal controls, and the result was the COSO model of internal controls, which was incorporated into financial auditing technical literature as SAS 78, *Consideration of Internal Control in a Financial Statement Audit*. Then the Sarbanes-Oxley Act (SOX) focused on an annual evaluation of the internal controls by management with an independent opinion of that evaluation by the financial auditors—Section 404 of the act. Again, if the purpose of SOX was to minimize fraud, internal control is the effective way to accomplish that goal. In fact, it could be argued that this aspect of the triangle is the only one that auditors can easily observe or control.

The opportunities to commit fraud are rampant in the presence of loose or lax management and (concomitant) inadequate attention to internal controls. When motivation is coupled with such opportunities, the potential for fraud is increased.

SCOPE OF FRAUD

How pervasive is business fraud? How likely is it to be discovered either by audit design or by accident? Research in the last 10 years has been able to reveal both the scope of fraud and the most effective means of detecting frauds.

The scope of fraud is such that almost all mid-size to large businesses are certain to have a fraud either currently being perpetrated or soon to be perpetrated. Virtually no small business is safe. Nor are not-for-profits or other types of organizations free from fraud's effects. Research by the ACFE reveals that the estimated level of fraud detected from 1996 to 2008 has been consistent in the U.S. economy—approximately 6 percent of annual revenues.[11]

Regarding financial frauds, a major study by COSO provides valuable insights. In 1998, COSO released its *Landmark Study on Fraud in Financial Reporting*.[12] The report covered 10 years of the Securities and Exchange Commission (SEC) enforcement cases, analyzing 200 randomly selected cases of alleged financial fraud investigated by the SEC—about two-thirds of the 300 SEC probes into fraud between 1987 and 1997. COSO examined certain key company and management characteristics, and the key findings were interesting: Most fraud among public companies was committed by small firms (well below $100 million in assets), boards of directors were dominated by insiders and inexperienced people, executive officers were identified as associated with financial statement fraud in 83 percent of the cases, and the average fraud period extended over a period of 23.7 months. The report went on to say: "The relatively small size of fraud companies suggests that the inability or even unwillingness to implement cost-effective internal controls may be a factor affecting the likelihood of financial statement fraud." COSO suggested external auditors focus on the "tone at the top" in evaluating internal control structures.

In 2009, KPMG released its fourth *Fraud Survey*.[13] In it, KPMG interviewed 204 executives in companies with at least $250 million in revenues. The report stated that the risk of fraud is increasing due to the economy and even the stimulus money. Of the respondents, 32 percent reported at least one of the categories of the fraud tree (corruption, asset misappropriation, financial statement fraud—see Exhibit 2.6 later in the chapter) was going to increase during the next 12 months in their organization. But 74 percent of employees reported they had personally observed wrongdoing in their organization in the prior 12 months. Also, 65 percent of executives reported that fraud and misconduct is a significant risk for their industry. The greatest concern was the potential loss of public trust, according to 71 percent of the executives. Executives believe that fraud will either stay the same (85 percent) or increase (74 percent) over the next 12 months. Inadequate controls or compliance programs enable fraud to go unchecked (66 percent). Areas that needed the most amount of improvement were employee communication and training (67 percent), technology-driven continuous auditing and monitoring techniques (65 percent), and fraud risk assessment (60 percent).

The ACFE tracks the trend in fraud and statistics on fraud regularly. It has been conducting surveys on occupational fraud and abuse since 1996 and communicating the results to the public via its *Report to the Nation.* In all five reports (1996, 2002, 2004, 2006, and 2008), the ACFE surveyed hundreds of certified fraud examiners (CFEs), who reported facts on a fraud from the previous year. The results show enormous amounts of fraud each survey. The reported losses due to fraud were 6 percent of reported revenues for 1996, 2002, and 2004; 5 percent in 2006; and 7 percent in 2008. Thus one measure of the scope of fraud is about 6 percent of the U.S. economy, or about 6 percent of the average firm. According to the most recent ACFE RTTN (2008), that figure would be $994 billion total (note the 2008 report estimated losses at 7 percent). By that estimate, fraud losses have more than doubled since the first survey in 1996. Financial frauds lasted a median of 30 months before being discovered (most categorizations place the median length at 24 months). For those entities subject to external audits, they went through at least one financial audit with the fraud going undetected.

The various ACFE RTTNs have also measured the common methods of detecting fraud. According to the reports, tips and complaints have consistently been the most effective means of detecting frauds, and are a much higher percentage than the methods ranked second. Tips and complaints accounted for 46.2 percent of the initial detection of occupational fraud in the 2008 report. Internal controls was second (23.3 percent), internal audit was third (20 percent), accident was fourth (19.4 percent), and external audit was fifth (9.1 percent). Interestingly, while generally the percentages have not changed much over time, internal controls has gained potentially suggesting the emphasis placed on controls (particularly including Sarbanes-Oxley) may be improving fraud detection. Thus the best detection methods are tips, internal controls, and internal audit. All of these are integral tenets of the Sarbanes-Oxley Act of 2002 and associated auditing standards.

PROFILE OF FRAUDSTERS

A key aspect of preventing and detecting fraud is to understand the profile of typical fraudsters, by type of fraud. Regarding asset misappropriation, the person is usually someone who was not suspected, oftentimes least suspected. The profile of white-collar criminals is very different from blue-collar criminals, or street criminals. This fact makes fraud even more difficult to prevent or detect.

Who Commits Fraud?

In view of the principles mentioned, one might conclude that fraud is caused mainly by factors external to the individual: economic, competitive, social, and political factors, and poor controls. But how about the individual? Are some people more prone to commit fraud than others? And if so, is that a more serious cause of fraud than the external and internal environmental factors previously discussed? Data from criminology and sociology seem to suggest so.

Begin by making a few generalizations about people:

- Some people are honest all of the time.
- Some people are dishonest all of the time.
- Most people are honest some of the time.
- Some people are honest most of the time.

Research has been conducted to ask employees whether they are honest at work. Forty percent say they would not steal, 30 percent said they would, and 30 percent said they might.[14] Beyond those generalizations about people, what can one say about fraud perpetrators? Gwynn Nettler, in *Lying, Cheating and Stealing,*[15] offers these insights on cheaters and deceivers:

- People who have experienced failure are more likely to cheat.
- People who are disliked and who dislike themselves tend to be more deceitful.

- People who are impulsive, distractible, and unable to postpone gratification are more likely to engage in deceitful crimes.
- People who have a conscience (fear of apprehension and punishment; that is, perception of detection) are more resistant to the temptation to deceive.
- Intelligent people tend to be more honest than ignorant people. Middle- and upper-class people tend to be more honest than lower-class people.
- The easier it is to cheat and steal, the more people will do so.
- Individuals have different needs and therefore different levels at which they will be sufficiently motivated to lie, cheat, or steal.
- Lying, cheating, and stealing increase when people have great pressure to achieve important objectives.
- The struggle to survive generates deceit.

People lie, cheat, and steal on the job in a variety of personal and organizational situations. The ways that follow are but a few:

1. Personal variables
   - Aptitudes/abilities
   - Attitudes/preferences
   - Personal needs/wants
   - Values/beliefs
2. Organizational variables
   - Nature/scope of the job (meaningful work)
   - Tools/training provided
   - Reward/recognition system
   - Quality of management and supervision
   - Clarity of role responsibilities
   - Clarity of job-related goals
   - Interpersonal trust
   - Motivational and ethical climate (ethics and values of superiors and coworkers)
3. External variables
   - Degree of competition in the industry
   - General economic conditions
   - Societal values (ethics of competitors and of social and political role models)

Why Do Employees Lie, Cheat, and Steal on the Job?

These 25 reasons for employee crimes are those most often advanced by authorities in white-collar crime (criminologists, psychologists, sociologists, risk managers, auditors, police, and security professionals):

1. The employee believes he can get away with it.
2. The employee thinks she desperately needs or desires the money or articles stolen.
3. The employee feels frustrated or dissatisfied about some aspect of the job.
4. The employee feels frustrated or dissatisfied about some aspect of his personal life that is not job related.
5. The employee feels abused by the employer and wants to get even.
6. The employee fails to consider the consequences of being caught.
7. The employee thinks: "Everybody else steals, so why not me?"
8. The employee thinks: "They're so big, stealing a little bit won't hurt them."
9. The employee doesn't know how to manage her own money, so is always broke and ready to steal.
10. The employee feels that beating the organization is a challenge and not a matter of economic gain alone.
11. The employee was economically, socially, or culturally deprived during childhood.
12. The employee is compensating for a void felt in his personal life and needs love, affection, and friendship.
13. The employee has no self-control and steals out of compulsion.
14. The employee believes a friend at work has been subjected to humiliation or abuse or has been treated unfairly.
15. The employee is just plain lazy and will not work hard to earn enough to buy what she wants or needs.
16. The organization's internal controls are so lax that everyone is tempted to steal.
17. No one has ever been prosecuted for stealing from the organization.
18. Most employee thieves are caught by accident rather than by audit or design. Therefore, fear of being caught is not a deterrent to theft.
19. Employees are not encouraged to discuss personal or financial problems at work or to seek management's advice and counsel on such matters.

20. Employee theft is a situational phenomenon. Each theft has its own preceding conditions, and each thief has her own motives.
21. Employees steal for any reason the human mind and imagination can conjure up.
22. Employees never go to jail or get harsh prison sentences for stealing, defrauding, or embezzling from their employers.
23. Human beings are weak and prone to sin.
24. Employees today are morally, ethically, and spiritually bankrupt.
25. Employees tend to imitate their bosses. If their bosses steal or cheat, then they are likely to do it also.

To be respected and thus complied with, laws must be rational, fair in application, and enforced quickly and efficiently. Company policies that relate to employee honesty, like criminal laws in general, must be rational, fair, and intended to serve the company's best economic interests. The test of rationality for any company fraud policy is whether its terms are understandable, whether its punishments or prohibitions are applicable to a real and serious matter, and whether its enforcement is possible in an efficient and legally effective way.

But what specific employee acts are serious enough to be prohibited and/or punished? Any act that could or does result in substantial loss, damage, or destruction of company assets should be prohibited. What is acceptable or considered substantial will vary by organization, but wherever the boundaries are defined, they must be well communicated, exemplified by upper management, and enforced as necessary.

The greatest deterrent to criminal behavior is sure and even-handed justice; that means swift detection and apprehension, a speedy and impartial trial, and punishment that fits the crime: loss of civil rights, privileges, property, personal freedom, or social approval. Having said all that, why is it that, despite the dire consequences of criminal behavior, it still occurs? Apparently, it is because the rewards gained often exceed the risk of apprehension and punishment; that is, the pains inflicted as punishment are not as severe as the pleasures of criminal behavior. The latter seems to be particularly true in cases of economic or white-collar crimes. Many times, if not most, when a fraud is detected, the extent of punishment regarding the perpetrator is to be fired, sometimes without even paying back the fraud losses. So while potential white-collar criminals may believe they might get caught, the ramifications are below some acceptable threshold.

High-Level and Low-Level Thieves

At high levels of organizational life, it is easy to steal because controls can be bypassed or overridden. The sums high-level managers steal, therefore, tend to be greater than the sums low-level personnel steal. For instance, according to the 2008 ACFE RTTN, executives average about $834,000 per fraud, managers about $150,000, and employees about $70,000. The number of incidents of theft, however, is greater at low levels of organizations because of the sheer number of employees found there.

The ACFE RTTN has put together a profile of fraudsters based on the information collected from CFEs in its surveys. The more *expensive* frauds, in terms of cost or losses, are committed by fraudsters who (a) have been with the firm a long time, (b) earn a high income, (c) are male, (d) are over 60 years of age, (e) are well educated (the higher the educational degree completed, the higher the losses), (f) operate in collusion rather than alone, and (g) have never been charged with anything criminal.[16] The most *frequent* frauds, however, are committed by fraudsters with a different profile. These fraudsters (a) have been an employee for about the same amount of time as the high-level thieves, (b) earn much less, (c) could be either male or female (gender doesn't matter), (d) are between the ages of 41 and 50, (e) have finished high school, (f) operate alone, (g) and have usually not been charged with any criminal behavior.

Hall and Singleton[17] provide a similar profile for a typical fraudster in general. These criminals are (a) in a key position in the company, (b) are usually male, (c) are more than 50 years old, (d) are married, and (e) are highly educated. This profile is similar to the one from the ACFE RTTN, and leads us to this overall conclusion: A white-collar criminal *does not look like a criminal!*

WHO IS VICTIMIZED BY FRAUD MOST OFTEN?

Controls to protect against fraud by either organization insiders or outside vendors, suppliers, and contractors must be adequate; that is, they must accomplish the goal of control—cost-feasible protection of assets against loss, damage, or destruction. *Cost-feasible protection* means minimal expenditures for maximum protection. Creating an organizational police state would be control overkill. A balanced perspective on controls and countermeasures is the ideal, and may require involving employees in creating control policies, plans, and procedures. A balanced perspective weighs the costs and benefits of proposed new controls. While a trusting culture breeds loyalty and honesty, a distrusting culture is often associated with frauds. However, absolute trust with no accountability is a seedbed for fraud.

Fraud is therefore most prevalent in organizations that have no controls, no trust, no ethical standards, no profits, and no future. Likewise, the more these circumstances exist, the higher the risk of fraud.

Empirical evidence shows that the most common factor in all frauds committed is the lack of segregation of duties with no compensating control—a situation frequently present in small business entities. Small businesses and organizations (e.g., charities) have a higher risk of fraud than any other size entity, because they are more likely to have one accountant, no segregation of duties, and no compensating control, and those factors are the most common in fraud. The 2008 RTTN shows that 38.2 percent of all frauds occur in the smallest size entity (less than 100 employees), and the second highest frequency is 23 percent in companies with 1,000–9,999 employees. Likewise, companies with under 100 employees lose an average of $200,000, and those with 100 to 999 employees report an average loss of $176,000. Therefore, the smallest size entities have a higher risk of occurrence and relative size loss than any other size entity, and are victimized by fraud most often, based on size.

FRAUD TAXONOMIES

Almost every fraud survey and major fraud author has a different system for classifying frauds. While some are similar, some also present problems in applying the taxonomy to antifraud activities. For the purposes of this book, we focus on frauds in financial statements and business transactions. The following are some of the ways fraud has been classified.

General Dichotomies of Frauds

There are numerous dichotomies of fraud and ways to categorize fraud. The key is to find a fraud taxonomy that can be effectively applied to antifraud programs, fraud investigations, and antifraud controls.

Consumer and Investor Frauds

Fraud, in a nutshell, is intentional deception, commonly described as lying, cheating, and stealing. Fraud can be perpetrated against customers, creditors, investors, suppliers, bankers, insurers, or government authorities (e.g., tax fraud). Consumer and investor fraud have their own literature.

Criminal and Civil Fraud

A specific act of fraud may be a criminal offense, a civil wrong, or grounds for the rescission of a contract. *Criminal fraud* requires proof of an intentional deception. *Civil fraud* requires that the victim suffer damages. Fraud in the inducement of a contract may vitiate consent and render a contract voidable.

The definition of a criminal fraud according to the ACFE is the one used in this book:

> Criminal fraud denotes a false representation of a material fact made by one party to another party with the intent to deceive and induce the other party to justifiably rely on the fact to his/her detriment (i.e., his injury or loss).

Fraud for and against the Company

Fraud can be viewed from yet another perspective. When one thinks of fraud in a corporate or management context, one can perhaps develop a more meaningful and relevant taxonomy as a framework for fraud auditing.

Corporate frauds can be classified into two broad categories: (1) frauds directed against the company, and (2) frauds that benefit the company. In the former, the company is the victim; in the latter, the company, through the fraudulent actions of its officers, is the intended beneficiary. In that context, one can distinguish between organizational frauds that are intended to benefit the organizational entity and those that are intended to harm the entity. This classification may also clarify the intent of the fraud, which as mentioned previously can be difficult to discern or prove.

For example, price fixing, corporate tax evasion, violations of environmental laws, false advertising, and short counts and weights are generally intended to aid the organization's financial performance. Manipulating accounting records to overstate profits is another illustration of a fraud intended to benefit the company but that may benefit management through bonuses based on profitability or stock prices in the market. In frauds *for* the organization, management may be involved in a conspiracy to deceive. Only one person may be involved in a fraud against the organization, such as an accounts payable clerk who fabricates invoices from a nonexistent vendor, has checks issued to that vendor, and converts the checks to his own use.

Frauds *for* the company are committed mainly by senior managers who wish to enhance the financial position or condition of the company by such ploys as overstating income, sales, or assets or by understating expenses and liabilities.

In essence, an intentional misstatement of a financial fact is made, and that can constitute a civil or criminal fraud. But income, for example, may also be intentionally understated to evade taxes, and expenses can be overstated for a similar reason. Top managers use fraud to deceive shareholders, creditors, and regulatory authorities. Similar frauds by lower-level profit-center managers may be used to deceive their superiors in the organization, to make them believe the unit is more profitable or productive than it is, and thereby perhaps to earn a higher bonus award or a promotion. In the latter event, despite the fact that the subordinate's overstatement of income, sales, or productivity ostensibly helps the company look better, it is really a fraud *against* the company.

Frauds *against* the company are intended to benefit only the perpetrator, as in the case of theft of corporate assets or embezzlement. The latter specific category of fraud is often referred to as misappropriation of assets. Frauds against the company may also include vendors, suppliers, contractors, and competitors bribing employees. Cases of employee bribery are difficult to discern or discover by audit, because the corporation's accounting records generally are not manipulated, altered, or destroyed. Bribe payments to favor one vendor's product over another are made under the table or, as lawyers say, "sub rosa." The first hint of bribery may come from an irate vendor whose product is consistently rejected despite its quality, price, and performance. Bribery may also become apparent if the employee begins to live beyond her means, far in excess of salary and family resources.

One logical thought process should be pointed out. In frauds for the company that involve executive management manipulating books, the fraud *eventually will be against the company*. Take any of the recent public scandals of Enron, WorldCom, or HealthSouth and follow the company after the fraud was discovered. All of them had a difficult time recovering from the fraud. Some companies do not recover but close their doors. So even though we classify financial statement fraud as for the company, that classification is only while the fraud goes undetected. Once detected, it becomes something against the company's very ability to survive.

Several other financial crimes do not fit conveniently into the schema here but also are noteworthy: arson for profit, planned bankruptcy, and fraudulent insurance claims.

Internal and External Fraud

Frauds referred to as corporate or management frauds can be categorized as *internal frauds* to distinguish them from *external fraud* (a category that includes frauds committed by vendors, suppliers, and contractors who might overbill, double bill, or substitute inferior goods). Customers may also play that game by feigning damage or destruction of goods in order to gain credits and allowances.

Corruption in the corporate sense may be practiced by outsiders against insiders, such as purchasing agents, for example. Corruption can also be committed by insiders against buyers from customer firms. Commercial bribery is often accompanied by manipulation of accounting records to cover up the payment and protect the recipients from the tax burden.

Management and Nonmanagement Fraud

Corporate or organizational fraud is not restricted to high-level executives. Organizational fraud touches senior, middle, and first-line management as well as nonmanagement employees. There may be some notable distinctions between the means used and the motivations and opportunities the work environment provides, but fraud is found at all levels of an organization—if one bothers to look for it. Even if internal controls are adequate by professional standards, one should not forget that top managers can override controls with impunity, and collusion is always possible as well. In addition, internal controls depend on human intervention and do not operate in a vacuum. Internal controls are measured by their effectiveness; they must be monitored constantly to ensure that they are functioning at the level designed and intended and not at some subordinate level due to ineffective use by the employee(s) responsible for executing the controls.

Specific Frauds and Categories

As stated earlier, fraud is intentional deception. Its forms are generally referred to as lying and cheating. But theft by guile (larceny by trick, false pretenses, and false tokens) and embezzlement sometimes are included as fraudulent acts. The element of deception is the common ground they all share. But *fraud* and *deception* are abstract terms. They go by many other names as well. For example, in alphabetical order, they might be called:

- Accounts payable fabrication
- Accounts receivable lapping
- Arson for profit
- Bank fraud
- Bankruptcy fraud
- Benefit claims fraud
- Bid rigging
- Breach of fiduciary duty
- Breach of trust
- Business opportunity fraud
- Bust out
- Cash lapping

- Check forgery
- Check kiting
- Check raising
- Collateral forgery
- Commercial bribery
- Computer fraud
- Concealment
- Consumer fraud
- Conversion
- Corporate fraud
- Corruption
- Counterfeiting
- Credit card fraud
- Defalcation
- Distortion of fact
- Double dealing
- Duplicity
- Electronic funds transfer fraud
- Embezzlement
- Expense account fraud
- False advertising
- False and misleading statement
- False claim
- False collateral
- False count
- False data
- False identity
- False information
- False ownership
- False pretenses
- False report
- False representation
- False suggestion
- False valuation
- False weights and measures
- Fictitious customer
- Fictitious employees
- Fictitious person
- Fictitious vendors
- Financial fraud
- Financial misrepresentation
- Forged documents
- Forged signatures
- Forgery
- Franchising fraud
- Fraud in execution
- Fraud in inducement
- Fraudulent concealment
- Fraudulent financial statement
- Fraudulent representation
- Industrial espionage
- Infringement of copyrights
- Infringement of patents
- Infringement of trademarks
- Input scam
- Insider trading
- Insurance fraud
- Inventory overstatement
- Inventory reclassification fraud
- Investor fraud
- Kickback
- Land fraud
- Lapping
- Larceny by trick
- Loan fraud
- Lying
- Mail fraud
- Management fraud
- Material misstatement
- Material omission
- Misapplication
- Misappropriation
- Misfeasance
- Misrepresentation
- Oil and gas scams
- Output scams
- Overbilling
- Overstatement of revenue

- Padding expenses
- Padding government contracts
- Payables fraud
- Payroll fraud
- Performance fraud
- Price fixing
- Pricing and extension fraud
- Procurement fraud
- Quality substitution
- Restraint of trade
- Sales overstatements
- Securities fraud
- Software piracy
- Stock fraud
- Subterfuge
- Swindling
- Tax fraud
- Tax shelter scam
- Technology theft
- Theft of computer time
- Theft of proprietary information
- Throughput scam
- Trade secret theft
- Understatement of costs
- Understatement of liabilities
- Undue influence
- Unjust enrichment
- Vendor short shipment
- Watered stock
- Wire fraud
- Wire transfer fraud

This list illustrates how difficult it is to create a taxonomy that can be applied to antifraud activities. There are several models for categorizing the numerous possible fraud schemes. Those models are discussed later and are presented together in Exhibit 2.8.

One way to view the pervasiveness and complexity of fraud might be to design a fraud typology by various groups involved (see Exhibits 2.2, 2.3, 2.4,

EXHIBIT 2.2 Fraud by Corporate Owners and Managers

Victim	Fraud Type
Customers	False advertising False weights False measures False labeling/branding Price fixing Quality substitution Cheap imitations Defective products
Stockholders	False financial statements False financial forecasts False representations
Creditors	False financial statements False financial forecasts False representations
Competitors	Predatory pricing Selling below cost

	Information piracy Infringement of patents/copyrights Commercial slander Libel Theft of trade secrets Corruption of employees
Bankers	Check kiting False application for credit False financial statements
Company/Employer	Expense account padding Performance fakery Overstating revenue Overstating assets Overstating profits Understating expenses Understating liabilities Theft of assets Embezzlement Conversion of assets Commercial bribery Insider trading Related-party transactions Alteration/destruction of records
Insurance carriers	Fraudulent loss claims Arson for profit False application for insurance
Government agencies	False claims Contract padding

and 2.5). An array of fraud characteristics may provide such insight. These lists of fraud perpetrators, victims, and fraud types summarize most frauds, but are far from exhaustive.

EXHIBIT 2.3 Fraud by Corporate Vendors, Suppliers, and Contractors

Victim	Fraud Type
Customers	Short shipment
Customers	Overbilling
Customers	Double billing
Customers	Substitution of inferior goods
Customers	Corruption of employees

Source: Adapted from Jack Bologna, *Forensic Accounting Review* (1984).

EXHIBIT 2.4 Fraud by Corporate Customers

Victim	Fraud Type
Vendors	Tag switching
Vendors	Shoplifting
Vendors	Fraudulent checks
Vendors	Fraudulent claims for refunds
Vendors	Fraudulent credit cards
Vendors	Fraudulent credit applications

Source: Adapted from Jack Bologna, *Forensic Accounting Review* (1984).

To summarize these typologies, a rough guide to classification appears as:

Insider Fraud against the Company

- Cash diversions, conversions, and thefts (front-end frauds)
- Check raising and signature or endorsement forgeries
- Receivables manipulations such as lapping and fake credit memos
- Payables manipulations such as raising or fabricating vendor invoices, benefit claims, and expense vouchers, and allowing vendors, suppliers, and contractors to overcharge
- Payroll manipulations such as adding nonexistent employees or altering time cards
- Inventory manipulations and diversions such as specious reclassifications of inventories to obsolete, damaged, or sample status, to create a cache from which thefts can be made more easily
- Favors and payments to employees by vendors, suppliers, and contractors

EXHIBIT 2.5 Fraud by Corporate Employees

Victim	Fraud Type
Employers	False employment applications
Employers	False benefit claims
Employers	False expense claims
Employers	Theft and pilferage
Employers	Performance fakery
Employers	Embezzlement
Employers	Corruption

Source: Adapted from Jack Bologna, *Forensic Accounting Review* (1984).

Outsider Fraud against the Company

- Vendor, supplier, and contractor frauds, such as short shipping goods, substituting goods of inferior quality, overbilling, double billing, billing but not delivering or delivering elsewhere
- Vendor, supplier, and contractor corruption of employees
- Customer corruption of employees

Frauds for the Company

- Smoothing profits ("cooking the books") through practices such as inflating sales, profits, and assets; understating expenses, losses, and liabilities; not recording or delaying recording of sales returns; early booking of sales; and inflating ending inventory
- Check kiting
- Price fixing
- Cheating customers by using devices such as short weights, counts, and measures; substituting cheaper materials; and false advertising
- Violating governmental regulations (e.g., Equal Employment Opportunity Act [EEO], Occupation Safety and Health Administration [OSHA], environmental securities, or tax violations standards)
- Corrupting customer personnel
- Political corruption
- Padding costs on government contracts

FRAUD TREE

The ACFE has developed a model for categorizing known frauds that it calls the *fraud tree*, which lists about 49 different individual fraud schemes grouped by categories and subcategories (see Exhibit 2.6). The three main categories are (1) fraudulent statements, (2) asset misappropriation, and (3) corruption.

Fraudulent statement fraud schemes typically are done by executives. They are the most expensive frauds but the least frequent ones. Executives who commit fraud are often driven by motives related to stock prices in the market (e.g., stock bonuses, pressure to keep stock prices trading high or higher, etc.). *Asset misappropriation* schemes typically are done by employees and include a large number of different schemes. They are the most common by occurrence (frequency) but the least costly per incident. Because the frauds tend to be immaterial, especially individual transactions, they are difficult for financial or

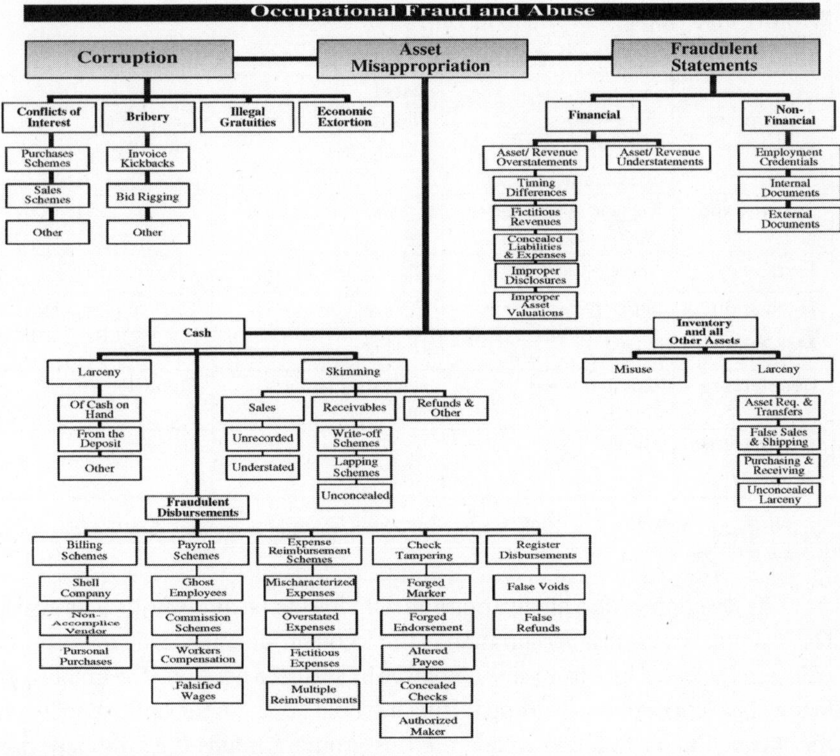

EXHIBIT 2.6 The ACFE Fraud Tree

Source: Report to the Nation, 1996. Institute of Certified Fraud Examiners. See the full report at www.acfe.com.

internal auditors to discover when conducting traditional financial and internal audits. *Corruption* involves a number of schemes, such as bribery and extortion, which usually involves a person inside the entity working with a person outside the entity, even though one might be considered an unwilling party. Corruption is therefore based on related-party transactions, and usually the relationship is not known (e.g., the Enron board of directors supposedly did not know that Fastow had a financial interest in the companies with which Enron was forming special purpose entities [SPEs]).

This book will use the ACFE Fraud Tree because of its ability to be applied to antifraud activities. To illustrate, look at some descriptors of fraud based on the category of fraud from the fraud tree and it is easy to see that they are unique among the groups (see Exhibit 2.7).

EXHIBIT 2.7 Application of Fraud Taxonomy/Fraud Tree

ACFE FRAUD TREE – CATEGORY CHARACTERISTICS			
Descriptors	**Fin-Fraud**	**Asset Misappropriation**	**Corruption**
Fraudster	Executive management	Employees	Two parties
Size of fraud	Largest: $1 million to $258 million	Smallest: $150,000	Medium: $538,000
Frequency	Least often: 10.6%	Most often: 91.5%	Medium: 30.8%
Motivation	Stock prices, bonuses	Personal pressures	Challenge, business
Materiality	Likely	Unlikely	Depends
Benefactors	Company and fraudster	Fraudster (against co.)	Fraudster
Size of victim company	Large	Small	Depends

Source: Report to the Nation, 2008. Institute of Certified Fraud Examiners. See the full report at www.acfe.com.

The descriptors also allow antifraud activities to be more easily addressed. For instance, asset misappropriation is the fraud group most likely to occur. It will be perpetrated by a front-line employee in a trusted position. The amount of loss will be less than other groups. Thus it would be best if the entity employed the internal audit function to address this group of frauds (i.e., they are not likely to be material, so do not rely falsely on external audit to detect them, they are likely to occur so do not ignore them, and review business insurance to assure recovery of losses).

The opposite would be true of financial statement fraud. It is more likely to be material and so audit committees should place an emphasis on external auditors detecting financial statement frauds. Whatever is motivating executives to commit financial statement fraud, stock prices usually become the center of attention. If it is bonuses, it usually is stock options and therefore the fraudster may need to cook the books to get the bonus (options), which is probably associated with the stock market or analysts' earnings per share (EPS) predictions. Once the executive accumulates large blocks of shares of stock, he then needs to continue to keep the stock price up so he will have value for that stock portfolio.

Since corruption deals with at least two parties, and since it relies on a related party, then attacking corruption schemes would focus on these factors. Look for related-party transactions, especially where the relationship was hidden. Have accountability for bids, contracts, and other transactions that are subject to influence or fraud (e.g., bid rigging, kickbacks, bribery, etc.).

EXHIBIT 2.8 Summary of Models/Typologies/Taxonomies

Source	Fraud Taxonomy
Bologna and Lindquist [2e]	Insider fraud against the company Outsider fraud against the company Frauds for the company
KPMG	Employee fraud Consumer fraud Vendor-related fraud Computer crime Misconduct Medical/insurance fraud Financial reporting fraud
Albrecht and Albrecht	Employee embezzlement Management fraud Investment scams Vendor fraud Customer fraud Miscellaneous fraud
ACFE	Fraudulent statement fraud Asset misappropriation Corruption

Other notable fraud taxonomies exist. KPMG used a different taxonomy in its fraud surveys. Albrecht and Albrecht use another one in their book on fraud.[18] Exhibit 2.8 summarizes these major taxonomies.

EVOLUTION OF A TYPICAL FRAUD

Most frauds follow a similar pattern in the life cycle of the processes or steps. There are differences to consider depending on the fraud. For example, a skimming fraud scheme is "off the books" and therefore requires no real concealment of the fraud. Likewise, the motivation for financial statement frauds is usually very different from that of asset misappropriation frauds. A general evolution of a typical fraud follows.

Step	Description	Explanation
1	Motivation (pressure, incentive)	Financial need, greed, ego, revenge, psychosis
2	Opportunity	Knowledge and opportunity to commit the fraud. Fraudster holds a

		position of trust, has tenure, and/or access to records or assets. Control weaknesses, lack of audit trail, lack of segregation of duties, no internal audit function, weak culture
3	Rationalization	Mentally juxtapose the crime against personal code of ethics to formulate intent without self-incrimination; e.g., "just borrowing the money," entitlement
4	Commit the fraud	Execute a particular scheme, usually the fraud escalates as time goes by and fraud goes undetected—larger amounts or add more schemes
5	Convert asset to cash	If necessary (not necessary if already cash), an official check is same as cash, sell inventory at reduced prices in a "black market"-type venue; financial statement fraud leads to stock options, which leads to cash out of stock
6	Conceal the crime	If necessary (not necessary if no one looking! Or if off-the-books fraud), false refunds/credits, use large volume accounts, rely on apathy, alter documents, destroy documents
7	Red flags	In the process of commit, convert, and conceal, fingerprints are left that are known as "red flags"; behavioral red flags could be a lifestyle change—true even for off-the-

		books frauds; transactional red flags are missing data or anomalies (e.g., unfavorable variances, unusual increases)
8	Suspicion or discovery	Tip, discovery of variance or anomaly including a sufficient analysis, discrepancies, internal controls, internal audit, external audit, accident
9	Predication determined	Before a fraud investigation can begin, predication has to be determined to exist; a fraud professional believes a fraud has occurred, is occurring, or will occur because of circumstances
10	Fraud theory	Unless the specific fraud is known, the fraud theory approach helps to identify the most likely schemes and how they are being perpetrated
11	Fraud investigation	Identify and gather forensic evidence, loss of assets confirmed, loss documented, interrogations performed, nonfinancial evidence acquired
12	Write a report	Almost all fraud investigations require a report at its conclusion, whether to victim's management, insurance company, or court officials/lawyers

(Continued)

13a	Disposition: Termination	Most often, the victim company extricates itself from the fraudster employee and hopes that ends the episode, employee terminated for cause, where possible insurance claim is filed to recover some or all of the losses
13b	Disposition: Prosecution	Either criminal or civil prosecution is sought by the victim entity, prosecuting entities may not even take the case, and may not successfully prosecute the case
14	Trial	Presentation of facts and testimony before trier of fact, use of expert witness, presentation of forensic evidence

Some of these items are covered in this chapter, at least by way of introduction to basic concepts. The remainder of the book focuses on this list, usually in the sequence listed.

SUMMARY

An understanding of the fraud principles is the foundation to any antifraud activity, whether it is developing a fraud policy, investigating a fraud, or designing antifraud controls. This understanding is particularly critical because some of the principles are counterintuitive to the naïve antifraud stakeholder. Therefore it is vitally important to know all one can about the fraud triangle, fraud tree, scope of fraud (it *can* happen here), profile of a fraudster, and other basic principles.

NOTES

1. Michigan Criminal Law, Chapter 86, Sec. 1529.
2. Joseph T. Wells, *Occupational Fraud and Abuse* (Austin, TX: ACFE, 1997).
3. *Southern Development Co. v. Silva,* 125 U.S. 247, 8 S.C. Rep. 881, 31 L. Ed. (1887).
4. The name of this tactic is attributed to forensic accountant Ralph Summerford of Forensic Strategic Solutions in Birmingham, AL.
5. Edwin H. Sutherland, *White-Collar Crime* (New York: Dryden Press, 1949), p. 234; Donald L. Cressey, *Other People's Money* (New York: Free Press, 1949), p. 30; Norman Jaspan and Hillel Black, *The Thief in the White Collar* (Philadelphia: Lippincott, 1960), p. 37; and Frank E. Hartung, *Crime, Law, and Society* (Detroit: Wayne State University Press, 1965), pp. 125–136.
6. Sutherland, *White-Collar Crime.*
7. Cressey, *Other People's Money.*
8. Jaspan and Black, *The Thief in the White Collar.*
9. Hartung, *Crime, Law, and Society.*
10. Association of Certified Fraud Examiners (ACFE), *Report to the Nation* (RTTN), 2008.
11. ACFE, *Report to the Nation,* 1996, 2002, 2004, 2006, and 2008.
12. Committee of Sponsoring Organizations (COSO), *Landmark Study on Fraud in Financial Reporting,* 1998.
13. KPMG, *Fraud Survey,* 1994, 1998, 2003, and 2009.
14. W. S. Albrecht, Gerald W. Wernz and Timothy L. Williams, *Fraud: Bringing Light to the Dark Side of Business* (New York: Irwin Professional Pub., 1994).
15. Gwynn Nettler, *Lying, Cheating, and Stealing* (Cincinnati: Anderson Publishing, 1982).
16. ACFE, *Report to the Nation,* 2008.
17. James A. Hall and Tommie Singleton, *IT Auditing & Assurance* (New York: Southwestern, 2004).
18. W. S. Albrecht and C. Albrecht, *Fraud Examination and Prevention* (New York: Thomson/Southwestern, 2004).

CHAPTER THREE

Fraud Schemes

INTRODUCTION

In order to prevent fraud, detect fraud, or investigate fraud, one needs to understand fraud schemes as much as possible. In Chapter 2, various classifications were presented to classify frauds. The authors believe the best classification (taxonomy) for understanding fraud schemes is the one used by the Association of Certified Fraud Examiners (ACFE). There are several reasons for this choice.

First, the ACFE is emerging as the primary antifraud organization. Its only purpose is the antifraud profession, whereas the American Institute of Certified Public Accountants (AICPA), Institute of Internal Auditors (IIA), and Information Systems Audit and Control Association (ISACA) have different primary objectives. Other groups have a similar goal, but none has the sole purpose of fighting fraud. As such, the ACFE's model serves as the de facto standard for the antifraud profession.

Second, the ACFE taxonomy has been stable over time. There are 49 individual fraud schemes classified in the ACFE fraud tree. That number has not changed over the years. Fraudsters find different or even new ways to carry out frauds, but most often it is one of the old-fashioned fraud schemes used by perpetrators (e.g., the Internet and other technologies open up new ways to perpetrate some of the exsisting frauds and not actually creating new schemes).

Third, the ACFE taxonomy has a limited number of schemes. Beyond the number, about 20 of the 49 schemes make up over 80 percent of all the frauds committed. Thus, the study of the most common fraud schemes enables a fraud auditor or forensic accountant to detect or prevent the vast majority of potential fraud schemes. While this trait is not unique to the ACFE taxonomy, it is worth pointing out for purposes of understanding the ongoing analysis of fraud schemes.

Fourth, the scheme categories are relatively distinctive in the ACFE fraud tree, especially when compared to the other taxonomies. Many classifications are categorized by vendor, customer, employee, and consumer. Yet some frauds involve both a vendor and an employee (e.g., kickbacks), so there is an overlap in classifying a single fraud.

Last, the ACFE model has understandable, usable, and unique characteristics for its three major categories that make it easy to apply to fraud audits, investigations, fraud prevention programs, and so on (see Exhibit 3.1). These unique characteristics and descriptors assist in customizing and tailoring fraud audits or controls for the antifraud environment.

EXHIBIT 3.1 ACFE Fraud Tree: Unique Characteristics of Each Category

Descriptors	Corruption	Asset Misappropriation	Fraudulent Statements
Fraudster	Two parties	Employees	Executive management
Size of the fraud	Medium: $250,000	Smallest: $93,000	Largest: $1 million to $ 258 million
Frequency of fraud	Medium: 30%	Most often: 92.7%	Least often: 7.9%
Motivation	Challenge, business	Personal pressures	Stock prices, bonuses
Materiality	Depends	Unlikely	Likely
Benefactors	Fraudster	Fraudster (against company)	Company and fraudster
Size of victim company	Depends	Small	Large

ACFE FRAUD TREE

The ACFE model for categorizing known frauds is referred to as the fraud tree (see Exhibit 3.2). It categorizes the individual fraud schemes into a classification model of categories, subcategories, and microcategories. The three main (top-level) categories are: (1) corruption fraud, (2) asset misappropriation fraud, and (3) financial statement fraud. These major categories are unique in their characteristics (see Exhibit 3.1). That is, the characteristics that describe or define a financial statement fraud are very different from those that describe an asset misappropriation, when using the same descriptors. Why is that important? A thorough knowledge of the

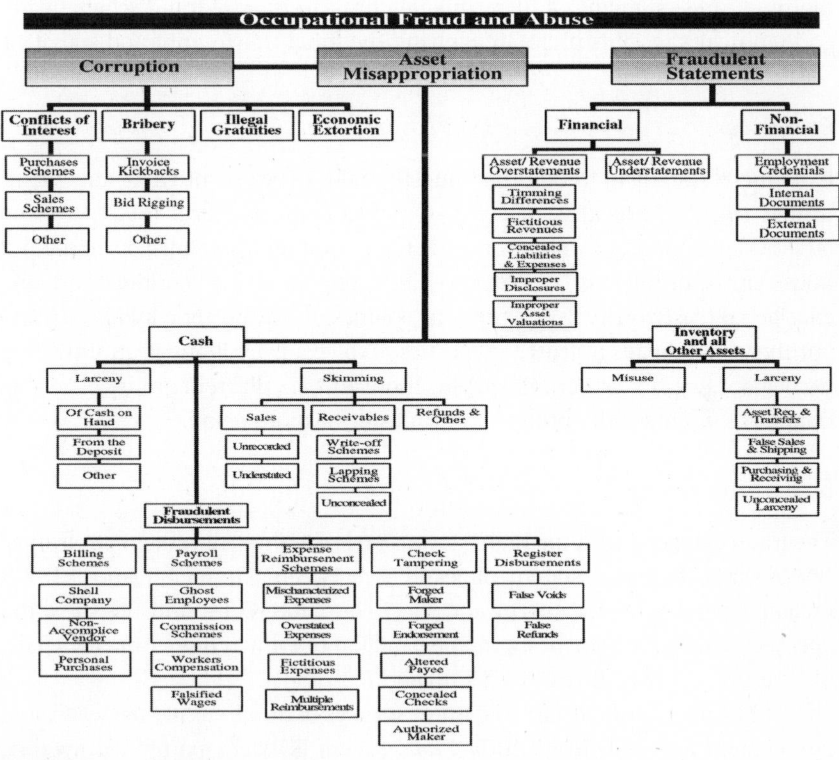

EXHIBIT 3.2 ACFE Fraud Tree

Source: Report to the Nation, 1996. Institute of Certified Fraud Examiners. See the full report at www.cfenet.com.

categories and their specific characteristics is crucial in the success of designing and conducting fraud audits as well as fraud prevention and detection programs.

The ACFE *Report to the Nation* (RTTN) has been providing statistics on frauds periodically since 1996. The reports continue to relay distinctive attributes of fraud schemes. The 2008 RTTN will be used in providing statistics for the analysis of descriptors in the fraud tree.[1] It should be noted that, while these statistics are an important tool to understand and to consider, they are not a panacea for preventing or detecting fraud.

Scheme Category Characteristics

Each of the three primary branches of the fraud tree have characteristics that when examined prove to be unique when compared to the other two. A thorough understanding of these unique characteristics of fraud scheme categories provides insights useful in applying the fraud tree in antifraud activities.

Fraudster

In financial statement frauds, the fraudster tends to be executive management, usually the chief executive officer (CEO), chief financial officer (CFO), or some other C-level manager. The fraudster who commits asset misappropriation, however, is usually an employee—albeit one in a key position and one considered trustworthy. In corruption schemes, the fraudster could be anyone but there are always at least two parties involved, even if one is an unwilling participant (e.g., extortion). Obviously, these are very different groups of people. Chapter 2 discusses the profile of a fraudster in more detail.

Size of the Fraud

The fraud category with the highest average loss is financial statement frauds. The average financial statement fraud is between $1 million and $257.9 million depending on the survey and year. The 2008 RTTN statistics show the average financial statement fraud at $2 million but it was higher in years past. (In the 2002 RTTN, it was $4.25 million.)

KPMG also conducts periodic fraud surveys of hundreds of businesses and government agencies. In its 2003 *Fraud Survey*, KPMG reported the average financial statement fraud was $257.9 million.[2] By comparison, the average fraud in the asset misappropriation category of the 2008 RTTN was only $150,000. The average corruption fraud was $250,000.

Frequency of Fraud

The category with the most frequent *occurrences* of fraud is asset misappropriation. Over 92 percent of all frauds are classified in this category. Financial frauds, by comparison, made up only 7.9 percent of all frauds by occurrence. Corruption made up 30.1 percent of frauds. The fact that these percentages add up to more than 100 percent is noteworthy. If a fraudster manages to hide a fraud for some period of time, it is not unusual to add another fraud to the nefarious affairs. Sometimes bold fraudsters start their crime with more than one type of fraud. Either way, it should be noted that some fraudsters not only occasionally conduct more than one fraud, but those frauds cross categories.

Motivation

In Chapter 2, there is a list of known motivations: psychotic, economic, egocentric, ideological, and emotional. These motivations tend to be associated with only one or two of these categories. Certain motivators are associated with financial statement frauds, and different motivators tend to be associated with asset misappropriation frauds. Such associations are extremely valuable in conducting fraud audits and fraud investigations, and they are *very* valuable in designing antifraud programs for management or the board.

Financial statement frauds tend to be motivated by *egocentric* motives. They also tend to be motivated by stock prices, directly or indirectly. For example, the first financial fraud recorded in accounting history was the South Sea Bubble scandal in England around 1720. This scandal is discussed in more detail in Chapter 1. The motive behind the fictitious profits was the market price of its stock. Three hundred years later, the motive behind financial statement fraud is basically unchanged, all the way up to and including Enron, WorldCom, and others of the last decade. Stock option bonuses are a double motive: First keep the stock price up to get the bonus, and second get and keep the stock price high so the options, or existing stock held, will be as valuable as possible. Performance bonuses, pressure from stockholders, and other pressures are indirectly linked back to stock price as well.

Asset misappropriation frauds, however, are usually motivated by *economic* pressures. White-collar crime researcher Donald Cressey called this type of motivation an *unshareable need*. For example, high debt, such as large balances on credit cards, and an inability to make further payments on debt bring considerable economic pressure. This pressure could also be driven by a gambling, drug, or alcohol habit whose fuel (cash) needs replenishing.

Fraudsters sometimes persuade themselves to commit an asset misappropriation fraud because of *emotional* motives, such as the challenge to beat the system or being disgruntled with management or the company.

Corruption frauds could be motivated by the same kinds of things as asset misappropriation is. However, corruption frauds often are driven by business motives (*economic*), such as the bribery scheme to gain access to otherwise inaccessible markets. Political motives can also be associated with corruption frauds.

Materiality

The fraud categories are also different in the area of materiality. Financial frauds often will be considered material to the organization. They are invariably in the millions, and occasionally billions of dollars (e.g., Enron and WorldCom). Asset misappropriation, however, is *most likely to be immaterial to the financial statements*. Corruption could be material, especially for frauds above the average cost of corruption frauds, which is $250,000. It could also be immaterial, depending on the size of the organization.

Benefactors

Financial statement frauds are perpetrated on behalf of the company, although usually because such frauds benefits the fraudster. In Chapter 2, this type of fraud is referred to as *frauds for the company*. Asset misappropriation and corruption, on the contrary, benefit the fraudster and are classified in Chapter 2 as *insider fraud against the company*. Corruption can also benefit the company in some schemes, such as some briberies.

Size of Victim Company

Because financial statement fraud is usually motivated by stock prices or something directly related to stock prices, the companies victimized by financial statement fraud tend to be publicly traded ones, which tend to be larger companies. Though such companies are more complex and difficult to control, they also tend to have more resources to apply to internal controls, internal audit, and antifraud programs. These companies also tend to be subject to other regulations, which generally lead to more controlled environments, and thus have a smaller risk associated with asset misappropriations, which are intrinsically harder to control.

EXHIBIT 3.3 Average Cost of Fraud per Employee

Number of Employees[a]	Average Fraud	Fraud Amount ($)/ Employee
<100	$200,000	$4,000.00
100–999	$176,000	$320.00
1,000–9,999	$116,000	$21.00
10,000+	$147,000	$13.36

[a]For average number of employees, we took the mean of the size, except for 10,000+, where we used 11,000.

The opposite is true regarding asset misappropriation and victim organizations. Because organizations affected by this kind of fraud tend to be small, they have either scarce resources to attend to prevention and detection of fraud or simply are unable to focus on it (do not care, are unaware of the risks, etc.). Often a small company has only one accountant and cannot justify proper segregation of duties. "An insufficient or absent segregation of duties is almost always associated with asset misappropriation schemes" (ACFE 2004 RTTN).

The ACFE 2008 RTTN confirms this supposition. Organizations were divided into sizes: 1 to 99, 100 to 999, 1,000 to 9,999, and 10,000 or more employees. The largest average fraud was found in the smallest size entity and averaged $200,000 per fraud. If these figures were used as a ratio of average fraud cost per average number of employees, the smallest organizations have a staggeringly higher ratio than the others, about 13 times higher than the second highest ratio! See Exhibit 3.3 for a comparison.

Fraud Tree and Who Audits Whom

Using Exhibit 3.1 and the preceding discussion, it seems intuitive as to which group of auditors should be considered primarily responsible for which types of frauds. This section discusses this issue in generalities, or what appears to be the natural association of each category. By no means are these associations absolute. For example, an effective antifraud program for a large publicly traded company would most likely include all three major fraud scheme categories and most likely be charged to the internal audit function by the audit committee.

Financial Statement Fraud: Financial Auditors The auditor group most likely to be most responsible for financial statement fraud is financial auditors. That is true for at least three reasons.

First, the amount of a financial statement fraud in total tends to lead to a material misstatement of the financial reports. The goal of financial audits is to ensure that the financial statements fairly present the financial health of an entity in all material respects. Financial audit procedures, therefore, are designed to detect material misstatements. And financial statement frauds often are material with respect to the financial reports. In addition, financial auditors must comply with SAS 99, *Consideration of Fraud in the Financial Statement Audit*, and internal control procedures that are aimed toward detecting material misstatements including those due to fraud. Likewise, because asset misappropriation and corruption tend to be immaterial, it is unrealistic to expect financial auditors to detect them. That caveat is compounded by the fact fraud audits are significantly different from financial audits. According to the ACFE 2008 RTTN, 9.1 percent of frauds are detected by financial auditors. The 2003 KMPG *Fraud Survey* reports less than 11 percent of frauds were detected by financial auditors, and that survey was done by a financial audit firm.

Second, financial statement audits are suited to detecting financial statement fraud. Procedures to detect fraud are very different from procedures used in financial audits to detect material misstatements, particularly in that financial audits often use statistical theory based on materiality and not fraud risk. Some fraud-specific procedures are required, namely SAS No. 99 procedures. However, since financial audit procedures are designed to detect material misstatements, and since the vast majority of financial statement frauds are material, and since financial audits are by nature concerned with financial statements, then financial auditors are naturally a prime defense against financial statement frauds.

Third, because executive management is involved with financial statement fraud, other parties internal to the company (such as other management, accounting, or the internal auditors) can be fooled or pressured into complicity. Management can override controls, but executive management can *really* override controls. The CFO can simply direct subordinates to manipulate the books. Executive management can use various other advantages in their positions to cajole internal auditors or CFOs into becoming coconspirators.

Internal auditors can be fooled or circumvented. For instance, Cynthia Cooper (chief audit executive for WorldCom) tells how she was locked out of the corporate computers and circumvented, with reports and transactions being generated clandestinely without her ability to see, review, or question them. She says she came back to work late at night and finally was able to gather evidence of the fraud. Other internal auditors from some of the most recent and infamous financial scandals have confessed privately to the authors that they were deliberately kept away from the real set of books, activities, and knowledge that would have disclosed the fraud, and it was the CEO or CFO who was behind that effort. A fraudster executive who is perpetrating a financial statement fraud can frustrate the best-intentioned internal auditor. But the independent external auditor should be in a better position to detect the financial statement fraud, especially if it is material.

Asset Misappropriation: Internal Auditors The auditor group most likely to be most responsible for asset misappropriation fraud is internal auditors. As stated, because asset misappropriation schemes tend to be immaterial, especially individual transactions, they are difficult for financial auditors to discover while doing traditional financial audits. They are also difficult for internal auditors to detect during *traditional* internal audits, for the same reason.

However, it is more reasonable to expect internal auditors to develop and execute antifraud programs and fraud audits than financial auditors. Effective antifraud programs are a necessity in ongoing programs. The internal audit function is better suited to oversee a continuous antifraud program, mostly because financial audit procedures are not designed to detect frauds, and internal audit can design programs and procedures to detect frauds. Those antifraud programs are usually initiated and overseen by either the audit committee or the CEO/CFO or both. Therefore, it makes sense for the internal auditor to execute those programs and report back to the audit committee, the board, or executive management.

Corruption: Possibly Either Internal or Financial Auditors Corruption fraud losses tend to be larger than asset misappropriation. If it becomes material, then clearly the financial auditors should have some responsibility, especially under SAS No. 99. These frauds sometimes involve breaking laws and violating regulations (e.g., bribery, kickbacks on government contracts, and extortion). Because of the legal aspect of certain corruption schemes, either compliance audits by an internal auditor—if the fraud is material—or financial audits by external auditors could be involved.

The primary responsibility for detecting corruption fraud lies with the external auditor and sometimes with the internal auditor. Most likely, the tasks and functions of the internal auditors involved with antifraud programs or fraud audits will be concerned primarily with asset misappropriation, but they may be interested in, or be charged with corruption and financial statement fraud, in particular if the program is initiated by the audit committee.

FINANCIAL STATEMENT SCHEMES

The category of financial statement schemes is broken down into two subcategories: financial and nonfinancial. The latter is fairly insignificant in terms of frequency, so this discussion is limited to the financial schemes. Six schemes are addressed in SAS No. 99, *Consideration of Fraud in a Financial Statement Audit*, as well. Most of the financial statement scandals involve some kind of revenue manipulation scheme, which is why SAS No. 99 stresses that financial auditors should *assume* this kind of fraud may be occurring in the client's books and deliberately look for this type of fraud *throughout* the audit process.

The most common financial statement fraud scheme is related to revenue overstatement. In some cases, companies simply invent revenues. (A credit to revenue and debit to accounts receivable produces miracles on the balance sheet and income statement.) There are five schemes under this subcategory in the fraud tree.

Timing Differences (Improper Treatment of Sales)

There are a variety of ways to perpetrate a timing differences scheme to exaggerate revenues for the current fiscal period. One way is to push excess inventory to salespeople or consignment whereupon the inventory is treated as a sale, knowing full well that much of it will be returned—but in a subsequent period. This method is known as channel stuffing. Sales also can be booked in other violations of generally accepted accounting principles (GAAP) (e.g., early revenue recognition). For instance, a three-year contract to provide services across the period can all be booked as revenue in the current year to inflate profits for the next set of financials, at the expense of future financials, and obviously not in compliance with GAAP and the matching principle.

Enron used a similar method in its special purpose entities (SPEs) to account for all of the revenue from long-term agreements in the current year. In another fraud, the CFO for a bankrupt company (as a result of a financial statement fraud) admitted in his deposition that many sales were booked before they were actually consummated. His reason: "If you knew in your heart it was a sale, then we booked it."

Fictitious Revenues

Fictitious revenues are created simply by recording sales that never occurred. They can involve real or fake customers. The end result is an increase in revenues and profits, and usually assets (the other side of the fictitious accounting entry).

For example, the infamous Equity Funding scandal used a fictitious revenues scheme to inflate both revenues and accounts receivable. Equity Funding was an insurance company, to be specific, a reinsurer. To create fictitious revenues, the CEO simply created phony insurance policies. After seven years, the fraud was finally exposed in 1973 by a recently fired and disgruntled employee. At that time, $2 billion of the $3 billion in receivables was phony.

Concealed Liabilities (Improper Recording of Liabilities)

One way to perpetrate this fraud scheme is to simply postpone the recording of liabilities in the twelfth month of the fiscal year so that the current year will have less expenses, and record that liability in the first month of the next fiscal year. It is precisely because of this possibility that financial auditors perform subsequent-period substantive tests—looking for invoices that are dated the year under audit but posted in the first month of the subsequent year.

Another way to commit this fraud is to move those liabilities somewhere else. If the company is large and has subsidiaries, this objective can be accomplished by moving the liability to a subsidiary, especially if that company is either not audited or audited by a different audit firm (an intentional decision to hide the fraud). This scheme probably is used often by companies. Our assumption is based on the fact that the shifting of liabilities is difficult to detect in audits. However, if it is occurring, there should be changes in certain ratios: earnings per share (EPS), debt/equity, and so on.

The fraudsters at Parmalat used this method to hide liabilities and perpetrate a financial statement fraud of more than $1.3 billion, moving liabilities to subsidiaries in the Caribbean, far from corporate headquarters in Italy, and to companies audited by a different financial audit firm. The executives at

Parmalat also invented assets and forged documents to back up entries for them, which illustrates the complexity of many frauds: The fraudster begins perhaps with a single fraud scheme but sometimes expands to multiple schemes. Adelphia used the same fraud method, moving liabilities to off-balance-sheet affiliates.

Finally, a simple failure to record liabilities accomplishes the same purpose. Without the liability, there is no additional expense, no reduction in assets, or no decrease in equity that normally occurs.

Improper Disclosures

One principle of fraud is that it is always clandestine. The fraudster will attempt to cover up for frauds in the books. (This is not necessary for off-the-book schemes.) This cover-up extends to disclosures.

While Enron was technically GAAP compliant in disclosing SPEs in the financial statements and annual report, it was fraudulent in handling the associated revenues, and it was clandestine in its disclosures. Enron did make disclosures regarding the SPEs, as required, but they were so obfuscated that even financial experts could not read them and understand exactly the financial ramifications of those SPEs, which is what was intended. Also, Andrew Fastow, CFO, reportedly hid his association with the SPEs from the board to further obfuscate their disclosure. Other methods include omission in disclosures of liability, significant events, and management fraud. An inadequate disclosure can be a way to hide evidence of a fraud.

Improper Asset Valuation

By inflating the amounts of assets (commonly receivables, inventory, and long-lived assets), capitalizing expenses, or deflating contra accounts (allowance for doubtful accounts, deprecation, amortization, etc.), the financials will show a higher than truthful equity and profit. HealthSouth exaggerated assets balances to cover insufficient profits over a period of years. A transaction that debits an asset and credits an equity or revenue account "magically" creates profits.

In the case of the WorldCom financial statement fraud, leases of telephone lines were clearly an expense. Yet WorldCom's CEO convinced accountants internally and financial auditors externally to treat them as assets. Thus by moving millions of dollars of expenses to the balance sheet, the income statement suddenly looked much better.

CORRUPTION SCHEMES

According to the ACFE 2008 RTTN, corruption schemes make up 27.4 percent of all frauds and the average loss was $375,000.[3] Corruption includes economic distortion, illegal gratuities, conflicts of interest, and bribery. Bribery includes three microcategories: kickbacks, bid rigging, and other. Kickbacks are undisclosed payments made by vendors to employees of purchasing companies to enlist their influence in gaining business with the entity, or in allowing the vendor to overbill. Bid rigging occurs when an employee fraudulently assists a vendor in winning a contact involving the competitive bidding process.

Corruption schemes are characterized by someone on the inside (i.e., employee of victim company) working with someone on the outside. This related-party activity is usually kept hidden from the management and auditors. Or if approval is sought and obtained, the fraudster will originally conduct business ethically but as time goes by and the approval is not reviewed or renewed, the fraudster will begin to get involved with a kickback or other corruption scheme. Thus a key to detecting corruption schemes is to look for undisclosed or unknown related-party transactions, specifically an undisclosed relationship between an employee inside the entity and someone or some entity outside the entity, which is doing business with the object entity.

Conflicts of Interest

A conflict of interest occurs when an employee, manager, or executive has an undisclosed economic or personal interest in a transaction that adversely affects the company. Conflicts of interest include three microcategories: purchases schemes, sales schemes, and other schemes. The difference between conflict of interest and other corruption frauds is the fact that fraudsters exert their influence (e.g., approving invoices or bills) because of their personal interest rather than because of a bribe or kickback.

Bribery

Bribery can be defined as the offering, giving, receiving, or soliciting anything of value to influence an official act or business decision. Bribery has been around for centuries. It is probably most often associated with politics. The famous Francis Bacon of England was promoted to the highest position in the king's court, Lord Chancellor, in 1618. A British landowner brought charges of bribery against Lord Bacon, and the subsequent investigation found an abundance of evidence that he had been taking bribes often to manipulate the judgments of cases. Bacon had to resign his office.

In the United States, President Warren G. Harding's administration was damaged by the Teapot Dome Scandal. In it, Secretary of Interior Albert Falls took bribes to allow private drilling of government oil fields and several other similar bribery schemes. But bribery is also prevalent in the business world when contracts and arrangements are involved.

Illegal Gratuities

Illegal gratuities are similar to bribes, but with illegal gratuities there is not necessarily intent to influence a business decision. For instance, a person of influence could be given an expensive gift, free vacation, and so on for her influence in a negotiation or business deal, but the gift is made *after* the deal is over. Because it is afterward, it is hard to prove. But accepting a gift is usually illegal in most political entities and is prohibited in large businesses, above some small minimal value.

Economic Extortion

Basically, economic extortion is the opposite of a bribery fraud. Instead of a vendor offering a bribe, the employee demands payment from a vendor in order to favor the vendor.

ASSET MISAPPROPRIATION SCHEMES

A clear definition of asset misappropriation is helpful in recognizing this type of fraud. The term *asset misappropriation* can be difficult to articulate; fundamentally, asset misappropriation is converting legitimate asset possession or influence into illegitimate personal gain. The definitions that follow further expound the meaning of asset misappropriation as used in this book.

Black's Law Dictionary defines *misappropriation* this way:

> The act of misappropriating or turning to a wrongful purpose; wrong appropriation, a term that does not necessarily mean peculation,

> although it may mean that. The term may also embrace the taking and using of another's property for sole purpose of capitalizing unfairly on good will and reputation of property owner.[4]

The definition in *Webster's Dictionary* is a little different, and more in line with the use of the term in this book:

> to appropriate wrongly (as by theft or embezzlement).[5]

Joe Wells defines misappropriation in this way:

> [Misappropriation] includes more than theft or embezzlement. It involves the misuse of any company asset for personal gain.[6]

By far, the most common frauds are asset misappropriations per the 2008 RTTN (88.7 percent of all frauds involve asset misappropriation). There are two subcategories (*Cash* and *Inventory and All Other Assets*), five microcategories (see Exhibit 3.2), 5 categories under the microcategory *Fraudulent Disbursements*, and 18 different schemes under them. Altogether, a total of 32 different individual fraud schemes are contained in this major category.

Cash

Cash schemes involve the taking of cash from one's employer. Cash schemes dominate the asset misappropriations cases, according to the statistics from the ACFE. In its 2008 RTTN, 85 percent of all asset misappropriation frauds involved the misappropriation of cash.

Cash schemes, in the ACFE fraud tree, are divided into three groups: larceny, fraudulent disbursements, and skimming.

Larceny

Joe Wells defines cash larceny as the intentional taking of an employer's cash (currency and checks) without the consent and against the will of the employer.[7] Said differently, cash larceny is the outright stealing of cash. Because the cash stolen by an employee in a cash larceny scheme has already been recorded in the accounting system, the absence of the cash ought to be more easily detectable than a skimming scheme, which is "off the books." For an employee to commit a cash larceny fraud, he or she must have been placed in a position in direct contact with cash somewhere along the company's cash path—cash coming in and cash going out. That also means the employee was considered trustworthy.

Cash larceny schemes fall into three groups: cash on hand, from the deposit, and other. According to the ACFE 2008 RTTN, 10.3 percent of all frauds are cash larceny, and the average loss was $75,000.

Fraudulent Disbursements

Fraudulent disbursement schemes are those in which a distribution of funds is made from some company account in what appears to be a normal manner but is actually fraudulent. The method for obtaining the funds may be the forging of a check, the submission of a false invoice, the doctoring of a time card, and so on. The key difference between fraudulent disbursement schemes and cash larceny schemes is in the former, the money is moved from the company in what appears to be a legitimate disbursement of funds.

Fraudulent disbursement schemes fall into five groups: billing, payroll, expense reimbursement, check tampering, and register disbursement. According to the ACFE 2008 RTTN, 63.9 percent of all frauds are fraudulent disbursements. The average loss in a fraudulent disbursement scheme was about $100,000. These frauds occur much more often than other types of cash misappropriation.

Billing Schemes Billing schemes use the company's accounting system to steal funds by submitting bogus claims in one form or another. If a vendor is on the authorized vendor list, and if an invoice has been approved by the proper person, the system will take care of the rest—it will generate and/or send a check for the perpetrator to intercept and cash. The same is true of payroll checks and employees. Billing schemes include shell vendor schemes (phony vendor), nonaccomplice vendor schemes, and personal purchases schemes.

According to the ACFE 2008 RTTN, 23.9 percent of all frauds are billing schemes. The average cost of a billing scheme was $100,000.

Shell Company Schemes A shell company scheme involves using a fictitious company, created for the sole purpose of committing a fraud, to generate checks from the company's resources that will be directed to the culprit, to her benefit. Usually the fictitious company has a fabricated name, and often the address is a post office box. Sometimes the culprit will use a derivation of a legitimate vendor's name to confuse those who might see the checks or the fictitious vendor's name. For example, if ABC Corporation was a legitimate vendor, the fraudster might use ABC Co. as the fictitious vendor's name.

A description of the shell company process follows. The fictitious vendor must be added to the authorized vendor list, an invoice must be approved, a check must be written to the shell vendor, and the check must be intercepted by the fraudster or an accomplice. (This could be as simple as mailing it to the fraudster's post office box.)

Often the perpetrator is in a control position with the authority to add a vendor. Also, often the perpetrator is in a position to approve the phony invoice. Or the perpetrator could be depending on "rubber stamping" or inattention to approval review. The perpetrator often also sets up a bank account in the name of the fictitious vendor, which is fairly easy to do. A check is processed and mailed, probably to a post office box. The perpetrator intercepts or receives the check, deposits it into the bank account, and writes checks out to whoever desired.

Pass-Through Schemes This scheme is a version of the shell vendor scheme in which the perpetrator sets up a company, but in this scheme, he actually buys products through the pass-through vendor. The perpetrator sells the goods to his employer, but at an inflated price. Paying excessive prices for goods is possible because the perpetrator is in a position to approve invoices or vendors for purchases. By marking up the prices to exorbitant levels, the perpetrator can siphon off funds from his or her employer to the pseudo vendor.

Nonaccomplice Vendor Schemes Unlike the previous two vendor schemes, the nonaccomplice vendor scheme involves a legitimate vendor. However, the vendor is not an accomplice but rather an innocent party being used by the perpetrator. The perpetrator could bill or overbill the company using the vendor's invoices, and either intercept the check for the invoice or send the check to the vendor and ask for a refund from the vendor and intercept that check. Another version of the scheme involves the perpetrator deliberately ordering merchandise not needed, returning the merchandise for credit to a legitimate vendor, and intercepting the refund check from the vendor.

Personal Purchases Schemes A personal purchases scheme is simply purchasing personal items with the company's money. With the advances in Internet technologies and purchase methods, it is much easier to perpetrate this kind of scheme. The General Accounting Office (GAO) did an audit of its e-procurement (electronic procurement) system and found thousands of dollars that had been misappropriated for everything from brothels to expensive country club memberships.

Payroll Schemes Payroll schemes are similar to billing schemes except instead of paying a vendor, the company is paying an employee. These schemes can be perpetrated in several ways: ghost employee, commission, false workers' compensation, or falsified wages.

According to the ACFE 2008 RTTN, 9.3 percent of all frauds are payroll schemes. The average cost of a payroll scheme was $49,000.

Ghost Employee Schemes In a ghost employee scheme, someone receives a paycheck but does not actually work for the victim company. The ghost can be fictitious or a real person in collusion with the perpetrator. For example, a controller for a university in Texas set up several ghosts in the payroll system, including her son and some of his friends. She would have them either bring her the checks or split the money between them. She stole several hundreds of thousands of dollars in the scheme over several months.

The ghost employee process is similar to the shell vendor process: The ghost must be added to the employee master file for payroll, a time card or salary must be approved, a check must be written to the ghost, and the check must be intercepted by the fraudster or an accomplice.

Commission Schemes In the commission scheme, fraudsters use several methods: generate bogus sales, overstate sales, increase the commission rate, or use some other means to gain more commission than was legitimately earned.

False Workers' Compensation Schemes The false workers' compensation scheme involves a worker faking an injury and collecting payment from the victim's insurance carrier.

Falsified Wages Schemes Fraudsters have sometimes used the falsified hours and salary scheme to pay employees enormous overtime or exaggerated pay rates.

Expense Reimbursement Schemes Expense reimbursement schemes are simple schemes: Submit a falsified business expense and gain a fraudulent reimbursement check from the victim company. According to the ACFE 2008 RTTN, 13.2 percent of all frauds are expense reimbursement schemes. The average cost of an expense reimbursement scheme was $25,000. Schemes that fall under expense reimbursement include mischaracterized expenses, overstated expenses, fictitious expenses, and multiple reimbursements.

Check Tampering Schemes Check tampering schemes are unique among the fraudulent disbursement schemes because it is the one scheme in which the perpetrator physically prepares the fraudulent check. In other cases, the fraudster causes the company to generate a check by submitting some form of false document to the victim company (e.g., invoice, time card).

According to the ACFE 2008 RTTN, 14.7 percent of all frauds are check tampering schemes. The average cost of a check tampering scheme was $138,000. This average figure makes this fraud scheme the most costly scheme or group of schemes of all the schemes.

Check tampering schemes include forged makers, forged endorsements, altered payees, concealed checks, and authorized makers.

Forged Maker Schemes A forged maker scheme involves the signing of another person's name to a check with fraudulent intent and the fraudulent alteration of a genuine instrument. A forged maker scheme usually starts with a blank check. The concern with forged maker schemes and checks is actually twofold. First, there is the concern over physical access to paper checks. The second concern is the digital access to check writing.

Forged Endorsement Schemes A forged endorsement scheme involves a culprit intercepting a company check intended for some other legitimate party and converting that check by forging the other party's name on the endorsement of the check. A forged endorsement check scheme starts with a completed check versus a blank check. For example, in a ghost employee scheme, the fraudster may use a real person, such as a former employee, as the ghost, intercept the check, and simply forge that person's name to cash the check. In a nonaccomplice vendor scheme, the fraudster usually intercepts a legitimate refund check from a legitimate vendor and forges the employer's endorsement on the back.

Altered Payee Schemes The altered payee scheme also involves intercepting a check written to another party, but in this scheme the culprit alters the payee designation so the check can be converted to himself or an accomplice. Sometimes the fraudster reverses the payee's name from the check, replacing his name with the original legitimate name, when the check is returned in the bank statement.

Concealed Check Schemes The concealed check scheme is a bold attempt to take advantage of "rubber stamping" or inattention to controls. The perpetrator prepares a fraudulent check and submits it along with legitimate checks to an authorized signer, whom the perpetrator hopes will sign it without a proper review. The perpetrator will likely wait until the check signer is busy or distracted before submitting the fraudulent check.

Authorized Maker Schemes An authorized maker scheme involves a perpetrator who has check-signing authority and makes out fraudulent checks to himself or herself for personal benefit. This kind of scheme is more difficult to detect because the person has check-signing authority. Obviously, this scheme succeeds only if controls are absent, circumvented, or too weak to be effective. In a small branch of a large chain of stores in Mississippi, the only accountant of the employer was an authorized maker. For three years, she wrote herself checks that went undetected. Someone at the employer's bank found a check signed by Mary, paid to Mary, endorsed by Mary, and deposited into Mary's personal account which was a little suspicious. The bank employee called the newly hired internal auditor of the branch and reported her suspicions. Eventually, over $250,000 worth of checks paid to Mary were uncovered. Remember, this business was a relatively small one.

Register Disbursement Schemes Register disbursement schemes involve the removal of money from a register, where the removal is recorded on the register's system (tape, computer file, etc.). These frauds are among the least costly and least frequent of all frauds. According to the ACFE 2008 RTTN, 2.8 percent of all frauds are register disbursement schemes. The average cost of a register disbursement scheme was $25,000. Register disbursement schemes involve two kinds of schemes: false voids and false refunds. Certain businesses have a higher risk for this fraud: restaurants, bars, street vendors, and any other cash business.

Skimming

Skimming is sometimes called front-end fraud, as funds are stolen *before* a booking entry is made. Thus it may be very difficult to detect a skimming scheme or to even notice that the money was stolen. Skimming is a common practice in cash businesses such as bars, restaurants, vending machines, home modernization contracting, gas stations, and retail stores. A good example might be the reported way Bugsy Seigel conducted business when he established casinos in Las Vegas. Supposedly Bugsy would take all of the cash from the day or week, "skim" off some for the Chicago mob to keep them happy and away from Vegas, skim some for himself (tax-free money!), and report what was left over as income. If the owner of a business, such as Bugsy, skims money from the incoming cash, then reports the balance to the books, it is *very* hard to catch such a fraud. In this example, who really cares if money is being skimmed? Maybe one or more government agencies, but they probably would have no way of knowing it was going on. The Crazy Eddie's fraud was exactly this kind of fraud. The family that owned the business skimmed millions of dollars from the electronics retail business.

Skimming schemes fall into three groups: sales (unrecorded sales, understated sales), receivables (write-off schemes, lapping schemes, and unconcealed schemes), and refunds. According to the ACFE 2008 RTTN, 16.6 percent of all frauds are skimming. The average loss in a skimming scheme was $80,000.

Skimming as a Sales Scheme

A type of skimming scheme is the sales scheme. Revenue skimming occurs at the point of sale. For instance, the cashier can ring up "no sale" and pocket the cash. It is sometimes possible that a point of sale person can exchange goods or services, be given cash payment, and pocket the cash. One motivation for skimming sales is to avoid paying income taxes on those sales.

Receivables: Lapping Scheme Lapping is a form of robbing one customer's payment to pay another's, because the latter's payment was stolen by the perpetrator. For example, a fraudster takes customer A's payment, steals it, and pays it back the next day with customer B's payment. Then in the next round, the fraudster steals from C and pays B's account with money from D, leaving C's and D's accounts overstated and unpaid on the books. The problem is that there often is a balloon effect from lapping. It is so easy to steal that the perpetrator takes a little more every time, and the balance grows larger and larger until the balloon bursts: There is not enough cash flow to sustain the scam any longer.

Several problems with the lapping scheme make it almost certain that the fraudster will get caught. First, eventually the customers' accounts get behind enough to be too problematic to hide. At that point, the fraudster may have to steal or alter customer statements to conceal the fraud adequately. Second, after several cycles of stealing, the fraudster also may have difficulty in knowing exactly which customers have sent in payments that have not been posted and how much the payments were. Sometimes a fraudster keeps a separate set of books, usually near her desk. Last, the fraudster cannot take much vacation or sick leave, as the fraud will unravel fairly quickly if someone else begins to handle receivables payments and customers' accounts. These facts present some ways to detect or look for lapping schemes (e.g., employees who do not take vacation). They also offer some preventive measures (e.g., force vacation to be taken, force rotation of duties).

Skimming as a Refund Scheme This skimming scheme is more rare than the other two. Usually, the perpetrator is in place to notice an overpayment by the company, and thus a refund is due. When the refund is paid back to the company, the perpetrator intercepts the refund and converts the check to cash for his own benefit. If the entity does not book refunds due, this scheme is fairly easy to conceal—do nothing!

Inventory and Other Assets (Non-Cash)

Schemes involving inventory and other assets are not nearly as common as cash frauds, but the two are almost identical in average losses. In the ACFE 2008 RTTN, 16.3 percent of the asset misappropriation frauds involved noncash assets and the average loss was $100,000.

An employee can misappropriate inventory and other assets (excluding cash) in basically two ways. The asset can be misused (e.g., borrowed), or it can be stolen.

Misuse

Misuse usually involves equipment, especially large and/or expensive equipment, such as backhoes, vehicles, and computers. Some surveys have estimated that over 50 percent of employees use employer's computers and company time for personal business (e.g., establishing and maintaining eBay accounts to sell merchandise online). But this problem can be systemic if the employee culture considers the use of employer's assets as part of their benefits.

For example, one forensic accountant was hired to examine the books for fraud based on multiple tips that the manager of a utility department for a municipality was abusing his position by employing a pass-through vendor scheme. In the process of interviewing people on site, he overheard one employee say to another late one Friday, "Did Joe get through with the backhoe?" The reply was yes. The first employee then said he was headed home and would be taking it. The forensic accountant approached the second employee and began to question him as to whether he understood what had just happened. The employee replied, "Oh, we do that all the time. Besides, Bill needs the backhoe for a job he is doing tomorrow." To his consternation, the forensic accountant was not able to convince the second employee that *anything* improper was happening. But clearly, the "borrowing" of the employer's equipment (especially to use in a side job for creating personal income) was a brazen, and in this case common, misuse of employer's assets. However, this example illustrates the fact that if misuse becomes a part of the culture, it may be hard to convince employees that this kind of fraud is really wrong. More important, rules against this type of misuse may be almost impossible to enforce. This example also proves that the existence of a policy, its communication, and its enforcement are critical steps in the deterrence of this type of fraud.

Larceny

Larceny of inventory is the simple theft of inventory from the employer's possession. In some cases, an employee may just steal inventory and make no attempt to conceal the theft in the accounting records. Or an employee may create false documentation to justify the theft, as if inventory had been sold, shipped, or moved internally.

For example, an employee of a campus bookstore found the bay in the back always had the door up to improve ventilation in an area that was stuffy and too warm. The employee simply carried books out that door, down the street to an off-campus bookstore, and sold them for pennies on the dollar. He made no attempt to conceal the crime, which was his undoing. After weeks and months of stealing books, the internal accountant complained to the manager that profits were low and something was wrong. The manager believed that someone outside had managed to infiltrate their security and was walking away with expensive books, so he hired a fraud auditor. The fraud auditor examined the excellent security measures *inside* the store, and then discovered the open door in the back of the storeroom. He immediately used the fraud theory approach and suggested to the manager that an employee might be taking books out the back door (inventory larceny fraud). The manager was almost insulted, claiming he had only honest employees and there had to be another explanation. The fraud auditor followed up on his belief, found the off-campus store a block away, and eventually uncovered sufficient evidence to prosecute the fraudster.

SUMMARY

Successful fraud auditors and forensic accountants know the fraud schemes very well. They know how they are perpetrated and the characteristics of the various schemes, which enables them to perform their investigation or fraud prevention programs effectively.

This discussion of fraud schemes is a major part of the critical knowledge it takes for fraud auditors and forensic accountants to be able to do an effective job. Another major part is the understanding of the red flags associated with these fraud schemes as presented in Chapter 4.

NOTES

1. ACFE, *2008 Report to the Nation*, pp. 6–36.
2. KPMG, *Fraud Survey*, pp. 3–7.
3. ACFE, 2008 *Report to the Nation*, pp. 10, 12.
4. Bryan Garner, *Black's Law Dictionary*, 8th ed. (New York: West-Thomson, 2004), p. 708.
5. *Webster's Dictionary Online*, www.m-w.com/dictionary/misappropriation, last accessed April 25, 2006.
6. Joseph T. Wells, *Occupational Fraud and Abuse* (Austin, TX: ACFE, 1997), p. 61.
7. Ibid., p. 130.

CHAPTER FOUR

Red Flags

INTRODUCTION

Red flags are used in this book as a synonym for fingerprints of fraud. When fraud occurs, there are traces of the criminal and crime left at the scene of the crime, or in the fraudster's life, much like fingerprints that may be left at a crime scene. Red flags have varying natures and include things such as an accounting anomaly, an unexplained transaction or event, unusual elements of a transaction, a person's behavioral changes or characteristics, or just characteristics commonly associated with known frauds, especially certain individual schemes or group of schemes.

The cornerstone of effective fraud prevention and detection is presented in Chapters 1, 2, and 3. The fundamentals in Chapter 1 provide information about the fraud investigation process itself. The concepts introduced in Chapter 2 help to explain the fraud basics, such as why fraud is committed (the fraud triangle), the scope of fraud, axioms of fraud, and the typical profile of a fraudster. These are of value in developing an antifraud program, in testing for fraud, or in conducting a fraud investigation. Using the fraud tree, fraud schemes were presented in Chapter 3 and are critical to detecting and preventing fraud. A fraud auditor or forensic accountant *must* understand the *specific* frauds that are perpetrated and *how* each fraud scheme usually is committed. But these things come together in studying, analyzing, and using red flags to prevent and detect frauds.

For example, the fraud theory approach starts with identifying the most likely fraud scheme and how it might have been perpetrated. Obviously such a thought process requires not only a good understanding of all the fraud schemes, but even which ones are more likely to occur in given circumstances: the industry, the state of internal controls, the size of the business, and so on. In order to prove or disprove the resulting theory, the fraud investigator looks for signs the identified fraud scheme is occurring. This process usually is based on the red flags of that particular fraud.

A careful analytical review of the fraud tree (schemes) and the fraud triangle brings to mind applicable flags. For example, in the fraud scheme of lapping, a person uses an elaborate method of taking some customer payments while applying payments from other customers in an overlapping fashion to those accounts stolen from earlier. It is easy to see that this type of fraudster cannot afford to take an extended vacation or else the scheme will be uncovered. Another example is the ghost employee scheme. Because the perpetrator usually has to intercept the check once it is printed, he cannot afford to *not* be there on payday. Thus a red flag in both of these frauds is the absence of extended vacation taken by an employee. In addition, red flags come to mind when analyzing motivators, based on the fraud triangle discussed in Chapter 2. One motivator is excessive debt. If a credit report shows that an employee has a high debt and a low credit score, that information is a red flag. In other words, the motivation leg of the fraud triangle is present for that employee. That does *not* mean that person is a fraudster or will commit a fraud, just that this circumstance is associated with frauds of the past.

It is quite important to remember that a red flag is just a red flag, and not necessarily indicative of a fraud. The forensic accountant and fraud auditor must not jump to conclusions; she should keep that mentality of "just the facts," and focus on proving or disproving a fraud has occurred rather than creating a checklist of red flags.

Identifying red flags is critical to the success of detecting and preventing fraud. Red flags lead naturally to the design of effective detection methods and processes. And these detection methods lead naturally to the design of good antifraud controls. Often a good detective control can simultaneously serve as a good preventive control.

PROFESSIONAL STANDARDS

Recent major fraud-related technical literature incorporates the concept of red flags. Most of the accounting professional organizations have followed the passage of the Sarbanes-Oxley Act (SOX) with the adoption of technical standards to accommodate the tenets of SOX, or the spirit of SOX, and they generally include red flags as a key to the guidance. Three examples of professional groups and their standards are the American Institute of Certified Public Accountants (AICPA), the Information Systems Audit and Control Association (ISACA), and the Institute of Internal Auditors (IIA). These were chosen because of their key role in auditing for fraud.

AICPA

The AICPA's Statement on Auditing Standard (SAS) No. 99, *Consideration of Fraud in a Financial Statement Audit*, which codifies much of the SOX tenets and certainly the spirit of SOX, incorporates a list of red flags. Much of the work in identifying those red flags is associated with the work of the Association of Certified Fraud Examiners (ACFE) and founder Joe Wells in particular. Wells and the ACFE contributed to the development of the red flags contained in the appendix of SAS No. 99. Those red flags are listed using a matrix of the three legs of the fraud triangle and the three major categories of the fraud tree (see Exhibit 4.1). Thus the SAS No. 99 appendix identifies *pressure* red flags associated with *financial statement* frauds (first cell in Exhibit 4.1), *opportunity* red flags associated with *asset misappropriation* frauds, *rationalization* red flags for *corruption* schemes, and so on, for a total of nine cells in the matrix. The list is fairly exhaustive and one that would be of value for all auditors, not just external auditors.

EXHIBIT 4.1 SAS No. 99 Red Flag Matrix

Triangle/Tree	Corruption	Asset Misappropriation	Financial Statement
Pressure			
Opportunity			
Rationalization			

ISACA

ISACA provides a similar list in its technical literature. The "Irregularities and Illegal Acts" guide (Standard 030.020.010) for "Procedures for Information Systems Auditing" became effective November 1, 2003. Section 4.1 provides a list of "Audit Considerations" that include red flags, among other issues, especially in the "Application of CAATs" segment.

IIA

The IIA literature is replete with examples of red flags. The IIA's technical and professional standards also address fraud. The IIA's *International Standards for the Professional Practice of Internal Auditing* states in section 1210.A2:

> The internal auditor should have sufficient knowledge to identify the *indicators of fraud* but is not expected to have the expertise of a person whose primary responsibility is detecting and investigating fraud. [Emphasis added.]

Professional Responsibilities

From the technical standards of these three organizations, it is clear that auditors are expected to be able to identify key indicators of fraud in the process of performing professional services. Because of this fact, it is necessary for auditors to be trained in aspects of fraud identification and detection using red flags.[1] It is also important for auditors to use training, articles, seminars, education, and other means to develop an effective mind-set related to fraud and especially to red flags.

One more comment is necessary about technical standards and professional responsibilities. A study of red flags will enable auditors of all types to be able to recognize a red flag when it comes across their desks, and ends up under their noses, in daily activities. For example, would the auditor be able to recognize a red flag if he were doing the audit trail verification and picked up an invoice for a service that is printed using an Excel-generated format? Here are at least two red flags: Shell company schemes usually bill for a service, and rarely do legitimate vendors use Excel as its billing system. This illustration could be told for countless other situations. But the bottom line is auditors need to have a high probability of recognizing an obvious red flag should they encounter one.

COMMON RED FLAGS

Generally speaking, some red flags are common to all frauds, or common to a major category of frauds in the fraud tree.

Financial Statement Frauds

A major class of frauds in the fraud tree is financial fraud. These frauds are generally perpetrated by senior management, for the organization (at least in part or indirectly), and for the benefit of the organization and the fraudster. In the end, it does not benefit the organization, but during the fraud it does.

For these frauds, some of the common red flags are different from those associated with fraudsters who commit asset misappropriation frauds or corruption frauds. Generally, red flags associated with financial statement fraud include:

- Accounting anomalies
- Rapid growth
- Unusual profits
- Internal control weaknesses
- Aggressiveness of executive management
- Obsession with stock prices by executive management
- Micromanagement by executive management

Of these red flags, the most common red flag of this category is the management style or character of key executives. Usually, a senior manager has a hard-to-observe weakness in personal ethics, but also exhibits an observable overly aggressive nature. For example, the executive could continually produce and approve overly optimistic financial goals. She could be domineering with employees, attempting to keep people under her thumb. She also probably would try to steer internal and external auditors around or away from those areas where the fraud would most likely be discovered. Being secretive or keeping certain financial information close to the vest is also a sign of this type of executive.

Asset Misappropriation

Those frauds categorized as asset misappropriation typically are perpetrated by employees, against the organization, for the benefit of the employee. According to Lux and Fitiani, general behavioral red flags include:

- Changes in behavior
- Inability to look people in the eye
- Increased irritability
- Irregular work history
- Character problems
- Consistent anger
- Tendency to blame others
- Change in lifestyle[2]

For persons with a higher personal code of ethics, the behavioral changes are more likely to occur (e.g., irritability, inability to look others in the eye); that is, their conscience will begin to bother them.

The last red flag, change in lifestyle, is perhaps the most common on this list. Of the fraudsters who get caught, most tend to escalate their crime by taking more with the same scheme each year that it goes undetected or by adding another scheme. That is, if a fraudster gets away with a $15,000 fraud this year, he tends to steal more, perhaps twice that much, the next year. If he gets away with $30,000 next year, he may double it again the next year. This influx of tax-free money usually is spent, and spent in such a way that those around the fraudster can notice an increase in his lifestyle. One fraud was revealed after an employee bought cars, boats, an expensive second home, and rounds of beer every week for the bowling team—all on a salary of $30,000 a year! A next-door neighbor, who also worked for the same company, was suspicious, because she did not understand how he could afford such a drastic lifestyle change. The fraudster claimed that a relative left him a lot of money. Not until months later, when a sharp internal auditor uncovered the fraud, did the neighbor realize that his change in lifestyle was because he had stolen over $1 million over a period of five years from their employer. Such a change in lifestyle is observable and is a red flag of frauds in general.

Other red flags could include employees who:

- Are disgruntled with employer or supervisor
- Never take a vacation or take it in short time frames (probable in lapping and ghost employee schemes)
- Have financial strains or debt problems
- Exhibit traits of psychotic problems
- Constantly complain about how the boss or company treats them

- Exhibit behavioral characteristics associated with egocentrics or those who need to control everything
- Reject transfers, promotions, or other job offers

Corruption

Frauds categorized as corruption are perpetrated by employees, against the organization, for the benefit of the employee. For corruption to occur, someone on the inside has to work with someone on the outside in such a way that the relationship is a detriment to the organization. Knowing how to identify this relationship is critical to fraud prevention and detection. Red flags include the general behavioral red flags and lifestyle change, but also watch for the following:

- Relationships between key employees and authorized vendors
- Secrecy surrounding this third-party relationship
- A lack of review on management approvals for known third-party relationships that exist (over time, the fraudster may begin to steal using that relationship if the entity gets comfortable with it)
- Anomalies in recording transactions (e.g., what is the debit for a bribe on the books?)
- Anomalies in approving vendors

SPECIFIC RED FLAGS

Other red flags are particular to a specific fraud. This section illustrates some of the known red flags for each of the major fraud schemes. These red flags facilitate the development of some potentially effective detective methods for that specific fraud. Auditors should become familiar with these red flags and possible identification methods in order to accentuate their fraud mind-set.

Financial Statement Schemes

This category is broken down into six specific frauds. These six schemes are addressed in SAS 99 as well. For a detailed and lengthy list of red flags associated with financial statement fraud, see the appendix to SAS 99.

Red flags that apply to all types of financial statement schemes include (most are taken from SAS No. 99):

- Threats to financial stability or profitability by economic, industrial, or internal operational conditions
- Excessive pressure on management to meet aggressive financial requirements
- Evidence that executives or board members have a personal financial dependence on the performance of the entity
- Highly complex transactions or relationships to third parties
- Ineffective monitoring of executives
- Complex or unstable organizational structure
- Deficient internal controls, especially significant deficiencies or material weaknesses
- Unreasonable increase in gross margin, especially when compared to the industry average
- Recurring negative cash flows from operations, especially when coupled with increasing profits and overall positive cash flow
- Unusual profits, especially if well above the industry average
- Rapid growth, profits that are above the Standard & Poor's (S&P) average
- Significant transactions with related parties, especially when the other party is not audited or audited by a different audit firm
- Significant, unusual, or highly complex transactions at the end of the fiscal year
- Significant volume of sales to entities whose substance and owners are not known
- Unusual growth in revenues by minority of business units

Timing Differences (Improper Treatment of Sales)

This fraud centers around booking sales that are either premature or will be reversed in a few weeks or months. Red flags for this scheme center around the ways such improper transactions would be perpetrated. For example regarding potentially illegitimate sales such as channel stuffing, a red flag would be a sale recorded before transacted (i.e., violation of GAAP). Channel stuffing red flags include excessive returns of merchandise, accompanied with sales credits, especially in the early days of a new financial reporting period (i.e., first few days of a new quarter or new fiscal year).

Fictitious Revenues

Fictitious revenues are created by simply recording sales that never occurred. Red flags associated with these types of transactions or their results include:

- Unusual increase in assets (the other side of the entry to create fictitious revenues)
- Customers with missing data (especially physical address and phone numbers)
- Unexplained changes in certain relationships or ratio trends (e.g., revenues grow but accounts receivable does not)

Concealed Liabilities (Improper Recording of Liabilities)

Profits can be inflated unethically by moving liabilities from one entity's books to another. Liabilities can also be concealed by not recording legitimate liabilities. Red flags associated with those types of transactions include:

- Excessive transfers from one entity to a related entity (e.g., a sister subsidiary)
- Unusual or unexplained transfers from one entity to a related entity
- The employ of different audit firms for different subsidiaries or related business entities
- Vendor invoices and other liability transactions that are not recorded in the books

Inadequate Disclosures

Improper disclosures can be the tactic of a fraudster to hide a fraud. Red flags include:

- Disclosure notes that are so obfuscated that it is difficult to determine the true nature of the event or transaction
- Discovery of undisclosed legal contingencies, or any other significant event
- Discovery of undisclosed fraud

Improper Asset Valuation

Profits can be inflated by increasing asset values. That increase can be the result of adding value to the original costs or by decreasing the contra accounts that go with a depreciable asset. Red flags include:

- Unusual or unexplained increases in book value of assets (inventory, receivables, long-lived assets)

- Unusual trends in ratios or relationships of assets to other parts of the financial report (e.g., consistent increases in number-of-days in receivables ratio, changes in the ratio of receivables to revenues)
- Violation of GAAP in recording expenses as assets
- Tendency of management to be unresponsive when internal auditors report assets that need to be removed from a balance sheet (because they have supposedly been retired, or transferred to a different business entity)

Asset Misappropriation Schemes

Asset misappropriation schemes are the most common type of fraud. They involve the theft or misuse of assets, normally cash. Altogether, a total of 32 different individual fraud schemes are contained in this major category. The schemes or groups of schemes to be discussed were selected because of the probability of their occurrence (i.e., they occur more frequently than others) or higher costs (the schemes include the top 14 individual schemes).

Cash Larceny

Cash larceny is simply the theft of cash from the employer, occurring *after* it was recorded in the books of records. It includes cash and checks. Red flags include:

- Unusual or unexplained drops in the level of deposits in the bank
- Unusual or unexplained differences between the accounts or reports of activities and bank statement information
- Change in lifestyle of an employee

Billing Schemes

Billing schemes are the most common type of asset misappropriation, based on statistics from the ACFE's various *Report to the Nation* reports. Thus it is important to be able to prevent and detect (recognize) these types of fraud schemes. This category also contains a number of different schemes.

Shell Company In a shell company scheme, the fraudster establishes a fictitious company as the means to divert checks from the employer to the fraudster. Usually the fictitious vendor is a fabricated name, and often the address is a post office box. Sometimes the culprit will use a derivation of a legitimate vendor's name to confuse those who might see the checks or the fictitious vendor's name.

Red flags include:

- Use of post office box (POB) for the only address of a vendor, or in place of a physical address
- Lack of sufficient contact data: missing phone number, and so on
- Use of Excel-generated invoices by a vendor
- Sequential invoice numbers from a vendor
- Address that matches an employee's address
- A vendor who only bills for services
- Use of round numbers for amounts on an invoice
- Use of unintelligible descriptions on invoices
- Odd items being purchased (e.g., gravel for an attorney)
- Lack of detail on invoice
- Irregular folds on invoices from same vendor (e.g., looks like it was delivered in a shirt pocket!)
- No employer identification number (EIN) or an improper one (i.e., does not fit the format of a proper EIN)
- No sales tax identification number or an improper one
- Unusual or unexpected increase in cost of goods sold
- Irrational ratios
- Vendor who consistently gets paid more quickly than other vendors
- Applicable tips and complaints, especially from employees who can observe the fraud or evidence of the fraud
- Notations for "extra" or "special" charges

Pass-Through Vendor A pass-through vendor scheme is similar to the shell company scheme. In the pass-through vendor scheme, the vendor actually does deliver product to the employer, but the price paid to the vendor is exorbitant. The fraudster sets up the pseudo vendor for the purposes of bilking the employer into paying much more for services or products than would be paid honestly in order to take the excess for himself.

Red flags include many of the same ones as for a shell company scheme, plus:

- Tips from employees that the entity is paying too much for certain goods or services
- Evidence that high prices are being paid for certain products or services
- Declining profits, increasing cost of goods sold
- Unfavorable variances on performance reports

- Poor internal controls, especially lack of segregation between adding vendors and approving contracts or invoices. (If the same person can do both, that is a red flag.)
- Amounts of invoices are just below an approval level, especially an excessive number of invoices below that amount by vendor or by employee who approved the transaction

Nonaccomplice Vendor In this scheme, the vendor is an innocent participant. In some manner, the fraudster entices a legitimate vendor to send a check, usually for a refund, to the employer. The fraudster intercepts that check and forges an endorsement to cash it for her own benefit. Red flags include:

- Use of invoice numbers outside the range of normal sequence
- Unusual or unexplained levels of purchases from a vendor
- Unusual or unexplained purchases of particular goods

Personal Purchases In personal purchases frauds, the fraudster simply has the company pay for personal items. In the case of a General Accounting Office (GAO) audit of e-procurement purchases, auditors could not properly examine records because of a lack of sufficient detail in their records. The auditors contacted the credit card companies and obtained a copy of their data from the financial institution's database. They then sorted the data looking at the merchandise codes and pulled those that were incompatible with normal use. Those codes included merchants such as brothels, country clubs, and Victoria's Secret. Thousands of dollars of unauthorized expenses were detected in this manner. It is noteworthy that unauthorized expenses can be made for normal merchants (e.g., airlines, hotels, car rentals in this case), and they probably would not be detected using this specific audit procedure.

Red flags include:

- Unusual or unexplained activity on corporate credit cards
- Purchases of unusual items
- Consistently over-budget employee
- Pattern of purchases just below review

Payroll Schemes

Payroll schemes involve conning the company into paying wages that were not earned. The manner of such frauds varies, but they all lead to an unauthorized increase in a paycheck or an unauthorized paycheck period. Specific schemes include the ghost employee, falsified wages, commission, and false workers' compensation.

Ghost Employee A ghost employee scheme is perpetrated by a fraudster who adds a person, fictitious or real, to the payroll files. Then the fraudster manages to get pay approved for the ghost and intercepts the check or has it mailed to an accomplice or her own POB.

For example, a property management company had decided to expand into a neighboring state. The managers of the family-owned business assigned the management of the newly opened remote facility to their best employee, a woman who had worked for them for several years, had a great personality, and was fiercely loyal. She was sent to the new property as the only full-time employee of the business and was given a part-time handyman. When the handyman quit, she decided to leave him on the payroll, continued to send in approved time, intercepted the paycheck when it came back, forged his signature, and thus increased her personal income. In this case, the ghost was a real person—a former employee.

Other ghost employee frauds use fictitious people. The facts behind how these frauds are perpetrated lead to the red flags, which lead to effective ways to detect the fraud.

Red flags include:

- Unexplained or unusual increases in wages expense
- Paychecks for employees who:
  - Never take a vacation
  - Never take sick leave
  - Have no taxes withheld
  - Have no deductions
  - Have no Social Security number (SSN) or an invalid one
  - Have a POB and no physical address
  - Have an address duplicated by another employee, or it is the address of a relative or friend
  - Have no phone number, or duplicate phone number, or the phone number is a work phone of the employer rather than a residence
  - Have a duplicate direct deposit number
  - Have a date of paycheck *after* termination of the employee

Commission Commission schemes involve the fraudulent manipulation of commissions paid, either the rate or sales. Red flags include:

- Unexplained or unusual increases in commissions expense
- Changes in commission rates over time
- Higher rate of returns or credits for one salesperson

Falsified Wages This scheme consists of legitimate employees recording illegitimate payroll data (hours worked, salary amount, etc.) Red flags include:

- Unexplained or unusual amounts of overtime
- Unusual changes in pay rates
- Unusual or unexplained number of hours paid

Check-Tampering Five check-tampering schemes make up the most costly of frauds. As such, they deserve extra attention in understanding them and in developing detection and prevention methods and controls. Check tampering essentially involves using the entity's checks in one manner or another to extract cash from the victim organization.

With the advent of electronic check clearing (Check 21) rules, many of the red flags (especially those associated with endorsements) became more difficult to observe, as checks are truncated by the banking system. Therefore, it is important to select the entity's bank carefully. Choose a bank that scans both the front and back of the check, and provides customers with access to both images (front and back) over the Internet.

Red flags include:

- Excessive number of voided checks
- Missing checks
- Nonpayroll checks made out to an employee
- Alterations to payee or amount on cancelled checks
- Altered or dual endorsements on cancelled checks
- Questionable payees or payee addresses (e.g., POB)
- Duplicate or out-of-sequence check numbers

Skimming Skimming frauds happen *before* a booking entry is made. Because it is an off-the-books fraud, it is one of the most difficult to detect. One methodology to detect skimming is to perform an invigilation. *Invigilation* is the creation of a pristine, fraud-free environment for the purpose of benchmarking the total receipts that should be normal. This pristine effect can be created by a high-profile investigation, where everyone knows that fraud auditors are coming to look for fraud. Add cameras for surveillance and anything else that will increase the level of attention to the fraud audit. The intent is to create such a high level of perception of detection that the fraudsters shut down their skimming temporarily so the fraud auditor can determine the level of normal sales. That benchmark then can be compared to actual sales to determine if, and approximately how much, skimming is taking place. The individual skimming schemes are related to sales (unrecorded sales, understated sales), receivables (write-off schemes, lapping schemes, unconcealed schemes), and refunds. Like some other schemes, skimming cannot typically be perpetrated in the long-term without discovery if internal controls are operating effectively.

Red flags include:

- Lower than expected revenues
- Actual profits that are less than projections
- Gross margins significantly less than projections

Lapping Lapping is skimming accounts receivable (AR) payments before they are posted. Lapping is more difficult to conceal than skimming cash in a cash business because the customer expects to be credited immediately with a payment on account. Red flags include:

- Customer complaints about payments being posted long after checks were mailed
- Growing delinquency in accounts receivable or specific customers, incremental increases over time in number-of-days in receivables
- Employees who put in a lot of time after hours—sometimes necessary to keep a separate set of books on the lapping system—Employees who never take extended vacation

Corruption Schemes

There are four corruption subcategories of fraud schemes, six microcategories, and a total of eight different individual schemes. Corruption schemes invariably involve two parties, even if one is unwilling. The most common corruption schemes are conflicts of interests, bribery, and extortion.

Conflicts of Interest

A conflict-of-interest fraud involves an employee with a relationship with a third party by which the employee and/or the third party gain a financial advantage. The fraudster exerts influence for the benefit of the third party because of this personal interest in the third party. Entities should have a policy (ethics or fraud) that specifically forbids this kind of activity. Red flags include:

- A large volume of transactions with a particular vendor
- The discovery of a relationship between an employee and a third party that was previously unknown
- Weak segregation of duties in assigning contracts and approving invoices

Bribery

Bribery frauds involve payments to influence an employee to send business to the vendor making the payments. The frauds in this group include kickbacks, bid rigging, and others. Red flags include:

- A change in lifestyle of an employee
- Discovery of a relationship between an employee and a vendor
- Weak segregation of duties in approving vendors and invoices

Economic Extortion

Basically, economic extortion is the opposite of a bribery fraud. Instead of a vendor offering a bribe, the employee demands payment from a vendor in order to favor the vendor. The red flags and detection methods are the same as for bribery.

FRAUD DETECTION MODEL

Auditors often come across transactions, accounting records, or accounting data that are not quite right, that constitute an exception of some kind. Primarily, the irregularities are exceptions to policies, procedures, or internal controls. Many times, if not most of the time, these events and transactions are minor glitches in the recording of the accounting event, due to a number of possible reasons including human error. But sometimes they are actually evidence of a fraud. Financial auditors can be at risk if they examine a transaction and find suspicion of fraud, and then choose to expand the sample, or ignore the transaction because of the immateriality of that single transaction. The transaction could be the tip of the iceberg. At least some forensic accounting experts in public accounting recommend bringing in a subject matter expert (SME) when the above occurs, rather than take one of the other two options.

Recognizing signs of fraud (red flags) at first is difficult because of their apparent benign nature, especially when considering a single transaction, document, or event. For example, an internal auditor is doing a file review of a vendor and picks up an invoice and finds a POB as the address and no physical address on the invoice. Many vendors want the check and remittance to be returned to a POB. But it is also true that a POB and no physical address on an invoice is a red flag for a billing scheme. So should it be ignored? By itself, does it mean anything? Maybe it does not, but it should not be ignored. A single anomaly or fact can hold together the thread of other circumstances together in explaining a fraud. Thus some model of accumulating and classifying anomalies (exceptions) would be beneficial to auditors and antifraud concerns.

The recommended response in this kind of situation is based on the concept similar to that of materiality in financial audits. When a financial auditor finds a misstatement that is not material to the account or class of accounts, she does not ignore the misstatement. Rather she puts that misstatement into a file to be accumulated with other misstatements. The purpose of the accumulation is to determine if the misstatements are material in the aggregate. The same process and goal should apply to fraud audits and anomalies (red flags in particular). That is, individual factors and evidence should be considered in the context of how they align with and contribute to cumulative evidence and possibilities.

If a number of auditors are involved in an audit, it is conceivable that each of them observed one or two red flags but dismissed them. Their reasons would be quite valid on an individual basis. But a number of anomalies larger than any one person's could be dismissed. The question that begs to be answered, therefore, is are these anomalies, these red flags, significant *in the aggregate*? There is no way to know without some formal process in the audit to accumulate anomalies.

SUMMARY

In order to have a high probability of detecting fraud, a fraud auditor or forensic accountant needs to understand as many red flags of fraud as possible. Fraud auditors, and especially internal auditors, need to understand the general red flags that are indicative of a fraud but not necessarily associated with a specific fraud scheme. These red flags include an employee's change in lifestyle or behavior and tips or complaints from other employees that something is not right. But an identification of those red flags associated with specific fraud schemes (the larger context of applicable evidence and fraud theories) is even more important. They are crucial to detecting fraud in the lives of auditors in their everyday activities, whether they are internal or financial auditors. A thorough understanding and analysis of known red flags is the basic building block of effective fraud prevention and detection methods.

NOTES

1. Joseph T. Wells, "Sherlock Holmes, CPA, Part I," *Journal of Accountancy* (August 2003), pp. 86–90.
2. Allen G. Lux and Sandra Fitiani, "Fighting Internal Crime before It Happens," *Information Systems Control Journal* Vol. III (2002), pp. 50–51.

CHAPTER FIVE

Fraud Risk Assessment

INTRODUCTION

Since Enron and other frauds near the same time, there has been a significant focus on fraud, internal controls, and the concept of fraud risk management including risk assessment. The passage of Sarbanes-Oxley Act (SOX) in 2002 brought both more attention to these subjects and put tenets related to them into federal law. The Securities and Exchange Commission (SEC) and its accounting arm the Public Companies Accounting Oversight Board (PCAOB) have been issuing guidance on this topic. The Committee on Sponsoring Organizations (COSO) has also made significant efforts in the area of risk assessment, producing its COSO Model for enterprise risk assessment. Nonetheless, fraud statistics (as relayed in Chapter 2) indicate relative consistency in the overall amount of estimated fraud and an increase in the amount of losses from fraud actually discovered.

The cornerstone and heart of effective corporate governance, internal controls, antifraud programs, or fraud investigations is a thorough risk assessment. Effective fraud risk assessment is dependent on knowledge of fraud concepts (the fraud triangle, red flags, fraud schemes, and accounting information systems), all considered in the applicable fraud environment (entity, time frame, effectiveness of current internal controls, etc.). While the term *risk assessment* may imply a periodic, point-in-time exercise, true risk management requires a continuous ongoing process. This chapter discusses risk assessment concepts and tools to aid in that process. While presented primarily from a perspective internal to the entity at hand, contents here are applicable to externally conducted fraud investigations and other external audiences.

TECHNICAL LITERATURE AND RISK ASSESSMENT

The notion of risk assessment has been part of the technical literature for audits, suggesting or outright requiring that audits incorporate risk assessment. Standards in recent years reflect increased coverage on risks. For public companies, the PCAOB's Auditing Standards No. 5 (AS5), *An Audit of Internal Control over Financial Reporting That Is Integrated with an Audit of Financial Statements* (adopted in 2007), built on the previously existing PCAOB standard No. 2 (AS2) predominantly by expanding the role of risk assessment. AS2 addressed risk assessments from a management and auditor perspective, and included coverage of risks at various levels (transactional, account, etc.). AS5 furthered AS2 concepts and emphasized the importance of a top-down, risk-based approach to internal control audits, and the importance of understanding the entity's environment (size, industry, etc.). Broadly speaking, PCAOB standards are infused with language, content, and suggestions regarding risk assessment.

The American Institute of Certified Public Accountants (AICPA) adopted the "Risk Suite" of standards, Statement on Auditing Standards (SAS) Nos. 104–111 in 2006. Broadly speaking, the Risk Suite addresses risk assessment in the context of financial statement audits and internal control. Like AS5, the Risk Suite includes an emphasis on a holistic, top-down, risk-based audit approach including a thorough knowledge of the entity's environment and its internal controls. More specific to fraud, the AICPA's SAS No. 99, *Consideration of Fraud in a Financial Statement Audit*, provides guidance for financial auditors, including brainstorming during the planning phase, and forced recognition of certain potential frauds, especially revenue manipulation. More broadly, the AICPA standard requires consideration of a host of organization-specific factors, such as industry, strategy, and so forth. Auditors are required to adjust the nature, timing, and extent of audit procedures if the circumstances warrant it, based on a risk assessment during brainstorming and subsequent knowledge and results from procedures.

The Institute of Internal Auditors (IIA) promotes the idea that all of the internal audit function audits and activities should begin with a risk assessment (e.g., sections 2010 and 2600 of *Standards of Professional Practice in Internal Audit* [SPPIA]). The Information Systems Audit and Control Association (ISACA) also has the same requirement in its technical literature. Statement on Information Systems Auditing Standards (SISAS), *Use of Risk Assessment in Audit Planning,* outlines certain requirements related to fraud for information technology audits. Many other ISACA standards address risk assessment as well, most notably SISAS 8, *Audit Considerations for Irregularities.*

RISK ASSESSMENT FACTORS

The fundamental concepts of risk assessment are probability (the chance an event will occur) and impact (the magnitude of the event if it occurs). However simple those concepts are, measuring and applying them is difficult. What factors should be considered? What tools can aid in assessing risks? How can risks be precisely measured?

Factors can be considered on many levels, including entity, people (behavioral), divisions, geographies, products or services, accounting or business processes, controls, or computerized systems. Typically, factors are considered first on an entity level, as the probability of fraud, theft, or embezzlement in any work environment is a product of the personality of the executive and employees, the working conditions, the effectiveness of internal controls, and the level of honesty therein (the organizational culture or environment). However the process begins, different perspectives should be included and/or examined in the risk assessment process, including how entity management incorporates risk management best practices.

Corporate Environment Factors

Employee fraud, theft, and embezzlement are more prevalent in some industries and some organizations than in others.

The Association of Certified Fraud Examiners (ACFE) 2008 *Report to the Nation* (RTTN) surveyed its members regarding frauds that were resolved, and a total of 959 cases were reported. One of the statistics relates to the industries represented by these cases. While the statistical results could indicate the type of industry that is most likely to hire a Certified Fraud Examiner (CFE) to investigate a fraud, the results also could indicate industries more susceptible to fraud. For those industries that are more susceptible to fraud, entities within those industries clearly have greater risk of fraud—something to consider in a risk assessment for those entities. That is, a risk assessment should take into account the level of assessed fraud risk in the industry of the entity. The 2008 RTTN results are:

Industry by Frequency:

- Banking/Financial services (14.5% of all cases reported)
- Government/Public administration (11.7%)
- Health care (8.4%)
- Manufacturing (7.2%)
- Retail (7%)

Industry by Median Loss:

- Telecommunications ($800,000/16 cases)
- Agriculture/Forestry/Fishing/Hunting ($450,000/13 cases)
- Manufacturing ($441,000/65 cases)
- Technology ($405,000/28 cases)
- Construction ($330,000/42 cases)

A risk assessment should also consider the current economy. In good times, people steal; in bad times, people steal more! A 2008–2009 survey by the ACFE asked 507 CFEs to report on the level of fraud since the beginning of the economic crisis. More than half indicated that the number of frauds had increased during that time. Also, 49 percent reported an increase in the dollar amount of the fraud losses during the same period. The theory is that one leg of the fraud triangle is what Donald Cressey referred to as "unshareable financial need" or pressure (as noted in Chapter 2) and people generally are under more pressure during an economic recession and in that sense there would be an expected increase in frauds.

In addition, conventional wisdom among members of the audit and security communities suggests that the organizations most vulnerable are those with the weakest management, accounting, and security controls. Organizations that are more vulnerable to employee occupational fraud and abuse can also be distinguished from those that are less vulnerable by the environmental and cultural contrasts shown in Exhibit 5.1.

EXHIBIT 5.1 Corporate Fraud Environment: Potential for Fraud

Factors	High Fraud Potential	Low Fraud Potential
Management Style	Autocratic, profit focused	Participative, customer focused
Management Orientation	Low trust X theory Power driven Management by crisis issues and personal differences are skirted or repressed	High trust Y theory Achievement driven Management by objective Issues and personal differences are confronted and addressed openly
Management Structure and Controls	Bureaucratic Regimented Inflexible Imposed controls Many-tiered, vertical	Collegial Systematic Open to change Self-controlled Flat structure, horizontal
CEO Characteristics	Swinger Braggart Self-interested Driver Insensitive to people Feared Insecure Gambler Impulsive Tight-fisted Number and things oriented Profit seeker Vain Bombastic Highly emotional Partial Pretends to be more than he/she is	Professional Decisive Fast-paced Friendly Respected by peers Secure Risk taker Thoughtful Generous with personal time and money Products and market oriented Builder Self-confident Helper Composed, calm, deliberate, even disposition Fair Knows who, what, and where he/she is
Authority	Centralized, reserved by top management Rigid rules strongly enforced	Decentralized, delegated to all levels Reasonable rules fairly enforced
Planning	Centralized Short range	Decentralized Long range
Performance	Measured quantitatively and on a short-term basis Critical feedback Negative feedback	Measured both qualitatively and quantitatively, and on a long-term basis Positive feedback Supportive feedback
Reporting	Routine reports only Everything documented—a rule for everything	Exception reporting Adequate documentation, but not burdensome—some discretion allowed

(*continued*)

EXHIBIT 5.1 *(Continued)*

	Formal, written, stiff, pompous, ambiguous internal communications	Informal, oral, clear, friendly, open, candid internal communications
Primary Management Concerns	Preservation of capital Profit maximization	Human, then capital and technological asset utilization Profit optimization
Reward System	Punitive Penurious Politically administered Mainly monetary	Reinforcing Generous Fairly administered Recognition, promotion, added responsibility, choice assignments, plus money
Business Ethics	Ambivalent: rides the tides	Clearly defined and regularly followed
Values and Beliefs	Economic, political Self-centered	Social, spiritual Group-centered
Internal Relationships	Highly competitive, hostile	Friendly, competitive, supportive
External Relationships/ Competitors	Hostile	Professional
Peer Relationships	Hostile, aggressive, contentious	Cooperative, friendly
Success Basis/ Formula	Works harder	Works smarter
Human Resource Problems	High turnover Burnout Grievances Absenteeism	Not enough promotional opportunities for all the talent
Financial Concerns	Cash flow shortage	Opportunities for new investments
Company Loyalty	Low	High
Growth Pattern	Sporadic	Consistent, steady

Source: Jack Bologna, *Forensic Accounting Review* (1985).

Internal Factors

Internal factors that enhance the probability of fraud, theft, and embezzlement include inadequate management controls or monitoring activities such as the following:

- Failure to create an honest culture

- Failure to articulate and communicate minimum standards of performance and personal conduct
- Inadequate orientation and training on legal, ethical, fraud, and security issues
- Inadequate company policies with respect to sanctions for legal, ethical, and security breaches; especially for frauds and white-collar crimes
- Failure to counsel and take administrative action when performance level or personal behavior falls below acceptable standards, or violates entity principles and guidelines
- Ambiguity in job roles, duties, responsibilities, and areas of accountability
- Lack of timely or periodic audits, inspections, and follow-through to ensure compliance with entity goals, priorities, policies, procedures, and governmental regulations; generally speaking, a lack of accountability over key positions of trust

Fraud Factors

Any risk assessment should also consider the fraud schemes that are more likely to occur in order to guide the antifraud program. Prevention and detection countermeasures are certainly more effective if they address the most likely fraud schemes to be committed.

For financial statement frauds, clearly the executives of the entity are the most likely would-be fraudster and thus a risk assessment would necessarily include those individuals. For asset misappropriation, an employee in a trusted position is likely to be the culprit. For corruption, it might be the same but it includes somebody outside the entity working with someone inside—a unique characteristic of corruption schemes.

The statistics from the ACFE RTTNs can provide some assistance in making these determinations, as can a productive brainstorming of a cross-functional team.

RISK ASSESSMENT BEST PRACTICES

If an entity has not done a formal risk assessment, it cannot effectively defend itself from those risks, or mitigate those risks for obvious reasons. In order to develop an effective risk assessment, management should take a conscientious, formal approach rather than an ad hoc approach. That approach includes the people and the process.

Leader(s)

The risk-assessment process should include an appropriate person or group, and ideally should include a team. For organizational management, the appropriate person normally would be someone who has sufficient independence, such as someone from the internal audit function, if one exists, and the ability to effectively support risk management. The value of having a person experienced and proven to be effective in assessing risk involved with any risk assessment function cannot be overstated. Neither can the support of the entity's audit committee and/or board of directors.

Team

The team should be chosen carefully. Although it should start with the internal expert and/or consultant, it must include a broad cross-section of the entity. That cross-section should involve different levels of the entity, especially levels of management. The team should represent all of the major business units (especially accounting and sales because most frauds occur there), business processes, key positions, and perspectives necessary to provide a quality risk assessment. People who think creatively, reason logically, understand the business and industry well, and can effectively play devil's advocate should be sought, regardless of their position.

Documenting risk assessments is critical, most particularly because the documentation can be reviewed afterward when the risk as assessed has or has not been realized. Documentation can then serve as a learning tool for more effective assessments and preventive measures; that is, lessons learned can help fine-tune future versions of risk assessment. Documentation also establishes accountability for persons involved in the process. Several tools can be used to conduct the risk assessment, which would serve a dual purpose of documenting it as well. Exhibit 5.2 provides a checklist to serve as one example of how to organize a risk assessment.

Frequency and Alignment with Finance

Formal risk assessment within an entity should be conducted regularly, probably every 12 to 24 months. An annual frequency would allow fraud risk assessments to align with the typical financial planning and/or financial reporting time frames. Financial planning entails future considerations overlapping finance and fraud. Financial reporting can include findings (adjustments, disclosures, control deficiencies, etc.) that might require future

EXHIBIT 5.2 Risk Management Checklist

	Yes	No	N/A	Ref
1. Does the organization have an adequate level of fraud awareness and are appropriate policies in place to minimize fraud risk? Specifically:				
a. Generic risk factors				
□ *Has each employee been assigned a maximum "opportunity level" to commit fraud; for each employee, has management asked itself the question, "What is the maximum amount of which this employee could defraud the organization, and does this represent an acceptable risk?"*	( )	( )	( )	
□ *Has a "catastrophic" opportunity level been set; that is, has management asked itself the question, "Have we ensured that no single employee—or group of employees in collusion—can commit a fraud that would place the organization in imminent risk of survival?"*	( )	( )	( )	
□ *Is it the organization 's policy to immediately dismiss any employee who is found to have committed a fraud?*	( )	( )	( )	
□ *Is it the organization's policy to report all frauds to the authorities and press charges?*	( )	( )	( )	
□ *For any and all frauds that the company has experienced in the past, have the reasons that led to the fraud been evaluated and corrective action taken?*	( )	( )	( )	
b. Managing individual risk factors (i.e., to promote moral behavior and minimize the motivation to commit fraud)				
□ *Does the organization have a corporate mission statement, which includes as an objective good corporate citizenship; that is, maintaining good standing in the community?*	( )	( )	( )	
□ *Does the organization have a written code of ethics and business conduct?*	( )	( )	( )	
□ *Does the organization conduct ethical and security training for new employees with periodic updates for existing employees?*	( )	( )	( )	
□ *Does management set the right example; for example, does it follow the corporate mission statement, code of ethics and business conduct, and other organization policies, and do the employees clearly see it doing so?*	( )	( )	( )	

(continued)

EXHIBIT 5.2 *(Continued)*

	Yes	No	N/A	Ref
☐ *Does the corporate culture avoid characteristics that promote unethical behavior; for example, high or even hostile competitiveness within the organization, pushing employees to burnout, rigid and/or petty policies, or over-centralization of authority?*	( )	( )	( )	
☐ *When hiring, does the organization, to the extent possible, seek out individuals of high moral character and weed out those of low moral character?*	( )	( )	( )	
☐ *For especially sensitive positions, are screening and/or testing procedures used; for example, background checks, psychological testing, drug testing, lie detector tests where legal?*	( )	( )	( )	
☐ *Does the organization provide and/or encourage counseling for employees with personal problems; for example, alcohol and drug abuse?*	( )	( )	( )	
☐ *Does the organization have fair employee relations and compensation policies; for example, salaries, fringe benefits, performance appraisal, promotions, severance pay? Do these policies compare favorably with competitors' and promote an environment that minimizes disenchantment and similar motivations to commit fraud?*	( )	( )	( )	
☐ *Are fair mechanisms in place for dealing with employee grievances?*	( )	( )	( )	
☐ *As a feedback mechanism on its policies with respect to employee relations, does the organization conduct exit interviews of departing employees?*	( )	( )	( )	
c. Management awareness				
☐ *Overall, does management exhibit an awareness of fraud and its possible manifestations; for example, signs of employee problems such as drug addiction, and low-paid employees who suddenly appear with trappings of wealth?*	( )	( )	( )	
2. Does the organization have an adequate system of internal controls? Specifically:				
a. Fraud integral to internal controls				
☐ *Has the need for fraud prevention been explicitly considered in the design and maintenance of the system of internal controls?*	( )	( )	( )	

	Yes	No	N/A	Ref
b. Control over physical and logical access				
□ *Does the organization have a policy and practice of locking doors, desks, and cabinets after hours and when unattended, especially for areas with valuable assets including files and records such as personnel and payroll, checks and. other accounting documents, customer and vendor lists, corporate strategies, marketing plans, and research?*	( )	( )	( )	
□ *Does the organization have a policy and practice of using IDs and passwords for general computer access?*	( )	( )	( )	
□ *For sensitive files and applications, does the computer system require additional access controls? For example, does the access control of each user ID limit him/her access? Are there additional layer(s) of access control for remote access (such as smart cards, temporary PINs, biometrics, etc.)?*	( )	( )	( )	
□ *Does the organization have a stated and enforced policy that access is restricted to those requiring it to perform their job functions, including a strict policy against employees allowing access to unauthorized personnel by loaning keys, sharing passwords, and so on?*	( )	( )	( )	
□ *For especially sensitive areas, are there additional computerized security and/or electronic surveillance systems?*	( )	( )	( )	
□ *To an impartial observer, does the workplace appear to have adequate access controls?*	( )	( )	( )	
c. Job descriptions				
□ *Does the organization have written and specific job descriptions?*	( )	( )	( )	
□ *Do employees and managers adhere to them?*	( )	( )	( )	
□ *Does the company have an organization chart that reflects and is consistent with the employee job descriptions?*	( )	( )	( )	
□ *Are incompatible duties segregated; that is, handling of valuable assets, especially cash and related records?*	( )	( )	( )	
□ *Is the purchasing function properly segregated; for example, to ensure that one individual cannot requisition goods or services, approve and make the related payment, and access accounts payable records?*	( )	( )	( )	

(continued)

EXHIBIT 5.2 *(Continued)*

	Yes	No	N/A	Ref
□ *Are especially sensitive duties duplicated; that is, the double-signing of checks over a specified amount?*	( )	( )	( )	
□ *Do job descriptions specify that annual vacations must be taken?*	( )	( )	( )	
□ *Overall, has the process of formulating job descriptions been an integrated one, giving adequate consideration to the importance of fraud prevention?*	( )	( )	( )	
d. Regular accounting reconciliations and analyses				
□ *Bank reconciliations, for all accounts?*	( )	( )	( )	
□ *Accounts receivable reconciliations (month to month, general ledger to subledger)?*	( )	( )	( )	
□ *Accounts payable reconciliations (month to month, general ledger to subledger)?*	( )	( )	( )	
□ *Variance analysis of general ledger accounts (budget to actual, current year versus prior year)?*	( )	( )	( )	
□ *Vertical analysis of profit and loss accounts, that is, as a percentage of sales, against historical and/or budget standards?*	( )	( )	( )	
□ *Detailed sales and major expense analysis; that is, by product line or geographic territory?*	( )	( )	( )	
e. Supervision				
□ *Do supervisors and managers have adequate fraud awareness; that is, are they alert to the possibility of fraud whenever an unusual or exceptional situation occurs, such as when a supplier or customer complains about its account?*	( )	( )	( )	
□ *Do supervisors and managers diligently review the work of their subordinates; for example, accounting reconciliations, and, where appropriate, even have the employee reperform the work?*	( )	( )	( )	
□ *For smaller businesses or where division of duties is not possible, is close supervision in place so as to compensate for the lack of segregation?*	( )	( )	( )	
□ *Is supervisory or management override (a manager or supervisor taking charge of, altering or otherwise interfering in the work of a subordinate) prohibited, and are others in the hierarchy alert to this situation as a fraud red flag?*	( )	( )	( )	

	Yes	No	N/A	Ref
f. Audit				
□ *Is there an internal audit function?*	( )	( )	( )	
□ *Does the internal audit function perform regular checks to ensure that fraud prevention mechanisms are in place and operating as intended?*	( )	( )	( )	
□ *Are external audits performed on a regular basis; that is, quarterly for larger businesses?*	( )	( )	( )	
□ *Does management fully cooperate with external auditors with respect to its work in general and fraud matters in particular; that is, through the audit committee?*	( )	( )	( )	
3. Has the organization addressed the following fraud prevention issues?				
□ *Promoting an ethical environment?*	( )	( )	( )	
□ *Risk financing?*	( )	( )	( )	

consideration. Ideally, risk assessments are a continuous process whereby central owners consistently monitor and adapt to the fraud environment with periodic "refreshes" of the risk assessment and plan for response. Public companies have SOX §404 as a mandated type of this iterative process.

RISK MANAGEMENT CHECKLISTS AND DOCUMENTATION

The checklist shown in Exhibit 5.2 is designed to assist accountants in assessing and managing the risk of fraud in their organizations and those of their clients. Generally, all "No" answers require investigation and follow-up, the results of which should be documented. Where there is such additional documentation, the purpose of the "Ref" column is to cross-reference the checklist to the appropriate source.

This checklist is intended for general use only. While the use of the checklist helps ensure adequate factors are considered, using the checklist does not guarantee fraud prevention or detection and the checklist is not intended as a substitute for audit or similar procedures. If fraud prevention is an especially vital concern or if fraud is suspected, a systematic assessment beyond a checklist should be performed and/or a specialist's advice should be sought.[1]

Fraud Schemes Checklist

Another approach to risk assessment is to use an appropriate taxonomy of fraud schemes. For example, the ACFE fraud tree could be used to determine at least the initial list of fraud schemes. This approach can work particularly well. The columns of this form of risk assessment include (see Exhibit 5.3):

- The fraud scheme
- An assessment of inherent risk for that fraud in the particular entity or business process
- The factor internal controls has in mitigating that risk
- The "residual risk" left over after the mitigation of existing internal controls related to this fraud scheme in this entity or business process
- Business processes, where the scheme is likely to occur, if it does occur
- Red flags, which could be used to detect this scheme

Different Entities to Assess

If an organization is large enough, a single risk assessment may not be as useful as separate risk assessments. In this case, it is recommended that a different assessment and team be used for each major business unit, each significant business process that crosses business units, the corporate unit (executives,

EXHIBIT 5.3 Fraud Schemes Risk Checklist

Fraud Schemes	**Inherent Risk**	**Controls Assessment**	**Residual Risk**	**Business Processes**	**Red Flags**
General antifraud					
Fraudulent statements					
Financial:					
Overstate revenues					
Timing differences					
Fictitious revenues					
Concealed liabilities					
Improper disclosures					
Improper asset valuation					
Asset/revenue understated					

etc.), and any other entity or element that the leaders and team identify. It is possible the company is so large that different layers may be necessary: for instance, business units rolled up to subsidiaries, rolled up to corporate, where higher risks are rolled up with specifics as to the unit associated with the specific risk. A potentially more effective, though more challenging, way to assess risk at a high level in large organizations is by accounting or business processes as these can more accurately reflect the fraud risks present and can more easily align with fraud schemes; for example, cash management, payroll, manufacturing product "X," or research and development.

Fraud Schemes

There are a variety of ways to determine the fraud schemes to list in the first column of Exhibit 5.3 (Fraud Schemes). However, one should start with some established taxonomy (see Chapter 2) and add or delete from that list as needed. Then, using other taxonomies, or good judgment about specific schemes that are risks to this particular industry or entity, one should make any necessary additions or deletions. Herein is the value of using brainstorming—teams using shared criteria to make sure that important schemes are not missed and that irrelevant schemes are not considered (at least for specific entities certain fraud schemes may be irrelevant).

Measures and Relationships

Measuring risk in a quantitative sense is usually quite difficult. Some base must be used as a corollary to the impact of potential losses of a *possible* fraud. What is a relevant, reliable, and representative indication of the risk needing measurement? Such a determination should be made and agreed on by the *team* according to shared, planned criteria. The critical and difficult job of measuring risks is again a testament to the importance of selecting a diversified, organization-encompassing team able to make logical decisions during the risk-assessment process.

Inherent Risk

The team should determine what the inherent risk is for this fraud scheme for this entity or business process. The assessment could be a probability (1 to 100 percent) or simply low, medium, or high risk. A number of factors can be considered here, some of which are industry, strategy, market volatility, and organizational structure.

Controls Assessment

Auditors and other key people on the team should determine what controls are in place to mitigate the specific fraud scheme. The assessment would, of course, match the method of assessing inherent risk (percentage or tier). One must be sure to consider that people in key positions can best evaluate weaknesses in internal controls and risks; but those same persons are potentially the ones to commit fraud in the given area.

Residual Risk

A simple mathematical function of subtracting the level of control mitigation from the inherent risk will leave the residual risk. Again, it would take the form of whatever was chosen for inherent risk. Residual risk will inevitably require one of two responses: no action, as the remaining risk is accepted, or action to mitigate or remediate through additional prevention or detection procedures (even potentially including the purchase of insurance). The response taken should be documented and tracked over time, in part to determine the entity's abilities to measure and manage risks.

Business Processes

This column is a notation column to identify which business processes (i.e., cash receipts, payroll, etc.) are involved with this scheme. The business process owner should be documented as the responsible party for the area and, if applicable, for responding to unacceptable residual risk. Considering the aggregated number and risk ratings of all schemes by business process can also shed light on fraud risk.

Red Flags

Here the team would identify the red flags that could be associated with the scheme. This documentation is a starting point for fraud prevention or detection procedures. Red flags are available from a variety of literature sources. They include:

- ISACA's standard 030.020.010 (SISAS 8), *Audit Considerations for Irregularities*
- AICPA SAS No. 99, *Consideration of Fraud in a Financial Statement Audit*[2]
- PCAOB Standards No. 5 and No. 2

- *Occupational Fraud and Abuse*[3]
- Corporate policies, procedures, and internal controls
- Actual fraud cases, especially the entity's

SUMMARY

Risk assessment is a critical starting point for audits in general. In this chapter, risk assessment is used as a tool for an entity's antifraud program, where the entity is trying to minimize its fraud risk. As such, this step does not occur during the fraud audit processes. Rather, it is a tool to identify the risks and address the most important ones. It is recommended that any business, especially a publicly-traded one, go through this exercise on a regular basis, and that fraud auditors consider these concepts and management's risk management abilities in the course of fraud prevention, detection, and investigation.

NOTES

1. Joseph T. Wells, *Principles of Fraud Examination* (New York: John Wiley & Sons, 2008).
2. AU316, pp. 30–34.
3. Joseph T. Wells, *Occupational Fraud and Abuse* (Austin, TX: ACEF, 1997).

CHAPTER SIX

Fraud Prevention

INTRODUCTION

When developing a fraud control system, it is very difficult to know what to protect and how to protect it if one does not first perform a risk assessment to see where the risks lie in the entity (except for a fraud that has already occurred!). That would include the assets with the most risk, the fraud schemes most likely to occur, related red flags, and the residual risk considering what controls are in place to mitigate the risks present. Fraud prevention and risk assessment (Chapter 5) both deserve a thorough discussion, so they are separated in this book.

The goal of any antifraud program is to prevent fraud, not just detect it. The old axiom of "An ounce of prevention is worth a pound of cure" is an understatement with regard to fraud. The passage of the Sarbanes-Oxley (SOX) Act of 2002 puts into law tenets intended to *prevent* fraud. Although detecting fraud is important, it obviously would be better if fraud could be mitigated or minimized—prevented to the degree possible. Detection is inevitably tied to prevention, and the two together provide the system of antifraud controls. This chapter presents the components of a successful antifraud control system.

PREVENTION ENVIRONMENT

A key to successful fraud prevention is to look at the entity's culture and try to change it, if necessary. Some activities and attitudes can help in achieving this goal. The important prevention elements that are discussed next are generally applied to an entity, and not necessarily directed toward a specific fraud.

Corporate Governance Structure

Prior to the passage of SOX, research had shown that weak corporate governance was associated with all of the major financial frauds. For instance, the COSO *Landmark Study* (1998) studied 200 of the 300 fraud cases handled by the Securities and Exchange Commission (SEC) from 1987 to 1997.[1] The researchers found a distinctive pattern of weak boards for those entities investigated. Seventy-two percent of the cases identified the chief executive officer (CEO), and 43 percent named the chief financial officer (CFO) as being involved with the fraud. In addition, according to *Wheel, Deal and Steal*, the vast majority of the boards are chaired by a former or current CEO.[2]

Weaknesses from the report were summarized as follows:

- Board members who were not independent
- Board dominated by insiders
- Board members with significant equity holdings
- Board members with little board experience
- Boards and audit committees that did not meet
- Audit committee members who knew little about finances or auditing
- No audit committee
- Audit committee did not meet
- Top executives involved in the frauds

From the weaknesses listed here, the basic elements of governance are clear and SOX addresses these issues by requiring more independence and expertise, as well as a number of other activities that relate to good corporate governance. For instance, audit committees are responsible for implementing an anonymous tips and complaints system and a whistleblower system. SOX also requires the audit committee to hire external audit firms and set its fee for the financial audit. SOX recommends a high level of interaction between the audit committee with both internal and financial auditors. In summary, good corporate governance includes active, qualified, and independent members of the board and especially the audit committee.

Tone at the Top

Regardless of the corporate governance structure, management's style sets the tone for the organization. Although it is a worn-out phrase, sometimes ignored, often misused, the tone at the top is still a key to preventing fraud. If one reviews the major scandals of recent years, in almost every case, an executive was involved. That executive typically mistrusted people and kept as much of the financial affairs as possible secreted away from auditors. Thus there was clearly no antifraud tone at the top in Enron, WorldCom, Tyco, and others.

If key managers, and the board of directors where it exists, continually talk about fraud, communicate fraud policies, and encourage everyone to be involved in preventing and detecting fraud, then the entity eventually will develop an antifraud culture. Without the emphasis and support of key management, it is almost impossible to have such a culture.

Realistic Financial Goals

Another common element of the major frauds was the overoptimistic goals set for corporate performance. In financial frauds of the past, almost every goal and strategy of the entity revolved around increasing profits to an abnormal level for that industry and/or that entity. If the entity's leaders, especially the board, can avoid setting unrealistic financial goals, there will be less pressure on the executives to cut corners to reach those financial goals. Balancing those goals with any negative impact they might have is a delicate task.

As discussed, one of the legs of the fraud triangle is *pressure (motivation)*, and unrealistic financial goals automatically create this leg. Management can always override controls or collude at some level, which is a second leg of the fraud triangle—*opportunity*. That situation means only the executive's ethics (*rationalization*—the third and final leg) will prevent that executive from committing a financial fraud, if unrealistic performance goals exist.

Policies and Procedures

Policies define entity objectives and principles, while procedures define actions the entity takes to ensure objectives are achieved. Policies and procedures document the actions and transactions determined to be unethical, as well as how violations will be treated. Therefore, the foundation for an antifraud culture and environment for any entity serious about preventing fraud is a fraud policy and carefully crafted procedures based on policy. SOX essentially requires publicly-traded companies to have an ethics policy. Companies without a written ethics policy must state so in their 10-K forms and explain why they do not have one. A fraud policy becomes the source document for developing fraud prevention measures, actions to detect fraud, and actions in response to a fraud, and thus influence the effectiveness of an antifraud culture or climate.

To have an effective antifraud culture, an entity should have policies and procedures that:

- Define *frauds*
- Describe publication and communication of policy
- Describe implementation of controls for antifraud
- Describe training
- Describe proactive fraud audit measures
- Describe testing of antifraud controls
- Define investigation policies and procedures
- Describe actions taken in fraud audit
- Describe the analysis of evidence
- Describe resolutions to frauds
- Describe incident reporting procedures

But the creation of a written ethics or fraud policy is insufficient by itself. Effective systems include a means of communicating that policy adequately to all involved. An example would be to include ethics and fraud in employee orientation programs. Crucial to the success of the policy is a monitoring and compliance system. In research conducted on frauds and cooperatives, it was found when all three—policy, communication, and compliance—are present, fraud instances were statistically significantly less than any other situation. Only about one-tenth of the entities with an ethics policy had any compliance mechanism in place.[3]

Ethics policies can be based on values or principles. Instead of a detailed list of policies and procedures, a handful of values are selected as symbolic of the entity. With this approach, employees must buy into the values, which must be engrained in the culture and reinforced by actions.

Importantly, entities must consider the human element of the organization's culture. Although a myriad of factors influence culture, some are more important than others. The people are a large component of culture. Building an antifraud culture that fits the people, the business operations, and the organization as a whole will ensure that fraud is mitigated to the degree possible.

PERCEPTION OF DETECTION

Antifraud professionals agree that perception of detection is at the top of the list of fraud prevention measures. In fact, based on years of law enforcement and criminal justice experience, crime experts say the best deterrent to crime, including fraud, is the perception of detection. Because white-collar criminals who commit fraud tend to have some personal code of ethics, this technique is even more effective in preventing fraud than it is for "street" crimes. The fear of jail, humiliation, or loss of family ties is enough of a deterrent for many potential fraudsters to cause them to stop, think, and decide it is not worth the total cost. The best thing any entity can do to minimize fraud is to find a cost-beneficial way to increase the perception of detection. Some ways to increase the perception of detection include:

- Surveillance
- Anonymous tips
- Surprise audits
- Prosecution
- Enforcement of ethics and fraud policies
- Catch me if you can!

Surveillance

In those places where assets are at high risk, such as mailrooms where mail that contains checks and/or cash is opened, surveillance cameras or other surveillance methods can be a good perception of detection method. If surveillance is going to be employed as a countermeasure against fraud, it is best to announce it to the world that it is in place. One must make sure to monitor the surveillance in such a way that people will believe someone is actually following up on suspicious activities. Unethical employees will test the effectiveness of surveillance to see if it is really monitored and used by someone to actually follow up on suspicious activities. It is possible to use "dead" or fake cameras but only in conjunction with live cameras with monitoring and expeditious follow-up.

Anonymous Tips

Tips have been shown to be the best method to date in detecting frauds. However, they are also a prevention measure. The reason is simple. If employees know there is an anonymous tips system and anyone who sees something suspicious can turn them in, then it begins to serve as a perception-of-detection preventive measure. Best practices for anonymous tip programs include appropriate involvement of management, independent handling of complaints by a third party, and using multiple communication methods (phone, letter, email, etc.). Above all, make it easy, convenient, and comfortable for employees to provide a tip.

Surprise Audits

Internal audit is the highest-ranked proactive method of detection (per the Association of Certified Fraud Examiners [ACFE] *Report to the Nation* [RTTN] statistics). But surprise audits by either the internal audit function or hired fraud auditors are even more effective. Not only can these audits serve a similar purpose in detecting frauds (which can then be considered for further preventive measures), but the fact the surprise audit was unannounced can create a perception of detection. Fraudsters do not know when the fraud auditor is going to show up, so they cannot prepare to fool the auditor. In fact, in at least one fraud, a fake announcement of a surprise audit (the internal auditor was attempting to play a joke) caused the manager of the business unit to confess to a fraud.

Prosecution

Enormous benefits can be gained by prosecuting fraudsters to the maximum extent of the law. It is true that there is some downside risk in a public trial, and even some risk that the prosecuting agency may fail to do its job effectively. But the upside is not merely obtaining justice for the single incident and justice for the fraudster. Prosecuting someone sends a strong message about perception of detection: If one commits a fraud and gets caught, this entity is going to seek prosecution and perhaps imprisonment. Most experts agree that prosecution is *key* to maintaining an effective level of perception of detection.

Think of the signal that was sent in this case. A bank vice president (VP) stole about $5 million from his bank in fraudulent loans, which he transferred to a Cayman bank. When caught, the bank decided it was in its best interest to not prosecute. The VP was fired and never paid a penny back to the bank. So what would a rational VP of this bank think about working for the employer?

Would she be deterred or would she decide that the fraudster VP had found a better retirement plan?

There are numerous stories of people who commit a fraud, do not get punished, and move on to commit another one at the next employer. This scenario is likely if an entity chooses not to prosecute but rather just fire the employee. That is, it is usually best for the business community and the fraudster for the victim to prosecute. But quite often the victim does not prosecute because it is not good for them—at least in the short term. This approach seems to contradict a famous philosophical statement: "The good of the many outweigh the good of the one or the few."

Enforcement of Ethics and Fraud Policies

The same philosophy is true for compliance with fraud policy, ethics policy, and corporate policy in handling frauds. An entity should have determined beforehand what it would do if a fraud occurred; in particular, what penalties would be meted out for what kinds of frauds and levels of fraud. Then the entity would need to make sure to monitor and follow through with its stated penalties for fraud. Failure to follow its own guidelines for punishment of frauds is worse than having no fraud policy at all. It is emotionally difficult to make these kinds of decisions ad hoc after a fraud has occurred, and those emotions may inhibit the best decision.

Catch Me If You Can!

Oddly enough, perhaps the greatest perception of a detection measure is to catch a fraudster, prosecute him, and highly publicize what has been done. A recently busted fraudster can significantly increase the perception of detection, as it serves as a living example and reminder that this entity is serious, capable of detecting frauds, and willing to prosecute. Additionally, rewarding employees who contribute to detecting fraud contributes to an antifraud culture.

CLASSIC APPROACHES

A review of the classic approaches to the reduction of employee theft, fraud, and embezzlement is helpful in developing an effective fraud prevention and control program. Here are the classics:

- *Directive approach.* The directive approach is confrontational and authoritative. It says: "Don't steal. If you do, and we catch you, you'll be fired."

When an entity does little or nothing to prevent fraud, it is probably taking this approach. If a fraud did occur and was detected, management would probably fire the employee—and probably would not prosecute the fraudster. Management probably also would be shocked that someone would perpetrate a fraud against the entity.

- *Preventive approach.* In the preventive approach, potential fraudsters are screened out using various means, including background checks for criminal records and credit reports. Internal controls can be used in the preventive approach. Namely, segregation of duties can mitigate the risk of fraud at least to the point where management must override controls or persons must collude to commit fraud, which are always possibilities.
- *Detective approach.* In the detective approach, management sets up accounting controls and an internal audit function to monitor potential frauds. The internal audit function periodically verifies the legitimacy of transactions and confirms the existence of assets. Between the periodic audits, management depends on the accounting controls to detect any fraud that might occur.
- *Observation approach.* The observation approach relies on physical observation of assets and employees. Management monitors employee conduct for suspicious behaviors or activities. The level of stocks of valuable and portable goods is also monitored in person or by other means, such as cameras. The goods include valuable and portable inventory, cash, and other such assets.
- *Investigative approach.* Based on investigative results, the investigative approach follows up on discrepancies. For example, the entity would follow up on allegations of theft. For unfavorable, or certain favorable, variances in inventory, goods, materials, supplies, and product costs, the entity would follow up to determine the nature and extent of the loss and who the likely culprits might be.
- *Insurance approach.* This approach depends on adequate insurance coverage to cover losses that might occur due to a fraud. Although this approach clearly does not reduce employee theft, it does soften the financial blow when fraudulent losses occur.

But employee theft may occur even if an entity adopts all of these classic approaches. Two types of frauds can always occur: collusion between two persons and management override of controls. Additionally, the nature of these frauds mean they can continue on a large scale undetected. That fact seems to be the experience of many firms today, as evidenced by the results of the ACFE

1996, 2002, 2004, 2006, and 2008 RTTN where each survey showed fraud costs were 5 to 7 percent of total revenues.[4] What other options are available to minimize the rate of fraud and the amount of loss from frauds?

OTHER PREVENTION MEASURES

Outside of the general (environmental, cultural, and corporate) prevention measures, specific prevention measures can be employed to minimize fraud. The key employees—those who have control or access over valuable and portable assets such as cash or checks—need to be the object of prevention measures and fraud countermeasures. An entity should consider the appropriate prevention measures that would hold these employees accountable for handling valued assets.

Background Checks

One potentially effective prevention measure is to use background checks for key employees. Although a background check can reveal potential problems, it is not a 100 percent effective means of identifying potential fraudsters and not always cost effective for all employees. A background check could reveal a criminal record and/or high debt. Either of them could be justification not to hire the person. The high debt is evidence that the *pressure* (economic or financial pressure in this case) leg of the fraud triangle is already present. The criminal record shows the history of committing crimes before and willingness to perpetrate a fraud (relates to rationalization).

However, according to the ACFE 2008 RTTN, only 7 percent of fraud perpetrators in the study had prior convictions, and only 12 percent had been previously terminated by an employer for fraud-related conduct. Another related, simple, and sometimes overlooked measure is calling potential employee's references. There have been instances noted where a fraudster made a mistake in the references or confidently assumed no one would check and a single, simple phone call had a big impact on the hiring decision.

Regular Audits

The fact that auditors are coming around on a regular basis can serve as a prevention measure. Though by nature regular audits are detective, they could increase the perception of detection and thus serve as a prevention measure. However, if the auditors use some effective audit tools and techniques to look for ongoing fraud aggressively, that would serve as a prevention measure. A key to the effectiveness of regular fraud audits is to identify, review, and analyze anomalies.

In at least a couple of the major financial frauds of recent years, the internal audit function was crippled and not allowed to do anything serious with financial information, but kept busy with other kinds of audits. The CEOs for those companies were taking no chances that some diligent internal auditor might stumble across their scams. That happened where one internal auditor came in late at night and secretly examined financial records to which she was not allowed access during the day by the senior executives. Eventually, she uncovered the financial fraud and exposed the fraudster CEO.

In a separate instance, a small university newspaper office had one accountant who did all of the accounting. A retired accounting professor was conducting regular audits of the newspaper accounts. In April of a certain year, the retired professor notified the university president that this year would be his last audit. He suggested that the president find a replacement or put an internal audit function into place. Up until this time, the university did not have an internal audit function. In mid-October, a university VP got a call from the newspaper printing vendor. The vendor representative said the company was not going to print the next issue of the university newspaper because it had not been paid in some time. The VP checked into the records and found the accounting clerk had stolen thousands of dollars. Oddly enough, she began to steal in May of that year. Clearly the regular audit had served as a perception-of-detection measure for her, but once removed, she was able to rationalize the fraud.

Internal Controls

The fraud triangle includes *opportunity*, which is basically a synonym for internal controls. Of the three legs, a fraud auditor or professional has little if any ability to affect *pressure* or *rationalization*, though management can create a positively influencing environment for those aspects. Pressure and rationalization aspects happen predominantly in one's mind and can be difficult to observe directly. Specific control activities can restrict the opportunity to commit fraud and are more easily observed. Thus the control environment, specifically antifraud control activities, can act as preventive fraud measures.

Historically, the most common flaw with regards to fraud in control activities (aligned with corporate governance as discussed earlier) is inadequate and unmonitored segregation of duties. Other internal controls include:

- Proper authorization procedures
- Adequate documentation, records, and audit trail
- Physical control over assets and records
- Independent checks on performance
- Monitoring of controls

If SOX is truly a compilation of best practices, then section 404 of SOX aligns with attempts to minimize fraud. Section 404 requires annual evaluations of internal controls over financial reporting. As discussed, SOX is a dually preventive measure in that the perception of detection exists for the annually recurring SOX audit, and control weaknesses may be identified which can then be strengthened to function as a preventive measure.

Invigilation

A variation of surveillance is invigilation. In invigilation, the fraud auditor creates a pristine environment that should be fraud-free. That is, it is a high-profile, well-staffed fraud audit. Because employees will be very careful to not commit fraudulent activities during such a time, the invigilation serves as a benchmark of what the entity *should* be earning in revenues. By analyzing the revenues during the invigilation against other time periods, a fraud auditor can determine if frauds are occurring regularly outside the invigilation.

Invigilation is particularly useful for off-the-books frauds for which normal detective methods are fairly useless. Invigilation provides a benchmark to verify existing revenues, for example, and enables management to determine whether skimming or some other off-the-book scheme appears to have been perpetrated.

ACCOUNTING CYCLES

One way to address prevention measures is to examine the accounting business processes in their natural cycles. Considering some of the common characteristics of frauds in these areas is a way to develop effective prevention measures therein. Here we present a few examples to illustrate preventive measures that might be affected.

Generalizations

First, it should be noted how accounting transactions and cycles are specific to any given organization. The specificity can be due to the industry, strategy, size, culture, organizational structure, capital structure, and various other factors. The important fact to glean from this is that to prevent or detect fraud, one must understand the underlying processes and the situational environment. No frauds occur within a vacuum.

Organizational size is one of the most important factors to consider in fraud control. Size greatly impacts segregation of duties, a critical area to fraud prevention and detection. Size is also a factor when it comes to the type and amount of fraud committed (as noted in Chapter 5). Size is a factor when it comes to the control method; large organizations are innately more complex, and therefore more difficult to control in most aspects, but have more control resources to expend. The opposite is true for smaller organizations. This generalization does not always hold true. For example, segregation of duties is hard to implement in small organizations as a preventive control but is easier to detect as the organizational structure is generally much thinner and more tightly connected. Again, the critical point here is to understand the organizational context and the fraud environment factors at hand.

Although each organization's accounting transactions and cycles differ, on some level they are the same. Only a handful of basic accounting cycles exist. Though fraudulent transactions therein take on many forms, their substance is the same. (See Chapter 10 for Accounting Information Systems [AIS] and more on cycles.)

Sales Cycle

One common scheme in the sales cycle is *lapping*. For a person to carry on a lapping scheme for an extended period of time, she cannot afford to take more than a day or so at a time off work. Two possible prevention measures for lapping are: (1) forced rotation of duties and (2) forced taking of vacation. Segregation of duties can help prevent frauds such as *larceny* and *write-off schemes*. In many cases, a simple independent authorization step needs to be added to the business process.

Purchases Cycle

In the purchases cycle, the highest percentage of frauds revolve around fraudulent disbursements. One common fraud is a *shell company*. To perpetrate this fraud, a party needs to add vendors to the authorized list. Again, many fraud schemes could be stymied by segregation of duties, often a simple independent authorization step. This measure should help prevent *check tampering, false voids,* and *false refunds,* for example. Transactions with related parties, both in prevention and detection controls, should be carefully scrutinized, as this situation is another common area for fraud in disbursements.

Payroll Cycle

In the payroll cycle, common schemes to consider include *ghost employees*. An independent party could be used to add employees to the authorized payroll file. Another prevention method is to cross-check payroll against human resource (HR) records periodically. A ghost employee will be in the payroll but not the HR file. Forced rotation of duties and vacations in the payroll manager area is probably a good prevention measure as well.

Another critical point is the attention to people in and associated with the organization. HR, of course, is highly focused on getting the right people and, after all, *people commit fraud*. A thorough hiring process can be an effective fraud prevention technique.

SUMMARY

It is obviously more desirable to prevent fraud than to detect it after it occurs. There are a limited number of prevention methods (e.g., perception of detection) an entity can employ, but they are essential to a fraud-free environment. There are environmental issues that can enhance those preventive methods. A careful analysis of the business processes in the accounting cycle provides valuable input into preventive measures. Together, the countermeasures and concepts herein should enable auditors to assist management in developing an effective antifraud program that can minimize frauds.

NOTES

1. COSO, *Landmark Study on Fraud in Financial Reporting*, 1998.
2. Daniel Quinn Mills, *Wheel, Deal, and Steal: Deceptive Accounting, Deceitful CEOs, and Ineffective Reforms* (Upper Saddle River, NJ: Financial Times Prentice Hall, 2003).
3. Tommie Singleton, Frank Messina, and Rick Turpen, "Waving the Red Flag," *Rural Cooperatives*, (July–August 2003), pp. 13–14.
4. ACFE, *Report to the Nation*, 1996, 2002, 2004, 2006, and 2008.

CHAPTER SEVEN

7 Fraud Detection

INTRODUCTION

The cornerstone of effective fraud detection is presented in the key concepts of Chapters 1 through 4. The fundamentals in Chapter 1 provide information about the fraud investigation process itself. The concepts introduced in Chapter 2 help to explain fraud with the fraud triangle and the fraud tree. They are important in effective fraud detection, which is *early* detection. The fraud schemes presented in Chapter 3 are critical to detecting fraud. Chapter 4 stressed the important role red flags play in antifraud activities. In fraud detection, one needs a substantial amount of knowledge on all four topics: fraud background, fraud principles, fraud schemes, and red flags.

For example, the fraud theory approach to detecting frauds starts with identifying the most likely fraud scheme and how it might have been perpetrated. But in order to prove or disprove the resulting theory, the fraud investigator will need to know the fraud schemes (fraud tree), the fraud triangle, something about controls, and a lot about red flags. Topics in this chapter include fraud detection axioms and methods, general and specific (note specific detection methods are organized in the same manner as red flags are presented in Chapter 4).

FRAUD DETECTION AXIOMS

There are several axioms concerning fraud detection that are important to remember when designing an antifraud program or activities. A key to fraud detection is to remember that frauds are more often associated with the absence of controls rather than weak controls; that is, a weak control is generally better than none. They are also more often detected by reactive measures rather than proactive ones; thus there is a lot of room for improvement. There is an overreliance on external audit to detect frauds (see Chapter 17 for differences between a fraud audit and a financial audit). Lastly, frauds are often detected by intuition, suspicion of investigators, managers, auditors, or an exception (anomaly) detected in the accounting records. However, frauds are most often detected by proven detection methods. This chapter is devoted to proven means of *early* detection of fraud.

COMMON DETECTION METHODS

Periodically, the Association of Certified Fraud Examiners (ACFE) conducts a study on frauds resolved in the previous 12 to 18 months and reports the statistics to the public in the form of a report entitled *Report to the Nation* (RTTN). The ACFE has issued a RTTN in 1996, 2002, 2004, 2006, and 2008. In each RTTN, the statistics show the more common detection methods. In all years, the most common detection method has been tips. In some years, tips accounted for about twice as much in percentage of detection as whatever method ranked second. In all years, the least effective detection method, other than law enforcement, is external audit. It is therefore not logical to rely primarily on external audit for an entity's detection method yet that is exactly what most entities that experience frauds are doing; the 2008 RTTN shows external audit as the most popular control employed by the victim entities (almost 70 percent of the entities were using external audit, 61.5 percent a code of conduct, 55.8 percent internal audit). Notably, the least frequently employed controls by fraud victims are those listed as the most effective; that is, fraud victims have their controls upside down. This control information is a valuable source of knowledge in detecting frauds. Exhibit 7.1 shows the results from the 2008 RTTN.

Effective General Methods

The ACFE's RTTN classifies fraud controls by efficiency to detect or prevent fraud. Specifically, the 2008 RTTN asked respondents to identify which fraud countermeasures were in place when the fraud being reported was discovered, as well as the amount of the loss. Then a simple ratio depicting fraud loss

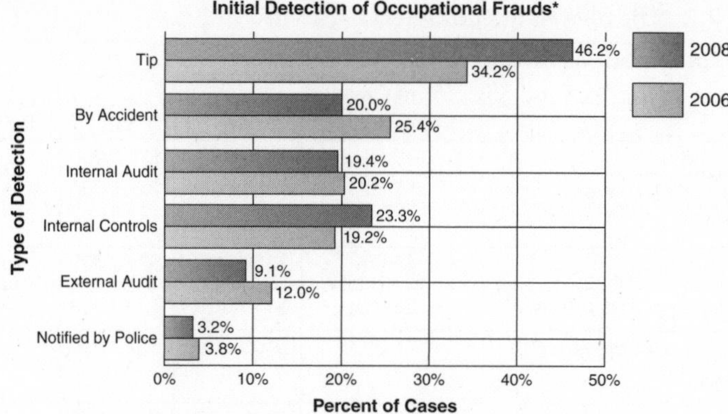

EXHIBIT 7.1 Most Common Detection Controls

Source: Report to the Nation on Occupational Fraud and Abuse, © 2008 by the Association of Certified Fraud Examiners, Inc., www.acfe.com/documents/2008-rttn.pdf.

reduction was calculated on each countermeasure, antifraud control, based on whether that control was in place ("yes") or not ("no"), and the average loss for each of the two groups.

Exhibit 7.2 depicts the analysis of the controls along with the ratio, which shows surprise audits as the most effective antifraud control, if measured in its ability to reduce the amount of losses incurred. It is followed by job rotation/mandatory vacation, anonymous hotlines (tips and complaints), employee support programs, fraud training for managers and executives, internal audit or fraud examination department, and fraud training for employees. Each of these controls reduced losses by at least 50 percent. Many of these methods would be considered detective controls, and would be useful in deploying antifraud controls that can provide *early* detection.

Other General Methods

Methods can be developed for frauds in general, or specific groups of frauds (e.g., a category), or even individual schemes. Some methods that could be used for general detection, regardless of the scheme, are:

- Internal audit function actively engaged in proactive antifraud activities
- Sarbanes-Oxley Act (SOX) section 404 results can lead to identification of weaknesses in internal controls that can cause a higher risk for fraud in that area or business process

EXHIBIT 7.2 Effective Antifraud Detection Controls

Median Loss Based on Presence of Antifraud Controls				
Control	**% of Cases Implemented**	**Yes**	**No**	**% Reduction**
Surprise audits	25.5%	$ 70.000	$207.000	66.2%
Job rotation/Mandatory vacation	12.3%	$ 64.000	$164.000	61.0%
Hotline	43.5%	$100.000	$250.000	60.0%
Employee support programs	52.9%	$110.000	$250.000	56.0%
Fraud training for manager/ executives	41.3%	$100.000	$227.000	55.9%
Internal audit/ Fraud Examination department	55.8%	$118.000	$250.000	52.8%
Fraud training for employees	38.6%	$100.000	$208.000	51.9%
Antifraud policy	36.2%	$100.000	$197.000	49.2%
External audit of internal controls over financial reporting	53.6%	$121.000	$232.000	47.8%
Code of conduct	61.5%	$126.000	$232.000	45.7%
Management review of internal controls	41.4%	$110.000	$200.000	45.0%
External audit of financial statements	69.6%	$150.000	$250.000	40.0%
Independent audit committee	49.9%	$137.000	$200.000	31.5%
Management certification of financial statements	51.6%	$141.000	$200.000	29.5%
Rewards for whistleblower	5.4%	$107.000	$150.000	28.7%

Source: Report to the Nation on Occupational Fraud and Abuse, © 2008 by the Association of Certified Fraud Examiners, Inc., www.acfe.com/documents/2008rttn.pdf.

- Horizontal and vertical analysis of financial reports, especially when comparisons are made between business units and their data
- Ratio analysis, especially trends over several years, and by business unit compared to other units and the entity as a whole
- Surprise audits and/or cash counts
- Anonymous tips and complaints system to which employees, vendors, and customers have access; comfortable, convenient, easy to use
- Data mining for applicable red flags using Computer-Assisted Auditing Tools (CAAT).

SPECIFIC DETECTION METHODS

This section describes some detection methods that are designed to detect specific schemes or groups of schemes rather than fraud in general.

Financial Statement Schemes

- Financial auditors' application of SAS No. 99
- Horizontal and vertical analysis of financial reports
- Ratio analysis, especially trends over several years
- Beneish's five earnings manipulation ratios (see Appendix 7A)
- Examination of generally accepted accounting principles (GAAP) tax rate versus cash tax rate
- Irrational price-to-earnings ratios: benchmark is 20 to 25, S&P average is about 36
- An audit committee that meets SOX requirements and is actively engaged in an antifraud program, especially in holding executives accountable
- Running background checks on executives
- External auditors maintaining a professional skepticism on *every* client

Asset Misappropriation Schemes

- Sending the bank statements to a person in the entity separate from accounts payable and any check-writing personnel, and having that person review the statement and cancelled checks, then forward them to the person responsible for the bank reconciliation
- Rotating duties or mandating vacation for key employees
- Examining all types of transactions that have a review/approval level, extracting all transactions just below that level, and classifying them by employee, vendor, and customer
- Reconciling inventory and confirming receivables regularly

Cash Larceny

- Investigating shortages in cash drawers, deposits, registers
- Investigating missing or altered sales records
- Having two people independently verify deposits on bank statements to postings in the general ledger
- Maintaining and reviewing daily cash availability amounts

- Having deposits delivered to the bank under dual control
- Secretly determining the deposit prior to its transmittal to the bank and then independently confirming with the bank the amount of the deposit
- Making sure deposits in transit are the first to clear on the next statement (flag associated with lapping deposits)
- Conducting surprise cash counts
- Reviewing cash and check ratio of daily bank deposits (for those who steal only cash)
- Reviewing timeliness of deposits from remote locations to central treasurer function
- Observing cash receipting at all points of entry

Billing Schemes

Shell Company

- Sorting payments by vendor, amount, and invoice number
- Expense exceeds budget, especially if it is exactly double (i.e., possibly producing two checks, one for the legitimate vendor, and one for the fraudster)
- Examining charges in largest expense account, as fraudsters often charge billing schemes to the largest account in an attempt to hide the crime
- Horizontal analysis
- Verifying service-only vendors' invoices
- Using a CAAT software tool to cross-reference employees' addresses with vendors' addresses
- Testing for turnaround time from receipt of invoice to payment
- Verifying that vendors are legitimate. While this test may appear daunting, it can become manageable by verifying only the vendors added since last audit, and only ones specific to the applicable business unit. Look them up in the phone book or in the online white pages. Use Google to search for the firm. Check with the local chamber of commerce. Contact others in the same industry.
- Reviewing cancelled checks
- Not paying a suspicious invoice/vendor and seeing who follows up on payment
- Taking special precaution with those employees who can add a vendor to the authorized list (segregate that duty if possible from invoice approval)
- Data mining for as many of the red flags as possible

- Verifying the legitimacy of any vendor who uses Excel-generated invoices
- Printing the vendor list alphabetically and searching for two vendors with nearly identical names and data

Pass-Through Vendor

- Examining all invoices just below the approval level, sorted by vendor or employee who approved the invoice
- Comparing market prices for prices on invoices, using a CAAT and some research
- Reviewing invoices for what is being bought and the prices

Nonaccomplice Vendor

- Sorting invoices by vendor and looking for unusual invoice numbers
- Classifying vendor by invoice amounts and looking for unusual amounts
- Verifying invoices that led to vendor refunds
- Requesting that the bank notify the proper person if someone endorses a check where the company is the payee, and use the stamp "For Deposit Only" for all endorsements

Personal Purchases

- Spot-checking expenditures on credit cards, looking for unusual vendors or items bought
- Surprise audits of employees who are authorized to use credit cards or sign checks
- Examining unfavorable balances on performance reports
- Vendor payment trend analysis
- Extracting all purchases with no purchase order, summarized by both vendor and employee
- Extracting all purchases just below the review/approval limit, summarized by both vendor and employee

Payroll Schemes

Ghost Employee

- Where feasible, reconciling employees in the payroll database with employees in the human resource (HR) database; the ghost should be missing in HR.

- Getting a copy of the Social Security number (SSN) file and, at least once a year, reconciling that file with your employees' SSNs
- Periodically and unannounced, distributing checks manually, requiring ID to pick up check
- Investigating any payroll checks with dual endorsements (a sign that an employee accomplice is working with a real person who is serving as the ghost)
- Rotating duties of handling printed paychecks, or requiring vacation timed with issuance of paychecks (pay day)
- Data mining payroll data looking for these red flags:
  - Post office box versus a physical address
  - Physical address matches that of another employee (i.e., a "duplicate")
  - Direct deposit account number that matches that of another employee
  - Missing phone number, or a phone number that matches either another employee or a work phone
  - Dates of paychecks compared to termination dates (employees being paid after terminated, and used as a ghost by an existing employee)
  - Employees who never take vacation or sick leave (if neither is taken, this is highly suspicious). (A fraud using a ghost employee, for example, would result in that fictitious employee having neither, unless the fraudster creates fictitious leave.)
  - Employees who have no deductions from paychecks
  - Employees with no SSN, invalid SSN, or duplicate SSN

Commissions

- Randomly spot checking all of the transactions involved in sales commissions for a pay period or a salesperson
- Investigating higher rates of returns or credits for a salesperson
- Creating and reviewing a linear correlation between sales and commissions paid, by employee
- Tracking uncollected sales by employee
- Creating exception reports for employees whose compensation has increased over last year by some unusual percentage
- Having a designated and independent official verify all changes in commission rates

Falsified Wages

- Data mining all transactions over a certain number of overtime hours (e.g., more than 20 hours per week)

- Creating exception reports for employees whose compensation has increased over last year by some unusual percentage
- Randomly verifying the pay rates in a pay period or for an employee over pay periods
- Having a designated and independent official verify all changes in pay rates
- Maintaining careful custody of time cards—after approval, process them immediately

Check-Tampering

- Periodically rotating personnel who handle and code checks
- Requiring dual signatures for checks over a designated threshold
- Using a positive pay system at the entity's bank
- Having the bank statement sent unopened to someone in management completely separate from accounts payable—in the case of smaller companies, perhaps the owner/manager. Review the statement and cancelled checks, even if it is online, before passing the statement on to the person who will do the bank reconciliation.

Skimming

Skimming frauds happen *before* a booking entry is made. Because it is an off-the-books fraud, this type of fraud is one of the most difficult to detect. One methodology to detect skimming is to perform an invigilation as described in Chapters 4 and 6. Individual skimming schemes are related to sales (unrecorded sales, understated sales), receivables (write-off schemes, lapping schemes, unconcealed schemes), and refunds. Suggested methods to use for this type of scheme are:

- Surveillance of employees at point of sale (e.g., cameras above registers and meal tables)
- Discovery of "markers" near registers (fraudsters use markers to keep up with the amounts skimmed; for example, a penny for $100, a nickel for $500)
- Investigating gaps in prenumbered receipts
- Checking registers for excessive no-sale transactions, voids, or refunds
- Posting a sign at the register or in plain view of customers: "If you did not receive a receipt, please contact the manager and your meal will be free."

- Using a trained secret shopper to look for signs of fraud
- Using an invigilation for an approximation of missing monies, or to determine if skimming is occurring
- Measuring variances in revenues by employee and by shift
- Creating a pro forma income statement, using cost of goods sold and standard markups to ascertain the level of sales that should exist, then comparing it to actual for an approximation of missing monies
- Performing surprise audits or cash counts just after closing out a shift

Lapping

- Conducting customer service phone calls: following up on customer complaints of delays in posting checks independent of the accounts receivable (AR) personnel
- Using a trend analysis of number-of-days in receivables, by business unit or AR clerk—following up on those above the standard or organizational average
- Getting independent confirmation of AR balances and aging in particular
- Conducting surprise audits and/or cash counts
- Classifying write-offs and credit memos by employee, and investigating any irregularities (i.e., transactions that are not randomly distributed)
- Conducting random, unannounced customer satisfaction surveys—specifically asking questions about length of time from check mailed to posted on account
- Watching for employees who put in a lot of time after hours
- Conducting a surprise "desk raid," looking for a second set of books (lapping system) kept in the desk
- Spot checking daily deposits to AR, verifying that names on checks match postings
- Comparing dates of AR postings to dates of checks or date payment was mailed

Corruption Schemes

- Classifying transactions by vendor and examining unusual, unexplained higher-than-expected volumes
- Random investigation of all vendors, including owners, major shareholders, and any relationship with employees
- Reviewing contracts and approval of invoices periodically, even if only a sample during each audit

- Verifying the authenticity of vendors as part of internal audits, even if it is only a sample
- Looking for related-party transactions where the relationship has been hidden
- Reviewing approvals for transactions with related parties annually

Bribery and Economic Extortion

- Rotating duties of approving contracts and/or vendors, and bid responsibilities
- Segregating duties of approving vendors and awarding contracts or approving invoices

SUMMARY

A study of the top fraud schemes, and the red flags of each, is a key success factor in detecting fraud. In fact, a thorough understanding and analysis of known red flags leads to potentially effective detective methods. A study of the ACFE's RTTN results also provides helpful insight into effective detection methods.

APPENDIX 7A: BENEISH'S RATIOS*

According to the research of Mesod Beneish, the following ratios have the poten-tial to distinguish between fraudulent financial reports and nonmanipulated financial reports. Notice that most of them are trend oriented, which provides insights into a key analytical procedure in detecting fraud—examining trends.

1. Days' Sales in Receivables Index

   $$\frac{(\text{Accts Rec}^{t}/\text{Sales}^{t})}{(\text{Accts Rec}^{t-1}/\text{Sales}^{t-1})}$$

   Nonmanipulators' mean index = 1.031

   Manipulators = 1.465
2. Gross Margin Index

   $$\frac{(\text{Gross Margin}^{t-1}/\text{Sales}^{t-1})}{(\text{Gross Margin}^{t}/\text{Sales}^{t})}$$

   Nonmanipulators' mean index = 1.014

   Manipulators = 1.193
3. Asset Quality Index

   $$\frac{(\text{Current Assets}^{t}+\text{Net Fixed Assets}^{t})/(\text{Total Assets}^{t})}{(\text{Current Assets}^{t-1}+\text{Net Fixed Assets}^{t-1})/(\text{Total Assets}^{t-1})}$$

   Nonmanipulators' mean index = 1.039

   Manipulators = 1.254
4. Sales Index

   $$\frac{(\text{Sales}^{t})}{(\text{Sales}^{t-1})}$$

   Nonmanipulators' mean index = 1.134

   Manipulators = 1.607
5. Total Accruals to Total Assets Index

   Δ (Working Capital – Cash – Current Taxes Payable) – Depreciation and

   Amortization / Total Assets

   Nonmanipulators' mean index = 0.018

   Manipulators = 0.031

   t = Current time period/Fiscal year (FY)

   t–1 = Last time period/Fiscal year (FY)

*Copyright 1999, CFA Institute. Reproduced and republished from the *Financial Analyst Journal* with permission from CFA Institute. All rights reserved.

CHAPTER EIGHT

Fraud Response

INTRODUCTION

The three basic phases of an antifraud program are prevention, detection, and response—similar to the P-D-C (preventive-detective-corrective) model used in Information Security (InfoSec), and controls design for accounting and auditing.[1] Obviously the prevention phase provides the highest leverage or return in that it prevents the fraud from happening. The response phase is necessary if a fraud is detected. Because an entity clearly wants to detect all frauds committed against it, management should think about what its response would be *before* a fraud actually occurs. Chronologically, this phase is likely to be the first or second (a fraud risk assessment may precede this step; see Chapter 5) to be performed in terms of planning and developing policies and procedures for an antifraud program.

FRAUD POLICY

Most likely, the best place to begin developing an effective fraud response is to develop an appropriate fraud policy. There are numerous reasons why this step should occur before a fraud ever occurs, and before developing specifics in an antifraud program, which will be brought out later.

There are several issues to consider addressing when crafting the fraud policy. First, a proper definition of fraud is important. As noted in Chapter 2, many definitions of fraud exist. If no definition is predetermined, employees may be confused, may misunderstand, or may disagree about what constitutes a fraud to the employer. In addition, an entity could find itself in litigation, where the definition would probably be subject to judge or jury interpretation, who also might not agree with a victim entity.

For instance, if an employee "borrowed" the employer's digital camera, makes pictures of his/her personal property, uses the entity's computers to set up an account at ebay.com, and to manage that account to sell his/her stuff, and does so on company time—is that a fraud? A judge or jury, absent a fraud definition agreed to by the parties, may struggle with the belief that it is a fraud. But if the entity had used the Association of Certified Fraud Examiners (ACFE) definition,[2] built it into its fraud policy, and had employees sign a copy indicating their agreement to adhere to that policy, there would be much less doubt in a courtroom about the definition of a fraud in that case. The same could be said about employees "borrowing" heavy equipment (e.g., backhoe) for the weekend to do some work for themselves or friends because it is not being used until next Monday. So the entity should determine what actions it would consider fraud and carefully craft a definition as a key part of the fraud policy.

Issues to consider in defining fraud would include:[3]

- Any dishonest or fraudulent act
- Violation of fiduciary responsibilities
- Misappropriation of funds, securities, supplies, or other entity assets
- Unauthorized use of the entity's assets; such as equipment for personal use, or computers used for personal gain
- Impropriety in the handling or reporting of money or financial transactions
- Profiteering as a result of insider knowledge of entity activities
- Disclosing confidential and proprietary information to outside parties
- Disclosing to other persons securities activities engaged in or contemplated by the entity
- Accepting or seeking anything of material value from contractors, vendors, or persons providing services or materials to the entity. Exception: Gifts less than $50 in value
- Destruction, removal, or inappropriate use of records (paper or digital), furniture, fixtures, or equipment

- Malicious activities directed at the entity's computers, systems, or technologies
- Any violation of a relevant illegal act
- Any similar or related irregularity

Management should include in the entity's policy how irregularities that are detected or suspected will be handled. The policy should stipulate who, what, where, when related to any tips, complaints, or whistleblowing, especially where such reports of suspicion should be reported. The policy should also discuss how to maintain the anonymity of tipsters. There should be some formal structure established to handle those reports and to make decisions on what to investigate, and how investigations will be handled. The policy should discuss how the entity will take care to avoid mistaken accusations, false accusations, or alerting suspects that an investigation has been undertaken. No information about the nature of any investigation or status of an investigation should be allowed except as authorized by management or required for legal reasons.

The policy should identify what unit will have the primary responsibility to carry out a fraud investigation of any suspected fraudulent acts as defined by the policy. That unit could begin with internal audit, an ethics unit, a special unit, an external consultant, a forensic accounting firm, or a legal firm. All investigations should be properly authorized and the policy should identify who that is and how that will be done.

The policy should convey the need to maintain the appropriate level of confidentiality, especially the protection of the rights of innocent employees who might get accidentally swept into an investigation, including whistleblowers and tipsters.

Management should consider addressing the repercussions a person will encounter if found guilty of violating the fraud policy. For instance, the entity should have some guidelines as to when it would pursue criminal prosecution, based on the amount of the loss, position of the employee, or whatever factors the entity believes to be key factors in pursuing prosecution. The same is true for civil litigation or termination of the employee. The latter is subject to human resource (HR) laws, such as states where employment is not "at will."[4]

The policy may also need to address when an attorney would be involved, which may be best in the majority of the cases, if not all cases. It could be that the entity has an attorney on retainer or internal legal counsel in which case that person would be consulted on each investigation, either at the beginning or during the investigation. Because of the possibility that *any* investigation may end up in litigation, criminal or civil, the employment of an attorney early in the investigation is usually wise.

Other similar investigative issues to be addressed by a fraud policy would include what circumstances under which management would involve forensic accounting subject matter experts (SMEs) as consultants, or digital/cyber forensic SMEs. Sometimes the best evidence is digital, or "hidden" in technology. Or the volume of data to examine is such that data mining tools and experts are necessary to develop competent, sufficient evidence that a fraud has, or has not, occurred. If it is possible one or more subject matter experts (SMEs) might be needed, the entity should identify possible candidates well before a fraud is discovered as these SMEs are often scarce and hard to find in cities other than the largest ones. Sometimes law firms have a certain forensic accounting firm they work with regularly, and that should be considered as well.

The policy should be communicated to all employees and, much like an ethics policy, should be signed by each employee to indicate his or her voluntary agreement to comply. Needless to say, the fraud policy should be communicated and promoted. For instance, a discussion of the fraud policy should be part of employee orientation upon beginning employment. It should be promoted and communicated in entity literature such as newsletters.

If an entity waits until a fraud occurs to think about these issues, and to make these kinds of critical decisions, at least some of the key people involved will be subject to the emotions of the moment. That is, the entity can probably craft a more effective response to fraud before it happens, when people have more time to think, the pressure of a fraud is not there, and emotions are not high. This possible mental and emotional impairment of responding to a fraud is one rationale for preempting it by developing a fraud response policy and plan *before* a fraud ever occurs.

The ACFE provides a sample policy to guide management in this key process (see Appendix 8A). Like other policies, management should provide a formal structure to monitor the policy's guidelines for compliance, and annually review the policy for possible revision.

FRAUD RESPONSE TEAM

Once management has developed a formal structure for handling fraud on paper, it needs to identify people, positions, or units to be responsible for the different procedures stipulated in the fraud policy. The ACFE has provided a tool to assist this part of fraud response in what it refers to as a "fraud policy decision

EXHIBIT 8.1 Fraud Response Team and SMEs

Legal/Litigation: prosecution, knowledge of potential effectual prosecutors, civil litigation
Legal/HR: legal termination of fraudster, legal issues in investigating an employee
Forensic accounting/CFE: fraud investigation, fraud/legal evidence, proper interviews
Digital forensics: data mining for evidence
Cyber forensics: evidence embedded in IT, hidden in IT, potential cyber sources of evidence
Internal audit: support the investigation, evidence gathering, controls remediation
Public relations: avoid publicity, manage publicity, craft public responses to fraud
Executive management: manage all key decisions of the process and followup

matrix" (see Appendix 8B). The fraud policy decision matrix illustrates how to determine the key elements, steps, and processes of handling a fraud if and when one does occur. The columns of that matrix can be used to determine the functions and/or members of the fraud response team (see Exhibit 8.1 for a list of SMEs and response team functions).

One key function of the fraud response team is legal oversight. As mentioned, legal counsel is needed in almost all, if not all, frauds detected. The team member or members would need to be SMEs in criminal matters. It is always possible that a detected fraud could lead to a criminal investigation.

However, criminal investigations can go awry for the victim. For instance, there are many instances when a fraud case was turned over to a law enforcement agency that did not prosecute. It could be that the amount of the fraud case is less than other cases and the district attorney or other agent, because of case load and scarce prosecutorial resources, decides not to pursue prosecution of the entity's fraud case. It could be that the agency chosen is not familiar or comfortable with handling white-collar crimes or prosecution of fraud, and because that agent's goal is a successful prosecution, he or she may decide not to prosecute due to the risk of losing the case.

Once a case is turned over to a law enforcement prosecution agent, the case is no longer under any control of the victim, and anything can happen. Therefore, if the victim entity wants a successful prosecution, they must carefully choose from among the potential prosecuting agencies, and that requires expert counsel. That person would be the appropriate SME such as an attorney, retired governmental investigator, and so on.

A similar need exists for civil litigation. The only legal recourse for some frauds will be a judgment from a civil proceeding. Thus that expertise needs to be represented on the fraud response team.

Another function of the fraud response team that must be represented is HR law and regulations, and the legal ramifications of actions taken toward a suspect. Issues will naturally arise upon the detection of a fraud because some employee will be involved and there are laws and regulations guiding the termination of an employee and other HR-related issues. In particular, the entity needs to protect itself from a "double dip" where a fraudster steals from the company and then because of an ill-advised action, is able to successfully pursue civil prosecution for illegal termination, unsuccessful prosecution, or some other related legal cause. This function may be represented by an attorney or HR SME.

The team definitely needs an SME in forensic accounting and fraud investigation. Some people make the mistake of thinking a fraud audit is the same as a financial audit, and that expert financial auditors or internal auditors will be able to successfully audit for evidence and/or conduct a fraud investigation. Nothing can be further from the truth. The approach to a fraud audit is drastically different from a financial audit, and a CPA who is not trained or experienced in fraud investigations will be impaired in his or her ability to successfully conclude a fraud audit or investigation. In fact, the double dipping described often happens because the entity chose to use an expert other than a qualified forensic accountant in prosecuting the fraudster only to lose the case in court, and then be back in court only in a different role—the defendant this time in civil litigation brought by the fraudster.

Accounting education, and traditional accounting and auditing experience generally do not provide a sufficient background, knowledge, or experience to identify all of the critical problems that can arise during a fraud investigation. This person needs to know the "land mines" of fraud investigation, such as approaching the suspect too early, handling evidence for litigation/prosecution, and proper interviewing techniques; improper methods could lead to *legal* issues! So the entity must be careful to include the appropriate SME on the response team in regards to fraud investigation, which would probably be a Certified Fraud Examiner (CFE) or comparable SME, and not just a traditional CPA.

Another function that should be included on a fraud response team is digital forensics. Digital forensics tools and techniques allow the expert to data mine a morass of data for fraud evidence. For instance, one fraud expert was called in to a case where a tipster provided the risk management director information that a shell vendor scheme was being perpetrated against the company. The problem was that the company had over 11,000 different vendors, and the director felt like she was looking for a needle in a haystack. When the data volume is large and evidence is likely contained therein, an SME in data mining would be essential to a successful conclusion to the investigation. That person would be expert in using data mining tools such as ACL, IDEA, Active Data, and other similar products that are capable of extracting relevant data from large data files. This SME also knows the techniques used to efficiently and effectively extract *fraud* evidence from large data files. Thus the proper SME not only knows how to use the tools but also understands fraud audit techniques—red flags, fraud schemes, and exactly what data characteristics to search for. An SME on digital data mining should be represented on the response team.

An aspect of fraud investigation that can be overlooked to the detriment of the entity that detects a fraud is cyber forensics. Each case will have its best evidence in a certain area: Most often, that comes from interview information or audit trail documents and/or data. But it could be that the best evidence is digital, embedded in technology. It may be difficult to impossible to know whether that is true unless the response activities include an SME's evaluation of that potential evidence.

This aspect of forensics is different from data mining. This SME is able to find latent ("hidden") data on a variety of sources including hard drives, cell phones, thumb drives, and other storage devices such as camera cards. Latent data is also found in electronic documents and system files. In fact, a benefit of having an SME on the team is that he or she will know which sources should be considered when looking for digital evidence, and will have the capability to extract that data, including data that is normally "hidden." The tools of the cyber forensic specialist are unique to the profession and not known by the general public or even the fraud and audit profession in general. Thus an SME on cyber forensics would be beneficial in making that determination, and more important, in being able to effectively and efficiently extract that evidence. One way to determine the qualifications of someone as an SME in this area is to find a person who is a Certified Information Systems Security Professional (CISSP).

Almost all responses to a detected fraud would involve the internal audit (IA) function. Thus the team should include someone to represent the IA function. IA would likely be involved in gathering audit evidence in terms of documents and data, and remediating the controls around the detected fraud to prevent such a fraud from happening again.

Perhaps nothing is more difficult to manage in a response to a fraud than the publicity and public relations aspect. In many cases, management will believe it is in their best interests to avoid any publicity. For example, a charity that detects a fraud may believe that if that fact becomes public, donors will stay away in droves. But a fraud may become public for some reason and then the entity has to manage the entity's image. The entity risks losing customers, losing prospective customers, losing market share, or tarnishing its public image. Thus an SME in public relations (PR) and publicity needs to be on the response team in case this need arises, either to avoid publicity or to manage a public fraud.

Clearly, executive management should be part of the response team. Senior management will need to be involved with the key decisions of the investigation, and will certainly want to follow up with some remediation activities to prevent fraud from happening to the entity again. One key duty of management would be to provide a strategic means to recover the monetary loss and assign responsibility of that process. However, in making the decision of who represents executive management, the entity should take into account the reality that a fraud, such as cooking the books in a financial statement fraud, could be perpetrated by a member of executive management.

Obviously, some of the team functions could be collapsed into one person who can perform multiple functions. For instance, it could be that internal legal counsel can handle litigation and HR legal issues. Also, the entity may find a person who is an SME in cyber forensics and digital forensics, or IA and digital forensics. The team could be constructed to collapse risk management with executive management. Some entities will not have all of the indicated units but the matrix is still valuable in providing a list of issues to review. It also demonstrates the need for segregation of certain activities where feasible.

RECOVERY

Part of the response phase is to recover monetary losses due to a fraud. The amount can not only be significant but difficult to recover. The latter is true because most often, the perpetrator has spent or hidden all or most of the ill-gotten gain, and there is little to recover from the fraudster.

According to the 2006 ACFE *Report to the Nation* (RTTN), 42 percent of all victims recovered nothing from a fraud. Another 23.4 percent recovered less than 25 percent of the loss. The median recovery of those who recovered all of the loss, approximately 16 percent of the cases, was $50,000. These numbers show that victims tend to recover nothing or a small percentage of a significant loss. Therefore, it is critically important for an entity to strategically develop an approach to make a full recovery. These facts also justify the need to develop a response plan well in advance of a fraud, because not having a response plan impairs the ability of the entity to recover financially from a fraud.

Recovery can be accomplished by business insurance/bonding, restitution agreements, or civil judgments. Obviously, the latter two are subject to many factors beyond the control of the entity that could impair the entity's ability to fully recover. Thus strategically, the most reliable recovery approach is some form of insurance or bonding of key employees. The question becomes how much insurance is needed to "fully" recover?

According to the 2008 ACFE RTTN, the average loss for a fraud was $175,000. Some industries are more susceptible to fraud and higher losses. All entities with antifraud controls that are missing or are very weak are also more susceptible. That means when trying to assess an amount of potential loss, a good place to start is to use $175,000 as a base and adjust it for conditions inherent to the entity, up or down for antifraud controls and industry risk (see Chapter 5 for more on risk assessment). The bottom line is the entity needs to protect itself from the potential monetary loss of a fraud and it cannot do that effectively unless some reasonable attempt is made to estimate that amount.

Management needs to choose the insurance provider that fits its desires about fraud investigations. Some insurance companies require the client to turn over the fraud investigation to the insurance company and its forensic accounting team, causing the entity to lose control over most of the response to fraud process; that is, management can still work on remediation and termination of employee but loses the opportunity to pursue prosecution and civil litigation in this situation. Sometimes the insurance company chooses to pay off the obligation without any investigation. Thus the entity needs to find a fit of the terms of the provider, the amount of coverage, and management's intentions about fraud response.

By combining the monetary risk assessment with a strategic approach to insurance, bonding, and litigation, the response has a higher probability of a full recovery. In fact, a good response plan probably includes both adequate insurance and aggressive litigation procedures in terms of recovery.

SUMMARY

Frauds are a bit like snowflakes—no two are alike. Each one needs to be treated as a separate case. Chronologically, frauds that are discoverable occur because preventive measures were absent or unsuccessful, then detected by some method, after which the entity must respond to the fraud and its effects. But chronologically, the first thing an entity should do in developing an antifraud program is develop the fraud response plan.

The development of an effective response plan includes an effectual fraud policy, the creation of an effectual and formal fraud response team, and a strategic development of a financial recovery plan. A study of cases and fraud surveys proves that those entities who are not prepared for a fraud (i.e., have no effective response plan) tend to suffer financial loss (recover little to nothing of the fraud loss), suffer public image loss, suffer less than an effectual investigation, and struggle with the emotions and mental anguish of the fraud, where the fraudster is usually a trusted employee. Therefore an effective response plan provides many benefits to entities willing and able to diligently develop one.

NOTES

1. The authors deliberately used this model in arranging chapters: Chapter 6/ Prevention, Chapter 7/Detection, and Chapter 8/Response.
2. "The use of one's occupation for personal gain through the deliberate misuse or theft of the employing organization's resources or assets."
3. Based in part on the ACFE Sample Fraud Policy.
4. "At will" means the state laws basically allow management to fire or lay off employees at will. Some states have legal restrictions about why an employee is fired or laid off.

APPENDIX 8A: ACFE SAMPLE FRAUD POLICY

Background	The corporate fraud policy is established to facilitate the development of controls that will aid in the detection and prevention of fraud against ABC Corporation. It is the intent of ABC Corporation to promote consistent organizational behavior by providing guidelines and assigning responsibilities for the development of controls and conduct of investigations.
Scope of Policy	This policy applies to any irregularity, or suspected irregularity, involving employees as well as shareholders, consultants, vendors, contractors, outside agencies doing business with employees of such agencies, and/or any other parties with a business relationship with ABC Corporation (also called the Company). Any investigative activity required will be conducted without regard to the suspected wrongdoer's length of service, position/title, or relationship to the Company.
Policy	Management is responsible for the detection and prevention of fraud, misappropriations, and other irregularities. *Fraud* is defined as the intentional, false representation or concealment of a material fact for the purpose of inducing another to act upon it to his or her (economic) injury. Each member of the management team will be familiar with the types of improprieties that might occur within his or her area of responsibility and be alert for any indication of irregularity. Any irregularity that is detected or suspected must be reported immediately to the Director of ______, who coordinates all investigations with the Legal Department and other affected areas, both internal and external.

(*continued*)

(Continued)

Actions Constituting Fraud	The terms *defalcation, misappropriation (of assets)*, and *other fiscal irregularities* refer to, but are not limited to: ■ Any dishonest or fraudulent act ■ Misappropriation of funds, securities, supplies, or other assets ■ Impropriety in the handling or reporting of money or financial transactions ■ Profiteering as a result of insider knowledge of company activities ■ Disclosing confidential and proprietary information to outside parties ■ Disclosing to other persons securities activities engaged in or contemplated by the Company ■ Accepting or seeking anything of material value from contractors, vendors, or persons providing services/materials to the Company. Exception: Gifts less than US $50 in value ■ Destruction, removal, or inappropriate use of records, furniture, fixtures, and equipment ■ Any similar or related irregularity
Other Irregularities	Irregularities concerning an employee's moral, ethical, or behavioral conduct should be resolved by departmental management and the Employee Relations Unit of Human Resources rather than the ______ Unit. If there is a question as to whether an action constitutes fraud, contact the Director of ______ for guidance.
Investigation Responsibilities	The ______ Unit has the primary responsibility for the investigation of all suspected fraudulent acts as defined in the policy. If the investigation substantiates that fraudulent activities have occurred, the ______ Unit will issue reports to appropriate designated personnel and, if appropriate, to the Board of Directors through the Audit Committee.

	Decisions to prosecute or refer the examination results to the appropriate law enforcement and/or regulatory agencies for independent investigation will be made in conjunction with legal counsel and senior management, as will final decisions on disposition of the case.
Confidentiality	The ______ Unit treats all information received confidentially. Any employee who suspects dishonest or fraudulent activity will notify the ______ Unit immediately, and should not attempt to personally conduct investigations or interviews/interrogations related to any suspected fraudulent act (see Reporting Procedures section). Investigation results will not be disclosed or discussed with anyone other than those who have a legitimate need to know. This is important in order to avoid damaging the reputations of persons suspected but subsequently found innocent of wrongful conduct and to protect the Company from potential civil liability.
Authorization for Investigating Suspected Fraud	Members of the Investigation Unit will have: ■ Free and unrestricted access to all Company records and premises, whether owned or rented. ■ The authority to examine, copy, and/or remove all or any portion of the contents of files, desks, cabinets, and other storage facilities on the premises without prior knowledge or consent of any individual who might use or have custody of any such items or facilities when it is within the scope of their investigation.
Reporting Procedures	Great care must be taken in the investigation of suspected improprieties or irregularities so as to avoid mistaken accusations or alerting suspected individuals that an investigation is under way.

(continued)

(*Continued*)

	An employee who discovers or suspects fraudulent activity will contact the ______ Unit immediately. The employee or other complainant may remain anonymous. All inquiries concerning the activity under investigation from the suspected individual, his or her attorney or representative, or any other inquirer should be directed to the Investigations Unit or the Legal Department. No information concerning the status of an investigation will be given out. The proper response to any inquiry is: "I am not at liberty to discuss this matter." Under no circumstances should any reference be made to "the allegation," "the crime," "the fraud," "the forgery," "the misappropriation," or any other specific reference. The reporting individual should be informed of the following: ■ Do not contact the suspected individual in an effort to determine facts or demand restitution. ■ Do not discuss the case, facts, suspicions, or allegations with anyone unless specifically asked to do so by the Legal Department or ______ Unit.
Termination	If an investigation results in a recommendation to terminate an individual, the recommendation will be reviewed for approval by the designated representatives from Human Resources and the Legal Department and, if necessary, by outside counsel, before any such action is taken. The ______ Unit does not have the authority to terminate an employee. The decision to terminate an employee is made by the employee's management. Should the ______ Unit believe the management decision inappropriate for the facts presented, the facts will be presented to executive-level management for a decision.

Administration	The Director of ______ is responsible for the administration, revision, interpretation, and application of this policy. The policy will be reviewed annually and revised as needed.
Approval	____________________ ________ (CEO/Senior VP/Executive) Date

Copyright © 2003 Association of Certified Fraud Examiners.

APPENDIX 8B: SAMPLE FRAUD POLICY DECISION MATRIX

Action Required	Investigating Unit	Internal Audit	Financial Accounting	Executive Management	Line Management	Risk Management	Public Relations	Employee Relations	Legal
Controls to prevent fraud	S	S	S	P	SR	S	S	S	S
Incident reporting	P	S	S	S	S	S	S	S	S
Investigation of fraud	P	S						S	S
Referrals to law enforcement	P								S
Recovery of monies due to fraud	P								
Recommendations to prevent fraud	SR	SR	S	S	S	S	S	S	S
Internal control reviews		P							
Handling cases of a sensitive nature	P	S		S		S		S	S
Publicity/Press releases	S	S					P		
Civil litigation	S	S							P
Corrective action/ Recommendations to prevent recurrences	SR	SR		S	SR	S			S
Monitor recoveries	S		P						

Proactive fraud auditing	S	P							
Fraud education/Training	P	S			S		S		
Risk analysis of areas of vulnerability	S	S				P			
Case analysis	P	S							
Hotline	P	S							
Ethics line	S	S							P

P = Primary responsibility
S = Secondary responsibility
SR = Share responsibility

Copyright © 2003 Association of Certified Fraud Examiners.

CHAPTER NINE

Computer Crime

INTRODUCTION

Technology plays various roles in the fraud environment. Systems and data can be used to prevent, detect, and investigate fraud. When technology is used to commit fraud, the mechanism used is typically a computer (broadly defined here as devices that perform calculations and store data). Technology, especially computers and servers, can even BE the target of the criminal. Technology increasingly integrates into society, it integrates into crimes including fraud.

Before there were computers, there was no computer crime, but there was crime—both the white- and blue-collar varieties. There were also crimes against people and crimes against property. The computer did not usher in a new wave of crime; it merely changed the form of older crimes.

Usually, computer-related crime is an occupational crime. That is, it is committed mainly by insiders, or former insiders, with the requisite skills, knowledge, and access. Unauthorized access can generally be gained more easily by organization insiders (employees) than by outsiders. Research on this subject finds about 70 percent to 80 percent of computer-related malicious acts are perpetrated by insiders,[1] despite mass media commentators, who often appear to portray the opposite.

HISTORY AND EVOLUTION OF COMPUTER CRIMES

Electronic computers were first introduced for commercial use in the United States in 1954, when General Electric (GE) became the first U.S. business to employ a computer. Before then, the few computers that existed were used for governmental purposes (for tabulating the national census, for military applications, and for scientific research). The history of computer crime begins in the mid-1950s.

Stanford Research International

Until 1958, no systematic tracking or tabulation of computer-related crime existed. That year, Stanford Research International (SRI) began tracking publicly reported incidents of computer abuse, some of which were criminal and others that involved the breach of civil laws, such as the copyright and patent acts. SRI grouped these incidents into four categories:

1. Vandalism (against computers)
2. Information or property theft
3. Financial fraud or theft
4. Unauthorized use or sale of (computer) services

The first year in which 10 or more of these incidents were reported was 1968. There were a total of 13 incidents that year. Reported incidents rose until 1977, but in 1978 they dropped dramatically. SRI discontinued tabulating such abuses after 1978 for several reasons. For one thing, the publicly reported incidents bore no relationship to all incidents. Many, perhaps most, incidents of computer abuse were not publicly reported.

Tabulating reported incidents by year could create the impression that computer abuse was growing or declining when, in fact, the reported incidents might not be fairly representative of all actual incidents of abuse. With more and more computers being used, one could expect an increase in the number of incidents of abuse. Figures of abuse would shed no light on the phenomenon itself or its causative factors. SRI elected to look at each case individually for whatever insights it could glean on causations and other variables, such as the mental dispositions of the computer abusers and the employment conditions that made abuse more likely—demographic characteristics of abusers.

Equity Funding Scandal

One of the earliest historic events regarding computer-related fraud was the Equity Funding scandal that was exposed in 1973. Managers at Equity Funding Corporation of America used a series of frauds beginning in 1964 to show false profits, thus increasing the company's stock price. The primary fraud was the use of phony insurance policies. Equity Funding used several tactics to perpetrate the fraud.

One was to use different external auditors in order to confound the audit process and prevent detection of the fraud. Another deceptive tactic was used during confirmation of receivables. When the external auditing firm tried to confirm receivables (policies) by phone, the Equity Funding switchboard operator simply patched them through to Equity Funding employees in the building. The most amazing fact of the case is that it went undetected for so long. Many people inside the company knew about the fraud, and yet the fraud was a closely held secret.

The fraud was exposed when a disgruntled ex-employee blew the whistle. In March 1973, the Securities and Exchange Commission (SEC) suspended trading of Equity Funding stock. The subsequent audit by Touche Ross was definitely not traditional. First, the auditors were trying to prove something (insurance policies) *did not* exist. Second, it was a fraud audit, not a financial audit. The audit took two years to complete. Touche Ross found about $2 billion of phony insurance policies—two-thirds of the policies Equity Funding claimed to have in force.

Because it was so pervasive, the fraud clearly should have been caught by the external financial auditors or the SEC. All bogus policies were coded to department "99." The auditors did not review the computer processes themselves but treated the computer as a black box (i.e., audit around the information technology [IT]). The SEC could be accused of some neglect as well. An SEC staff member wrote memos 15 months prior to Equity Funding's collapse reporting rumors of irregularities, to no avail.

The popular press treated the fraud as a computer fraud, but it was really a management fraud using the old familiar fraudulent statement scheme (similar to Ivar Kreuger, Enron, Waste Management, and numerous others before and after). Equity Funding management probably could not have perpetrated the fraud without the use of computers. In this case, therefore, the computer was a tool used by the fraudster to perpetrate a financial statement fraud.

The public's perception of the part that the computer played in the fraud caused a new wave of interest in audit procedures (i.e., electronic data processing [EDP]/IT audit procedures) where computers were a component of the accounting system. The prevailing belief at this time was that traditional audits (those that audited around the computer) were sufficient to detect the existence of large frauds. Others, primarily IT (EDP) auditors, had espoused the need for auditing through the computer. These people were now receiving attention from accountants, auditors, and management. Equity Funding did more for the rise of IT auditing (i.e., more IT auditor jobs) than any other single event up until the passage of the Sarbanes-Oxley Act (SOX).

Recent Statistics on Computer Crime

Statistics in computer crime are difficult to accumulate and assess. For starters, many crimes go unreported. The 2005 Federal Bureau of Investigation (FBI) Computer Crime Survey indicated that while 90 percent of surveyed participants reported security incidents, only 9 percent reported the incident to law enforcement.[3]

Costs of crimes that are reported are inherently hard to quantify due to the intangible nature of losses such as time, customer loyalty, and confidential information. Nonetheless, crimes are clearly costly. Respondents in the 2008 Internet Crime Report reported losses totaling $456 million,[4] but nationwide estimates run much higher. A 2007 report to Congress by the Government Accountability Office (GAO) referenced five surveys that estimated costs of computer crime in billions of dollars (see Exhibit 9.1).

Trends vary in the type of computer crime like estimates of costs; nonetheless some trends are clear. Identity theft continues to escalate, as suggested in Exhibit 9.1 by the estimated $49.3 billion cost in 2006. E-mail continues to evolve both as a method of committing crimes (identity theft, phishing, viruses, etc.) and as evidence of crimes (e-mail discovery in litigation). Several viruses, such as the Love Bug, Code Red, and Slammer, individually have estimated costs in the billions. Auction fraud and non-delivery of goods combined for about 58 percent of incidents reported in the 2008 Internet Crime Report provided by the Internet Fraud Complaint Center (IFCC). The two primary mechanisms by which fraudulent contact took place in those crimes was e-mail (74 percent) and web pages (29 percent), indicating the fact these are computer crimes. In fact, statistics from the 2008 IFCC indicate a rapid growth in computer crimes (see Exhibit 9.2).

EXHIBIT 9.1 Estimated U.S. Computer Crime Losses

Estimated Loss	Methodology	Source
$67.2 billion	Survey projected annual loss to U.S. organizations because of computer crime in 2005.	2005 FBI Computer Crime Survey
$49.3 billion	Survey of 5,000 U.S. adults projected that 8.4 million consumers suffered losses due to identity theft in 2006.	Javelin Strategy & Research 2007
$56.6 billion	Survey of 5,000 U.S. adults projected that 8.9 million consumers suffered losses due to identity theft in 2005.	Javelin Strategy & Research 2006
$8.4 billion	Survey of 2,000 households with Internet access determined U.S. consumers' losses due to viruses, spyware, and phishing in 2004–2005.	*Consumer Reports* State of the Net 2006
$2.13 billion	Survey of 5,000 U.S. adult Internet users estimated phishing-related losses between April 2003 and May 2005.	Gartner Research

Source: "Cybercrime: Public and Private Entities Face Challenges in Addressing Cyber Crime," Government Accountability Office Report to Congressional Requestors, June 2007. Online at: http://www.gao.gov/new.items/d07705.pdf.

EXHIBIT 9.2 Computer Crimes

Criminal Activity	2001	2008
Complaints received	50,412	275,284
Referrals	4,810	72,940
Loss	$17.8 million	$264.6 million

Source: 2008 IC3 Annual Report, www.ic3.gov.

COMPUTER CRIME THEORIES AND CATEGORIZATIONS

Computer crime can be regarded as either a crime against computers or using computers to perpetrate a conventional fraud or crime (e.g., fraudulent disbursement, fraudulent financial statements, etc.). This view highlights the fact that fraud principles, such as the fraud triangle and the fraud tree, apply to computer crimes as well. One theory of computer-related crime, which is similar to the fraud triangle but specific to computer crime, is a concept known as MOMM.

Computer Crime Theory: MOMM

MOMM is an acronym for *m*otivations, *o*pportunities, *m*eans, and *m*ethods. Notice the first two terms come from the fraud triangle (omitting only the rationalization leg). Means is closely related to opportunities and internal controls, with the addition of technology. Methods applies the systems model to computer-related fraud, but with clear inferences to the fraud tree for the schemes being committed using those methods. The computer-related theft can be depicted as an iterative process (see Exhibit 9.3).

Economic motives indicate that perpetrators have money as a main purpose. They have a need or desire to secure a financial gain from the crime. The object of the fraud does not have to be money, just something that can be converted into or exchanged for money.

Ideological motives are demonstrated when perpetrators feel compelled to seek revenge against someone or when they believe something is oppressing or exploiting them, not necessarily involving any economic motive. For example, acts of stealing classified information for foreign entities is often conducted for political and ideological reasons. Sabotage against computers by disgruntled employees is another example. Such criminals may think that computer technology threatens their economic and political survival or well-being, or may simply be seeking revenge.

Egocentric motives are those associated with egos, power, and pride. Most frauds include this motive to some degree. Young enthusiasts who seek the thrill of the challenge to commit computer frauds or crimes exhibit egocentric motives.

Psychotic motives include a distorted sense of reality, delusions of grandeur or persecution, and exaggerated fears of computers. There have been few reported incidents of computer abuse where psychotic motives were attributed to perpetrators.

Environmental conditions that have provided motives for computer-related crime and abuse include both the internal environment of the firm that operates a computer and the external environment (the world or marketplace in general). Internal influences that can add to the motive for computer-related crime and abuse include:

- Work environment
- Reward system
- Level of interpersonal trust
- Level of ethics in the entity's culture

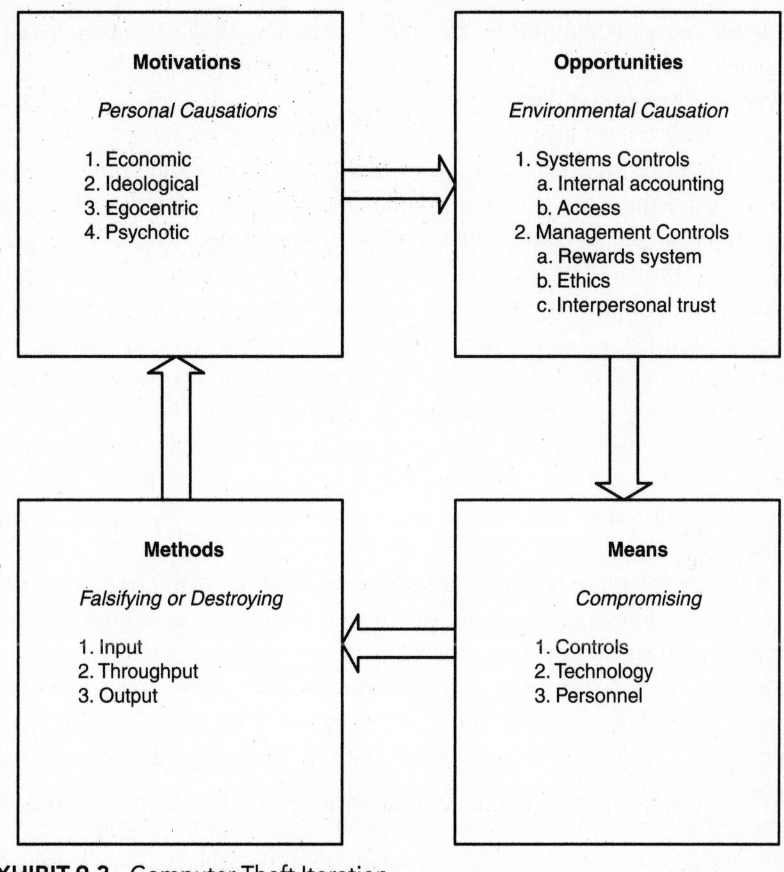

EXHIBIT 9.3 Computer Theft Iteration

- Level of stress (pressure for performance)
- Level of internal controls effectiveness

Externally, motives for computer-related crime and abuse may be provided by the current morals and social values of society, competitive conditions in the industry, and economic conditions in the country or the world.

Computer Crime Categorizations

The computer could be the target of the offender (destroying computers, denial of service, etc.), instrument used to commit the crime (online identity theft, fraudulent second set of accounting records, etc.), or incidental to the crime.

Computer crimes could also be classified by the loss to data (confidentiality, availability, or integrity), type of loss caused (financial, physical damage, etc.), or type of crime (fraud, larceny, etc.).[5]

Computer crimes can also be grouped into three simple categories that parallel the three stages of data processing: input, process, and output. Input crimes involve the entry of false or fraudulent data into a computer; data have been altered, forged, or counterfeited—raised, lowered, destroyed, intentionally omitted, or fabricated. Processing crimes encompass the altering of computer processing for fraudulent means (such as the infamous schemes portrayed in *Superman* and *Office Space* where programs round interest calculations and route the remaining amounts to personal accounts) or attacks such as denial of service that alter systems processing to affect losses to the victim. Output crimes, such as theft of computer-generated reports and data files (customer mailing lists, research and development results, long-range plans, employee lists, secret formulas, etc.) seem to be increasing in this era of intense competition.

Another meaningful categorization of fraud crimes is internal and external. Internal crimes are far greater in number. In fact, the most common type of computer crime is probably theft of assets by employees. They have fraud opportunity from being inside the organization; with some pressure to steal (personal cash flow problems) and weak personal ethics, the fraud triangle is complete. If a weakness exists in the controls, the temptation can become too great for the employee to resist stealing from the organization. Then there are those who break in from the outside to steal data, sabotage systems, or spy. Others bring a system down and make it unavailable to users. Whatever the damage, these actions intentionally bring about losses and as such are computer-related crimes.

CHARACTERISTICS OF THE COMPUTER ENVIRONMENT

Computerized accounting systems are a natural progression from manual accounting systems. Still, they have special characteristics that make them more susceptible to crime. To understand the potential impact and extent of computer-related crime, it is necessary to understand these characteristics.

Connectivity

Computer communications may be defined as the ability to transfer messages between independent devices. In order to communicate, the computer devices must, of course, be connected in some way. *The increase in connectivity of information technologies has increased vulnerability to computer crime, in short because the connectivity that facilitates the desired benefits facilitates the undesired crimes.*

The Internet exacerbates risk as it opens the network up to anyone in the world with the knowledge and opportunity to commit computer fraud. All that needs to be true for a computer fraud to occur is for one of these computer experts to become motivated to attack an organization's computer. The basic value proposition of the Internet is the opportunity to connect, almost any time, from almost anywhere, to millions of computers (and therefore data and people) around the world. The downside to the Internet is increased complexity in systems, attacks, and the ability to discern who did what, when, and how.

The idea of connecting computers continues to take on new forms. Networks are now connected wirelessly, through a virtual private network, via (VPN) intranets and extranets, with numerous types of other networks and "clients" (devices to connect to a network such as a BlackBerry or Personal Digital Assistant [PDA]). In many ways, distributed computing allows for more risk exposure than the traditional mainframe computer environment, as (parts of) applications and databases are integrated, although separately stored on multiple servers in distant locations. In other ways, risk can be better controlled by segregating access, requiring multiple authentication layers, and situating the most significant systems far from the network entry points or in environments that can be more narrowly and deeply monitored. Inevitably, trade-offs in systems management always occur between convenience and security.

Networks increase the vulnerability of computer systems by opening them to the Internet or external systems. Information can be stolen by copying it through a workstation or by tapping into communication mechanisms. There can be unauthorized entry through public telephone lines or Internet access. Data can be downloaded remotely to a nearly invisible flash drive. And once any undesired event occurs, the viral nature of computers means the impact can be exponential.

Concentration of Data

Data stored in computers is increasingly being considered an asset capable of effecting the transfer of money. Data transfers allow for monetary transactions to occur in a variety of ways, quickly, any time, and remotely.

But data also has value in another sense because of its concentration. Although data are not a negotiable instrument (as is a bank check), they nonetheless have intrinsic value. Digitized objects constitute confidential programs, scientific data files, programs a company can sell for a profit, and confidential financial information.

Computer systems collect and combine data from all departments within an organization. These data are processed and typically centrally stored. Centralization for security purposes can be advantageous for certain risks, but the location of data *in one location* makes data vulnerable to other risks. In some cases, simply by obtaining the appropriate password, excessive unauthorized access, or ability to override controls, a person can access any or all of a company's financial data or other digital records.

Data also suffers from physical loss due to human error or system failures, which can destroy records forever if a contingency plan is not in place or does not work.

Positions of Trust

By the very nature of their jobs, database administrators, programmers, and data entry clerks are in a position to manipulate records. A high degree of trust must be placed in the people in these positions, but the positions and people present a high degree of risk. For a fraud to occur, generally speaking, the person had to first be trusted.

Many computer analysts and programmers are not knowledgeable about accounting controls or the general principles of internal control. Thus most systems are designed without adequate controls, usually because they are standardized, not customized to the organization's structure and processes. In addition, many programs that have been operating for a long time have undergone extensive changes, with changes poorly documented. The "patched" programs can be hard to understand, and it is possible that only a few personnel are able to support them. If systems are current, they are probably still maturing and have extensive program changes, data conversions, and other projects occurring. Either way, anyone with sufficient knowledge of the given computer area conceivably *could* manipulate or change programs and/or data to their benefit without the change being discovered.

Other significant characteristics of the computer environment are as follows.

- *Obscure audit trail.* The sheer volume of transactions, together with the online access and networks available on many systems, may result in confused or incomplete audit trails.

- *Complex technology.* Understanding the substance and integration of technology is difficult and requires knowledge of and an ability to see through the technical aspect of systems.
- *Built-in insecurity.* Much of the hardware and software in use today was designed without much real security, and even secure technology constantly must be updated.
- *Instant access.* Access to systems is abundant, constantly available, and challenging to maintain.

INFORMATION SECURITY (INFOSEC)

One aspect of the *m*eans iteration of the MOMM computer-related fraud theory model is "compromising technology." Another is "compromising controls," which are increasingly embedded in, or dependent upon, systems. In MOMM, all of the *m*ethods are computer-related as well. Therefore, the systems' security and operations has become a dominant aspect of computer fraud and crime. Protecting the technologies, systems, and information is a critical success factor in the advanced technological environment of today.

The Computer Security Institute (CSI), in partnership with the FBI, conducts an annual survey of computer crime and security. The twelfth annual survey polled 494 U.S. corporations, government agencies, financial and medical institutions, and universities. It reported that about 46 percent of respondents detected computer security breaches in the past year. Survey respondents said they lost at least $350 million as a result of computer crime, compared with $168 million the previous year. Eighteen percent of those who suffered one or more kinds of security incidents also reported targeted attacks. Financial fraud was the number one crime in terms of financial losses.[6]

Critical issues in information security are:

- Ethics
- Access controls
- Data integrity (accuracy, validity, and completeness of data)
- Proprietary information theft
- Counterfeiting
- Piracy
- Social engineering
- Embezzlement
- Logging and monitoring

Risks and Threats

A critical organization policy is the security (or information security [InfoSec]) policy. Management needs to establish fundamental security objectives tied to business objectives and identify assets that need protection from identified risks. A good policy is contingent on a proper and thorough risk assessment.

One goal of the security policy is to emphasize to all stakeholders (employees in particular) that information and data are assets that have a value, and are not just computer files. A security policy will remind employees of the importance and value of information they handle and the risks or exposures that exist. That is, it will help to make a corporate culture that is security conscious. SANS (SysAdmin, Audit, Network, Security) presents a good overview of developing an effective InfoSec policy on their web site.[7]

Somewhat surprisingly, the greatest risk is from the organization's own employees. Disgruntled employees, recently terminated employees, embezzlers, former contractors or consultants, and others may be bent on revenge and be motivated to perpetrate an attack. In fact, a recent study found that vengeful employees are now the biggest security worry for 90 percent of executive managers.[8] Gartner (experts in computer and technologies research) estimates that more than 70 percent of unauthorized access to information systems is committed by employees, as are more than 95 percent of intrusions that result in significant financial losses.[9] *All businesses must examine the risks associated with their own employees* when developing an effective protective system against attacks.

PROFILING INTERNET FRAUDSTERS

Profiling is a common technique used by criminal investigators to identify criminals. Using whatever evidence is available, investigators compile what they know into a criminal profile, which is a list of characteristics that a criminal may exhibit. The profile aids in evaluating a suspect's probability of guilt and in the search for more evidence. Profiling is particularly necessary with Internet crime due to the invisibility, untraceability, and, often, lack of evidence.

According to the Commission on Critical Infrastructure Protection, an estimated 19 million people worldwide have the skills to engage in malicious hacking.[10] These malicious intruders usually begin cyber attacks at a young age. For example, Mixter (a self-proclaimed white hat hacker[11]) started learning computers at age 6 and began malicious activity at age 14.

A host of other profile considerations can be relevant. Knowledge of the criminal's background, associations, tendencies, culture, strengths, and weaknesses aids greatly in investigations with predicting and confirming malicious activities. Criminal intent (motivation) is clearly a helpful determination. When coupled with the type of crime, a portrait of the criminal begins to build on paper, which is just the first step. It is true that "Knowing is half the battle." The other half of that sentence should be: "The other half is synthesizing and following through."

Criminal Intent

Intent can be used effectively to profile computer fraudsters. Groups of criminals with shared objectives are, in technical terms, hackers, crackers, and script kiddies. Although hackers are the group most frequently mentioned, the term is not portrayed as it should be.

True hackers ("white hats"[12]) actually try to do a service for the Internet community. They look for vulnerabilities and weaknesses, then communicate the "hole" to the entity. These people enjoy the intellectual challenge of their activities. Traditionally, the term *hacker*[13] carried a positive connotation; it was a badge of honor regarding one's technical expertise.

People almost always refer to the "bad guys" as hackers because they are ignorant of the *technical* definitions. Bad guys are technically *crackers*[14] (sometimes referred to as "black hats") whose intent is to steal or destroy. Crackers in noncomputer terms are outlaws, armed and dangerous. Approach with caution.

The term *script kiddie* originated as a reference to young computer enthusiasts who download malicious code (e.g., viruses, denial of service [DoS]) generated by crackers, rather than author it, and conduct mischievous exploits. Kiddies are mostly not malicious, just bored. They are similar to street gangs who have created a way to tag the Internet (viral code) and invented their own form of graffiti (Web site defacements). They have gang wars online (using thousands of remote computers controlled by Internet relay chat [IRC] bots) and are immature.[15]

Steve Gibson's Web site (grc.com) was attacked by a vengeful teenage script kiddie, and his system defended itself against hundreds of thousands of distributed denial of service (DDoS) attacks per day for several days. Finally, Steve wrote an open letter to the teen cyberterrorist and admitted that his Internet system could be brought down at any time by a sophisticated attacker. Shortly thereafter, the attacks stopped. This type of story has been played out over and over again. *Any entity on the Internet is subject to this kind of threat or risk.*

Another example is a female (rare among script kiddies) from Belgium who authored Sharpei, one of the first ".Net" viruses. She says writing these viruses and DDoS programs is "a form of art, just like other hobbies. Also, it's a fun way to practice programming."[16] This statement reflects the attitude of, and demonstrates the problem with, attackers. They do not see themselves as being harmful to their victims, they are only enjoying the personal pleasure it brings.

Types of Computer Crimes

Computer crimes can take on many forms, including intellectual property theft or violations, software piracy, child pornography, online gambling, hate crimes, and espionage. While covering all types of computer crimes is not feasible, the following list represents the types of crimes.

Identity Theft

Thieves steal the typical physical items, credit cards or their data, or they steal login credentials for financial accounts, or even someone's identity. There are various ways a criminal might steal someone's identity, including data theft through cracking, excessive access, or social engineering, spyware, or sniffing (software programs that capture Internet messaging). The problem of identity theft continues to grow and will continue to grow into the foreseeable future.

Blackmail

Internet blackmail has been an area of high criminal activity, with targets such as online casinos, security and technology companies, and who knows what others, because victims generally do not report a blackmail publicly. The mafia, street gangs, and swindlers have increasingly migrated to computer-based operations, and often use blackmail or other threats. Ransoms from these attacks have been reported in the millions of dollars. If this type of crime is encountered, one must seek the help of a technology specialist and a lawyer immediately.

Denial of Service Attack

A DoS attack is intended to harm victims in a different way. Like most attacks, variants of DoS exist, and include DDoS and reflection DoS attacks. All of these malicious objects attempt to bring computer systems, specifically online web servers that provide e-commerce, to a rapid halt. When firms such as eBay, Amazon, and Yahoo! are down, not only do those entities have no means of conducting business operations during that time, but they are high-profile businesses, and criminals will gain publicity from their acts.

E-Mail Attacks

Criminals might use a variety of nefarious e-mail attacks, including spamming, spoofing, viruses, and spyware. *Spam* is unsolicited e-mail or junk e-mail. Spamming techniques can be used to clog an e-mail server to the point it locks up. One of the first so-called viruses was the Christmas Virus released into IBM's computers. A Christmas card message was sent that contained programming code to replicate the message to everyone in the recipient's address book, locking up IBM's systems for quite some time. Spamming the right system with the right code can work much like a DoS attack.

Spoofing is pretending to be someone else or some entity. The intent is to deceive the other party into taking action resulting in embarrassment or harm. Spoofing has been associated with *phishing*,[17] but now applies to the broader misrepresentation of self as someone else. Spoofing is often a gateway crime, opening up bigger and better fraud opportunities.

Viruses are a very significant threat to businesses in terms of resources lost. Experts estimate U.S. corporations spent about $12.3 billion to clean up damage from computer viruses in 2001, and many viruses cost over $1 million per virus. A virus can erase or disable system data, the operating system, or application software. One cybercriminal almost destroyed a business by erasing all of its data for existing projects. The business was a consulting firm that kept the project files on its network. The perpetrator had inside information that the business did not have a current backup, and by sending a virus to erase key files and drives on the network, the firm lost all current information on projects and had a serious problem of reconstructing work performed to date. The business almost collapsed.

Spyware continues to proliferate as a criminal medium. According to pcwebopedia.com, *spyware*, also called *adware*, is any software that covertly gathers information through the user's Internet connection without his knowledge, usually for advertising purposes.[18] Spyware ranges from harmless pop-up ads to the ability to record anything that happens on a computer and transmit that data to a remote site. For example, WinWhatWhere software can record all keystrokes on a personal computer and send them to some remote location on the Internet.[19] Spyware applications are sometimes bundled as a hidden component of freeware or shareware programs that can be downloaded from the Internet, and sometimes are placed on "hacked" computers. Once installed, the spyware monitors user activity on the Internet and transmits that information in the background to someone else. Spyware can also gather information about e-mail addresses and even passwords and credit card numbers.

InfoSec Controls and Activities

Access control systems are the beginning layer of protection for systems and information. They are used to authenticate and verify, usually by using one of three basic approaches to security: (1) something you have, (2) something you know, and (3) something you are.[20] Specific controls range from access cards/readers (something you have), to passwords or PINs (something you know), to biometrics (something you are). The more risk that exists, the greater the need to consider a higher level control or multifaceted access controls in order to maintain adequate security. That is, it takes more access security than just an ID and password to secure sensitive data or systems.

The most general authentication, authorization, and verification controls are password systems, firewalls, and occasionally access cards or biometrics. The weakness of the first two security methods is that they have been compromised, and intruders have caused great harm and significant financial losses. The latter approach, biometrics, has the potential to provide the greatest level of security because it involves something you are, and because it can be more reliable than the passwords or firewalls, especially stand-alone password or firewall systems. Cost and precision (too many false positives) keep biometrics from being everyday access control.

The difference between verification (authentication) and identification (authorization) needs to be emphasized. *Authorization* is the recognition of a specific individual from among all the individuals enrolled on the system. That is, the token or ID/password are valid and that ID is authorized to have access to the system. *Authentication*, however, is the process of confirming that the person carrying the token (e.g., badge, card, or password, which is the claim of identity) is the rightful owner of the token. Ideally, access control systems would do both.

Passwords are the first line of defense in authenticating access to systems and data, and serve as a reasonably effective preventive system. One strategy is to create multifaceted passwords, especially where remote access is frequent or e-commerce is employed. One more sophisticated approach is to generate a temporary password (PIN) that lasts for a very short time frame, sometimes less than a minute. When remote users log in, they check a beeper for the most recent PIN and can log in only with both their password and the temporary PIN.

Although they appear to be much less expensive than biometric systems, password systems cost an organization. This cost usually happens in two ways: passwords that are forgotten and passwords that are stolen. The former requires time and resources to reset passwords. The latter is a security breach and can be much more costly, if the system is compromised. Since the human brain is not a perfect storage system when it comes to complicated or long password, the more sophisticated passwords might be forgotten. In such situations, the password needs to be reset and a new password must be created. According to Mandylion Research Labs, resetting a password security system of a company with 100 workers would cost $3,850 per year. If the company has 1,000 authorized personnel, the same process would cost up to $38,500 per year.[21]

The most common biometric devices used for access control are fingerprint scanners, although facial and iris scanners and voice recognition systems are increasing in use.[22] Fingerprint scanners come in a variety of formats, from stand-alone devices to readers built into keyboards and mice. They are unobtrusive, inexpensive, and, essentially, they work. For example, the Public Benefits administrators in Texas and New York claim fingerprint identification has virtually eliminated fraud in their programs.[23] Computer models are readily available with integral biometric fingerprint readers and biometric mice.[24]

Another emerging trend is toward "layering" account security software or tools on top of applications. These solutions to security loopholes can be necessary for a variety of reasons and serve a variety of purposes; for example, a security package such as ACF2 may be layered on top of an older (legacy) mainframe system that does not include any inherent security (password or account management). Solutions include implementing security software (such as RACF, or Blockade), a "host" server that requires separate secure credentials (e.g., Citrix), or custom scripts (e.g., UNIX) or miniprograms that perform authentication checks.

Careless information security procedures are a big problem. First there is the problem with accounts that remain in the firm's systems. IDC estimates that 30 percent to 60 percent of accounts in large corporations are no longer valid.[25] These accounts serve as magnets to would-be insider employees and to outsider hackers, crackers, and intruders. Another problem is stale passwords, or passwords that are left unchanged for long periods of time. The entity might not have a password policy and procedure for changing passwords, or the policy goes unenforced, leaving the corporation vulnerable.

Many other potentially significant InfoSec activities exist. These include change control processes, periodic configuration reviews, penetration and attack simulations, managed security-related software services, data monitoring and reconciliation, and data encryption. Change control processes ensure changes to applications, scripts, databases, and other systems are authorized and tested prior to implementation as appropriate. Reviewing the configuration of software (application, operating systems, databases, etc.) and hardware (routers, firewalls, etc.) against established corporate security policy or best practices can identify potential control weaknesses. Penetration and attack simulations, often conducted with a specialized, outside expert, include attempting to penetrate supposedly secured systems or successfully attack them with denial of service, viruses, and so on. Managed security-related software services centrally manage updating security-related software with patches or other updates (such as updating operating system service packs, application patches, antivirus definitions, or local computer security policies). Data monitoring includes programs that monitor and send automated alerts around data changes; reconciliations attempt to match data from two sources to ensure processing between the two occurred completely and accurately. Data encryption tools, whether in storage or in communications, masks the data to unauthenticated users or allows for remote deletion or automatically enabled deletion.

SUMMARY

Computers can be used to commit frauds, and can be the victim. Computer *crimes* include a variety of things beyond the kinds of *fraud* schemes associated with internal frauds. Because computers are so pervasive and likely to hold data that could be used to perpetrate fraud, and IT itself can be used to perpetrate a fraud, and can be used to obtain information about the fraud, it is important to understand computers systems' place in the fraud environment. Many of the concerns over InfoSec are similar to fraud, and many of the computer crimes have similar characteristics to fraud crimes. Thus it is important to understand the similarities and the links between fraud and computer crime.

NOTES

1. Michael Cangemi and Tommie Singleton, *Managing the Audit Function,* 3rd ed. (Hoboken, NJ: John Wiley & Sons, 2003), p. 98.
2. Donn Parker, *Criminal Justice Resource Manual,* 2nd ed. (Washington, D.C.: National Institute of Justice, 1989), p. 2.
3. "New Computer Crime Survey," Federal Bureau of Investigation, January 18, 2006. Online at: www.fbi.gov/page2/jan06/computer_crime_survey011806.htm.
4. "2008 Internet Crime Report," Internet Crime Complaint Center. Online at: www.ic3.gov/media/annualreport/2008_ic3report.pdf.
5. Michael Kunz and Patrick Wilson, "Computer Crime and Computer Fraud," (College Park, MD: University of Maryland, 2004). Online at: www.montgomerycountymd.gov/content/cjcc/pdf/computer_crime_study.pdf.
6. CSI Survey 2007, "12th Annual Computer Crime and Security Survey," Arlington, VA.
7. SANS. Online at: www.sans.org/security-resources/policies/.
8. Kevin Cunningham, "Cyberterrorism: Are We Leaving the Keys Out?" *SC Magazine* (November 2002). Online at: www.scmagazine.com/scmagazine/sconline/2002/article/51/article.html.
9. Ibid.
10. According to Computer Emergency Response Team. See Elsa Lee, "Combating Cyberthreats: Partnership between Public and Private Entities," *Information Systems Control Journal* (2002).
11. A *white-hat hacker* is a hacker who works for an entity to improve its information security. A *black-hat hacker* would be a hacker who attacks computer systems without permission.
12. They are called *white hats* because (a) they have obtained prior permission to "hack," (b) hacking is a part of their job description and they are an employee, (c) they have a contract to conduct a pen test (specific domain, specific time frame), and (d) they have an engagement letter to conduct the pen test.
13. See technical definition of *hacker* at: http://pcwebopedia.com/ TERM/h/hacker.html.
14. See technical definition of *cracker* at: http://pcwebopedia.com/ TERM/c/crack.html. Likely a reference to safe crackers.
15. According to ZDNet associate editor Robert Vamosi. See "Can We Stop Script Kiddies? Yes! Here's How," *ZDNet Reviews* (May 15, 2002). Online at: www.zdnet.com.
16. Tommie Singleton, "Managing Distributed Denial of Service Attacks," *EDPACS* (November 2002), pp. 7, 9–20.

17. *Phishing* is a term used to describe social engineering, con artist, or plain old "fishing expedition"-type activities. The perpetrator usually sends an e-mail and asks for information under the pretense of some official or legitimate cause. The purpose is usually to steal either your identity or access codes to a computer system.
18. This paragraph is taken from the definition of spyware provided by pcwebopedia at http://pcwebopedia.com/TERM/s/spyware.html.
19. Available from www.trueactive.com/default.asp.
20. Simon Liu and Mark Silverman, "A Practical Guide to Biometric Security Technology," IEEE Computer Society. Online at: www.computer.org/itpro/homepage/Jan_Feb/security3.htm.
21. T. Singleton, "Biometric Security Systems: The Best InfoSec Solution?" *EDPACS* (March 2003), pp. 1–20.
22. "The Lowdown on Biometrics," *Government Computer News*, August 9, 2002 http://gcn.com/articles/2002/08/09/the-lowdown-on-biometrics.aspx?sc_lang=en.
23. Mark Kellner, "Digital Security," *Government Computer News*, August 9, 2002. Online at: http://gcn.com/articles/2002/08/09/digital-security.aspx?sc_lang=en.
24. Julian Ashbourn, "Biometrics: Making the Right Impression," *SC Magazine* (June 2002), pp. 58–63.
25. Ibid.

10

CHAPTER TEN

Fraud and the Accounting Information System

INTRODUCTION

Except for certain limited off-the-books schemes, fraud transaction data are almost always contained in the accounting information system, even if the fraudster destroyed the paper trail. Therefore, a proper understanding of the accounting cycles (business processes) and the accounting information system is critical to successfully preventing, detecting, and investigating fraud. The discussion of the accounting system here will delve further into the concepts of fraud control in accounting cycles discussed in earlier chapters.

Notably, accounting information systems can take on a manual or computerized form. Though few in number, completely manual accounting systems exist and no accounting system can be absolutely automated. Systems fall somewhere in between, automating in areas where efficiencies can be attained and using manual procedures where risks, preferences, or technological limitations make it necessary. Clearly, the trend is toward automation, but computer technology cannot replace some human capabilities.

This chapter discusses the fundamentals of accounting information systems and unique aspects of an automated accounting information systems environment relevant to a fraud audit or forensic investigation. In either context, it is particularly important to know what accounting processes dictate accounting systems and records. In automated systems, it is also important to understand the key systems personnel, hardware (media storage), and software. Understanding other concepts such as segregation of duties, reconciliations, and audit trails, better enables fraud auditors and forensic accountants to prevent and detect frauds.

ACCOUNTING CONCEPTS

Accounting is often classified by underlying business processes (accounting cycles). These processes include revenue and receipts, purchases and payables, payroll, fixed assets, financing, and the financial reporting close (general ledger). Several cycles are basically variations of others, thus the core accounting cycles of revenue, expenses, and financial reporting close are discussed next.

Revenue and Receipts Cycle

The revenue and receipts (sales) cycle includes all systems that record the sale of goods and services, and receive and record customer remittances (see Exhibit 10.1). The details of a product sold for a price, or of professional services rendered for a fee, are set out in a document called a sales invoice. Details of all sales invoices are listed in the sales journal.

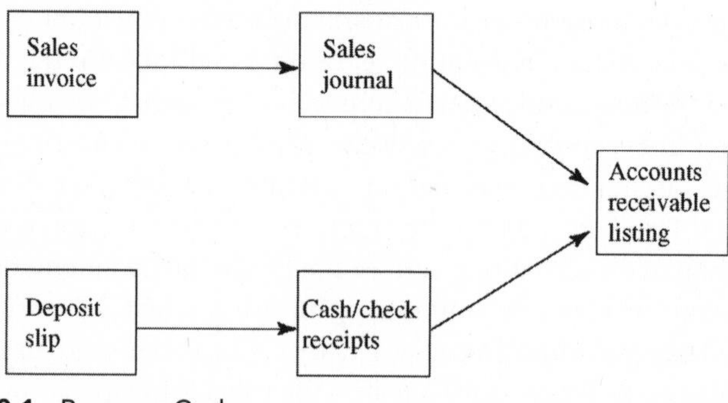

EXHIBIT 10.1 Revenue Cycle

When the customer pays, the company records the payment on a deposit slip ultimately listed in the cash receipts journal or receives notification of an electronic funds transfer (EFT) payment. Business organizations keep a list of those customers who owe money, produced by comparing the sales journal and the cash receipts journal. For customers who purchase on credit terms, transactions are recorded in the accounts receivable journal. It is usually prepared monthly and shows, for each customer listed, the balance owed and the aging of the receivable—that is, if the customer has owed the money for 30, 60, 90, or more than 90 days. Customer ledgers are used to depict a specific customer's sales and payment transactions and are often analyzed for critical customers or customers whose account is significantly aged (especially over 90 days past due).

The system of sales, receipts, and receivables constitutes the revenue cycle of any company. The primary documents are the sales invoice (evidence of the sale to the customer) and the deposit slip (evidence of the customer's payment to the company). The best evidence of payment is a customer's cancelled check. With the advent of electronic check clearing (Check 21), checks are truncated at some point of the banking system and not physically returned to the payer.

Purchases and Payables

The purchases and payables cycle (also known as the expenditures or disbursements cycle) includes all systems that record the acquisition of goods and services for use in exchange for payment or promises to pay. Exhibit 10.2 charts this cycle.

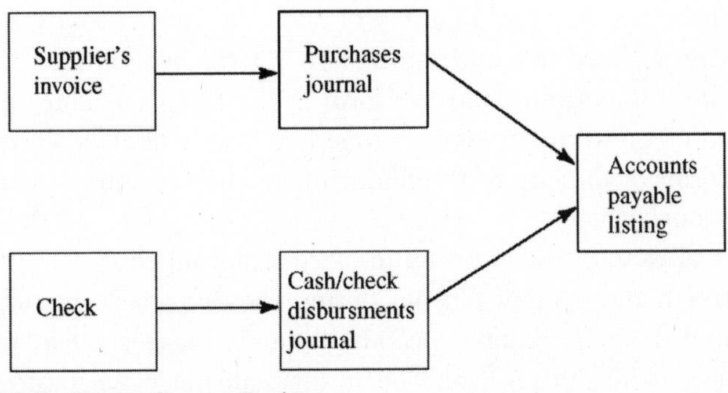

EXHIBIT 10.2 Expenditures Cycle

In order to produce its product for sale, a company makes various types of expenditures. These may be for acquiring land, buildings, and equipment; purchasing materials and supplies; and paying company employees. Purchases are made from many different suppliers. A supplier's invoice is evidence of a transaction. This invoice is sent to the company and sets out the details of the transaction. The company lists certain details of the supplier's invoice in the purchase journal.

If the company has the funds available, the supplier usually is paid within 30 or 60 days (according to payment terms set by agreement or in the invoice). This payment is evidenced by the company's cancelled check. All checks are recorded in the company's check disbursements journal when they are issued. This journal is simply a list of the checks paid to the various suppliers and other creditors and individuals doing business with the company.

Most companies attempt to keep track of what they owe suppliers. The company prepares an accounts payable listing by comparing what is recorded in the purchases journal with what is recorded as paid in the check disbursements journal. This list may detail how long various suppliers have been owed (e.g., 30, 60, or 90 days). Accounts payable listings for specific vendors are known as vendor ledgers.

The most common group of asset misappropriation frauds is fraudulent disbursements. Therefore, this cycle is ripe with possibilities of fraud detection in the average organization, if a fraud occurs. These frauds often involve collusion or override of controls, so monitoring and supervision are key to control.

General Ledger and Financial Reporting

Transactions listed in each of the four journals (sales, receipts, purchases, and disbursements) are totaled and entered into the general ledger. General ledger reports can be organized in a variety of ways: by journal totals, by primary accounts (assets, liabilities, and equity) and in total, by month or other cross-sections. More important than the form is the fact that adjusting journal entries and other transactions are sometimes made directly to the general ledger account or directly to the financial statements and not through the applicable journal.

Nearly all systems have a way to place a journal entry into the general ledger through the general journal during the financial reporting process. Mistakes and errors do occur in accounting and to correct them, an entry is made in the general journal. Even if no mistakes are made, the nature of certain transactions or the design of accounting processes lend themselves more efficiently to journal entries. For example, estimate transactions, such as the allowance for bad debt and associated expense, are often calculated based on data from the general ledger, prevailing market conditions, and other judgmental factors, which can be difficult to automate or due to dependencies lend themselves to journal entries. An example of business process design around journal entries is outsourced payroll where the entity receives a detailed report of payroll expenses, but for various reasons including efficiency, records the total payroll expense through a journal entry.

Traditionally, the general ledger served as the complete set of financial statements for financial reporting. However, statements are more complex today and many companies produce their financial statements by extracting data from the general ledger and entering additional transactions in spreadsheets or other methods outside the system. The risks associated with edits to financial statements outside the general ledger are similar to journal entries.

While most entries made in these manners are perfectly legitimate, such entries potentially bypass several steps in the accounting process. Normally, sales occur that will be related to receipts; those receipts and the process of matching sales to receipts provide a paper trail. The sale gives credibility to the receipt and vice versa. The process and credibility of general journal entries is dependent on the effectiveness of the controls for adjusting entries.

Adjusting entries should set out a documented explanation for the correction, supporting evidence, and normally evidence of management approval. A list of recurring journal entries and other typical transactions to record during the "close" (financial statement production) process should be documented and approved. Exhibits 10.3 and 10.4 illustrate the components and end product of the general ledger.

Due to the critical role the general ledger plays in producing financial statements and other reports, *entries to the general ledger present a significant fraud risk*. Financial statement frauds often employ journal entries either to create fictitious revenues or assets or to cover up the fraud. Normally, valid and invalid adjusting entries occur at the end of fiscal years or other time periods (months, quarters, etc.). Frauds have been discovered many times when managers, especially executives, booked fictitious revenues in the last quarter of the year to increase the profits of the organization. From an internal perspective, controls over all adjusting general ledger entries should be strong and firmly in place. From a fraud audit perspective, inspection of journal entries can be an effective technique for detecting frauds.

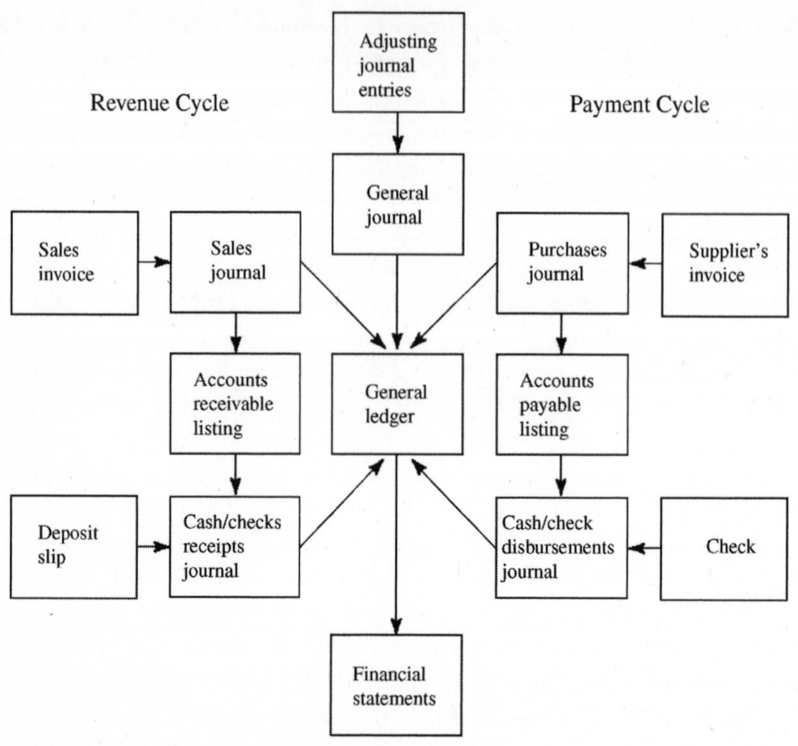

EXHIBIT 10.3 Documents in the Revenue Cycle

Cash Path and Reconciliations

In regard to fraud, the asset misappropriation type of fraud (generally perpetrated by employees) is almost always associated with cash coming in or cash going out of the business. Theft of inventory or other "liquid" (easily convertible to cash) assets is a small percentage of asset misappropriation frauds. Therefore, the positions that employees hold along the trail of cash coming in and going out are key positions and critical control points to prevent and detect fraud. The employees who hold these positions generally are believed to be trustworthy. Organizations should continuously consider if adequate controls are in place over cash (background checks, bank reconciliations, secondary approvals of wire transfers, etc.).

Reconciliations are comparisons of two sources of data and subsequent resolution of any differences. Reconciliations occur in many places in the

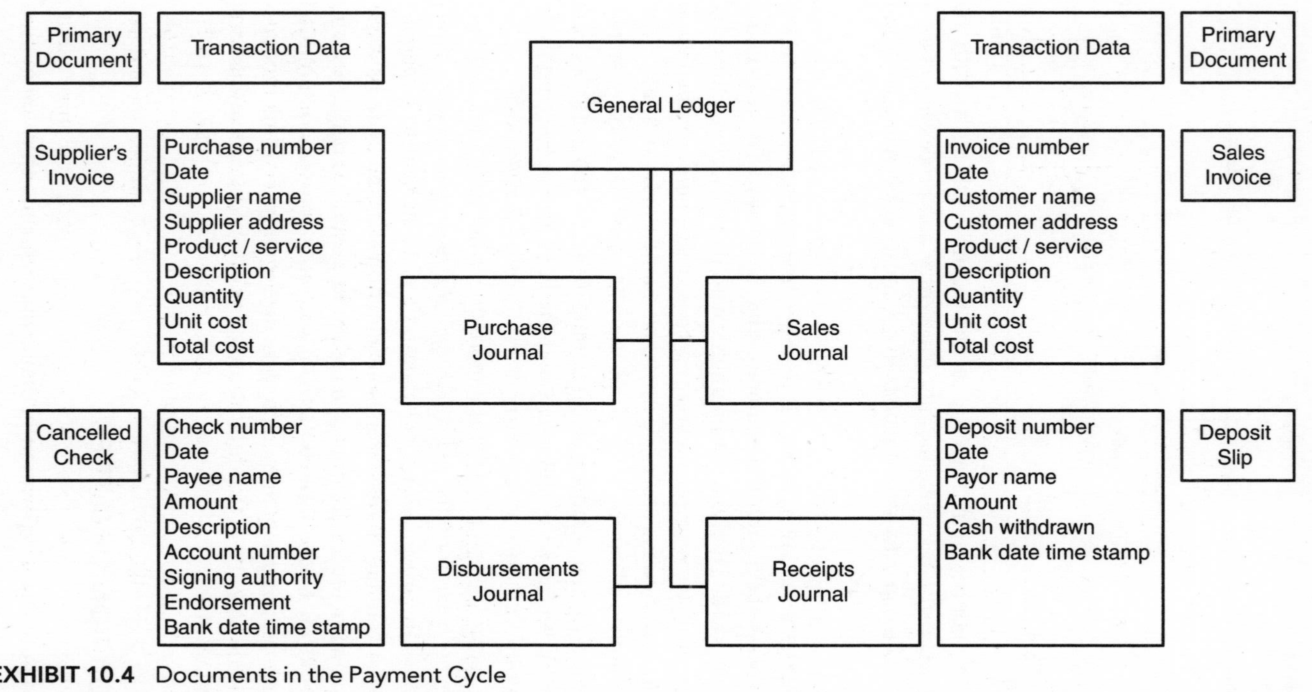

EXHIBIT 10.4 Documents in the Payment Cycle

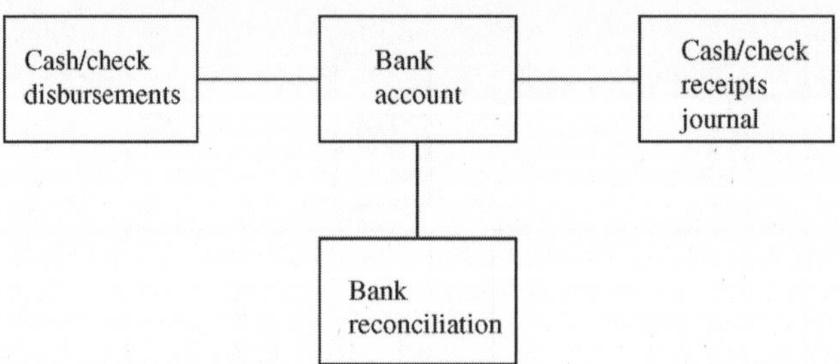

EXHIBIT 10.5 Bank Reconciliation

accounting information system. Typically entities reconcile subledgers with the general ledger to ensure complete and accurate entry and processing of data occurred. The reconciliations most understood and most closely related to fraud are bank reconciliations.

The monies the company receives (as recorded in the cash receipts journal) and the monies the company pays out (as recorded in the check disbursements journal) are processed through the company's bank account. To ensure that the transactions recorded in these journals agree with those shown on the bank statement, a monthly bank reconciliation is prepared. The bank reconciliation accounts for the transactions processed by the bank and those executed by the entity but not processed by the bank as of the statement date (for example, uncashed checks sent to vendors) in the comparison of the entity's bank balance according to the bank statement and the bank balance according to the accounting information system. Exhibit 10.5 charts this process.

The bank reconciliation is one of the more important functions management can oversee, because *in the end, frauds typically involve monetary transactions, the money must go somewhere, and it always leaves a trail in the accounting system*. The most common frauds are disbursement frauds, and the bank reconciliation can often reveal the fraud. Too often, however, the bank reconciliation is not performed, is performed by the perpetrator, or goes unmonitored by management. Management should consider segregating the bank reconciliation step from other steps in the disbursement cycle, or personally reviewing the bank reconciliation.

SEGREGATION OF DUTIES

Segregation of duties is a separation of conflicting interests that mitigates a person's ability to subvert the intended process. For example, entities typically require a check signature from a person who does not authorize payments to mitigate the risk of false disbursements. If a person could authorize payment and sign the check, what is to stop this person from authorizing a fraudulent check?

An analysis of the cycles shows where segregation of duties should be employed. Specifically, within a cycle, the steps in that cycle (initiating, authorizing, recording, reviewing, etc.) should be segregated as much as possible. When not possible or feasible, the compensating control of *formal* supervision and monitoring is necessary to help mitigate the risk of fraud. The illustration of sending bank statements directly to management or internal audit for their review is one type of formal supervision that could be used.

ACCOUNTING INFORMATION SYSTEMS

Essentially, there are three basic elements in an accounting information system that is automated as opposed to manual:

1. *Key personnel:* management, security, database management, and change control
2. *Computer hardware:* physical equipment that includes processing and communications units (mainly various types of servers, network devices, and personal computers) and peripheral devices from keyboards to laptops, mobile phones and PDAs
3. *Computer software:* programs or instructions that enable the computer to perform a business function (including protecting and managing other computer systems and data) using the data input by personnel

It is important to note that these elements are over and above those in conventional (manual) accounting systems, where the normal procedures are presumed to be in place. The major difference is fewer personnel are directly connected with the actual use of data in a computerized system, since programs and stored data are used to automate manual processing. From a risk perspective, it is important to note automation may shift risks in the environment to a degree, while basic risks such as unrecorded or inaccurately entered transactions cannot be eliminated.

Auditors and accountants have to understand the technology, the process, and the control to prevent, detect, and investigate fraud. As many users have access to data through applications, the process for granting user access to software is quite important. However, many applications in today's market are intranet, extranet, or Web applications, especially intranet applications. Often user access to the network automatically grants access to the software program, which again authenticates the user and authorizes the person to have certain privileges or permissions in the given application. When this scenario is the case, access to the network *almost completely* reduces the possibility of users who were removed from the network gaining access. This situation is just one example of how the systems infrastructure can affect security over data; *each system is unique. Fraud auditors need to truly understand the process and controls in order to effectively conduct a fraud audit using the accounting information system.*

KEY PERSONNEL

Specifying the typical information systems, or information technology (IT), department is difficult, but some generalizations can be made. While some decentralization usually exists, most organizations have a centralized IT department servicing the entire organization. The employees in that department are technology specialists of some kind, with regards to security, administrators, databases, software, or systems projects. The IT department develops, maintains, and supports systems and data for the rest of the organization especially end (systems) users and business owners. This section briefly describes the jobs in the IT department.

Management

Both systems and business management over the accounting system are important in regard to fraud for two reasons:

1. The importance of culture cannot be understated and management creates that culture in the environment it manages.
2. Management ultimately controls what happens within its department; management can always override controls that do not reach above the given management's level of authority.

Security

The gatekeepers to networks, systems, applications, and, most important, data, are security personnel. Besides managing physical access, they manage user access (adding, editing, and removing) to systems (logical access). Controlled physical access, except in unique industries and government, is not normally as essential to security as controlled logical access.

Depending on the information system infrastructure (hardware, software, data, and communications devices), different areas of physical and logical access are high risk. Defining access can be difficult, due to several reasons including lack of security concerns by business management requesting access and lack of business knowledge by security staff, complex access permission options, and access groups (profiles) or privileges that are not well defined or periodically reviewed. Even if defined properly, *keeping user access up to date is critical* and study after study has found neglecting to do so greatly increases the possibility of fraud.

Periodic reviews of user access, especially when aimed at high-level and terminated users, are the best single control related to unauthorized access when done thoroughly; reviews should reconcile access privileges with user responsibilities and consider segregation of duties. To maintain access to data, an effective line of communication must exist, well-defined processes and procedures must be in place, and personnel responsible for reporting changes to user access must understand the importance of this area and act accordingly.

Security personnel also manage parameters, settings, and technology related to security. Parameters and settings refer to the options available to customize security in infrastructure components. For example, security management software has parameters and settings for the use of password requirements.

Experienced security personnel know best practices for passwords—such as length (requiring six to eight characters), complexity (including a capital letter and a number or special character), expiration (enforces a change of password after a set number of days), and lockout (after a set number of failed attempts to access the system, the user will be locked out for a set time period). Experienced security personnel also know that end users have to be aware of the importance of passwords and know how to protect them, especially by not leaving them in the drawer right beside the computer or, even worse, written on a sticky note attached to the computer screen. It happens too often!

Most IT departments have specialized security personnel who manage the integrity of networks, critical applications, and other high-risk areas specific to the organization. They deal with issues such as encryption of data, remote access (VPN), application and data security, and surveillance and monitoring. These types of personnel perform the technical security work; for example, selecting a firewall, customizing it to the business process and needs, and monitoring it. They may also assist in developing, testing, or monitoring systems, as well as probing them for weaknesses. Security personnel are in a good position to relay any system weaknesses, although they are also in a good position to attempt to defraud systems.

Administrators

The term *administrator* is used quite loosely but generally means someone who oversees, or literally administers, some kind of system or data such as a network, operating system, application, or database. For example, database administrators oversee a database or association of databases to ensure the data has integrity. Database administrators help maintain database structures, jobs (small, automated, and usually programs that run automatically to edit or communicate data), data types, settings, relationships, access to, content in, and other aspects of databases.

Any kind of administrator has what is often called "power-user access." That generally means administrators can manipulate the system within their domain however they please. For example, an Application Access Administrator could potentially (depending on controls in place) create a fictitious account with high-level privileges, enter fraudulent transactions, and subsequently delete the fictitious account and possibly the audit trail of activities conducted. Administrator access must be balanced with monitoring through technology and through output of the system; controls here would include monitoring of automatic alerts and log changes made by administrator users and detailed review of reports on the data under administration.

Change Control

The change control department provides quality assurance over the process of changing programs, databases, settings, and infrastructure components. Change control is critical because program changes affect how applications or jobs (tasks) manipulate data, and changes directly to data values are difficult to automatically record and subsequently monitor. Change control should, at a minimum, ensure that:

- Change requests are approved and valid.
- Testing is performed and documented.
- Changes are moved into production (the version currently in use) by the appropriate person.

End Users and Business Owners

The end user inputs all of the data to be processed by the computer. Data in an accounting context are usually classified as being processed in batch or in real time. With batches, data accumulate and assimilate into groups over a period of time when transactions take place; later, at some specified time or when users send a command, the batch is sent to be processed. Real-time processing, simply put, process data in real time, as it is entered into the program. End users, especially those with a lot of experience in a given area, know software rather well and could be a good source of understanding how it does and does not operate and the intended business purpose, when relevant.

The term *business owner* refers to the employee responsible for the system. The designation is usually made departmentally. For example, the vice president of finance at a bank would be responsible for a capital management and forecasting system. Business owners are helpful in understanding the specific functions of a business process. Generally, business owners are at a high enough level of management to override controls, and the culture they create is an important factor in antifraud program activities. Additionally, business owners often play critical roles in controls such as approving or reviewing access, administering application access, approving and testing program changes, and involvement in broader IT projects.

Project Management

Managing IT projects is one of the most difficult jobs in systems. Project management is the body of knowledge that leads to successful implementation of a new or highly revised component of the organization's IT system to fulfill some specified business need. Projects are susceptible to failures on functionality, deadlines, and costs; in fact, most projects fail on at least one of these measures. This project risk is one reason why project management is important to an organization and may become important in a fraud audit.

Project management best practices result in a substantial degree of documentation throughout the project; approvals by business owners and other appropriate persons at project milestones, testing results with a comparison of expected to actual results, and user acceptance of the final product. In order to ensure success, the project management processes should be followed diligently. Personnel such as system analysts and designers, developers, and quality assurance specialists all play key roles in those processes.

The systems analyst works with the various user departments to determine how their needs can best be met, what data must be entered, what processing must be carried out on the input data, what output must be produced, and with what frequency. Systems designers convert those needs into system specifications. From the specifications, the programmer writes, debugs, and documents the new system components. Developers are expected to document new programs in detail and to update the documentation when programs are changed. Quality assurance staff members examine and evaluate all of the project steps to date and thoroughly test the system to ensure it is working as intended.

Other Personnel

Computer operators mainly exist in mainframe environments, where they direct the execution of various mechanical tasks by means of a console terminal. When operators are in place, they usually deal with a significantly important application, operating system, and/or server. Operators schedule tasks for the system to complete and are responsible for the proper use of input and output devices. Operators monitor for any problems and perform backup activities. They should be required to document key, if not all, activities, if automated logging is not in place.

The librarian stores and retrieves programs and data, usually at a location away from the computer site. Programs and data normally are stored on magnetic tape or disk and serve as a backup if the original software or transaction files are destroyed. The librarian also maintains, under normal circumstances, a log of tapes being checked out from and back into the library.

COMPUTER HARDWARE

Computer equipment may be online or offline. An online system permits the operator to access and manipulate information in the computer, changing the database immediately and receiving information from the computer immediately. In contrast, offline systems involve an intermediate step of some kind before processing takes place.

Generally, computer hardware includes: (1) equipment for preparing data for processing, (2) input devices, (3) a central processing unit (CPU), (4) output devices, and (5) communications devices. All of these devices provide some convenience at the cost of risks exposed by their presence; these risks do not change anything from a fraud audit perspective, but potentially provide new means to perpetrate a fraud.

Data Preparation Equipment

This equipment is used to convert the data into a machine-readable format. Data are almost always entered directly into systems via online computers, but offline systems and associated data conversions are still found in operation and present unique risks.

Input Devices

Input equipment includes such components as keyboards and video screens that show what is being entered, display instructions, and formats for inputting. Modern computer screens respond to touch. A wireless, optical "mouse" is often used in conjunction with data entry. Scanners, cameras, and video can bring imaging to every desktop and cell phone. Tablet personal computers (PCs) take the convenience of a small laptop to a whole new level and can store a vast amount of data. Computer software is available that will respond to a range of voice commands as input. New technologies are developing constantly and potentially provide new vehicles for fraud, especially the transport or storage of data.

Central Processing Unit

The CPU is the heart of the computer; it contains a series of operating programs and a translator that converts data into machine language (binary) on which the CPU itself operates. It stores programmed instructions and data; reads, writes, and moves data and instructions; interprets and performs programmed tasks; and synchronizes all of these activities. The CPU is really the technological processor, managing itself and processing according to mathematical functions. Software is the business processor, processing data according to business functions.

Output Devices

Output equipment includes printers, video display screens, and plotters. The technology of output as well as input devices is constantly being improved, because these devices constitute the interface between human beings and computers. Note that output devices, to date, do not edit data and therefore are not particularly relevant to fraud audits.

Communications Devices

A host of communication devices exist in the typical organizational systems infrastructure. Routers connect networks, switches and hubs connect devices within a network, modems and communication protocols ensure interoperability, and e-mail servers process countless messages per day. Cell phones, two-way radios, and PDAs, all with Internet capabilities, have flooded corporate America, and there is likely to be more portable devices and a concomitant increase in fraud risk. Again, with regard to fraud audits, the point is that there are more means available to commit fraud.

COMPUTER SOFTWARE

Software is the generic name for computer programs and their documentation. A program is a set of instructions that directs the computer to perform a task. Software is divided into two main classes: operating and application.

Operating systems (OS) software consists of the programs that keep the computer running as automatically as possible. They coordinate computer functions between the application software and the computer hardware (e.g., printing a check from a payroll application). OS can also control access to file directories ("paths") and directly to files, although limited security exists in most operating systems. Actually, most OS are constantly sending out upgrades ("patches") to fix identified security weaknesses and thus outdated systems increase the chance of fraud.

Applications software consists of computer programs that apply the computer to the user's needs by carrying out an organizational task the user wants performed (e.g., processing a payroll). The normal four-step sequence of instructions in an application program is:

1. Read the information entered.
2. Process it (add, subtract).
3. Update existing files in the computer's memory with new information.
4. Output the new information by displaying, printing, or storing it (or all three).

Applications have increasingly taken on networked forms, meaning application software is often accessed and used over the Internet, extranet, and most popularly through the intranet. As intranet applications are internal to the organization, they provide more security than other "Web-enabled" applications. Intranet software presents some unique risks, especially in "multilayered" applications, where different parts of the program reside on different computers and interact in a more process-oriented and hierarchical fashion. Again, what is important in the context of a fraud audit is to understand the new ways fraud can be perpetrated.

NEW FORMS OF MEDIA

The trend in new forms of media has been toward portability—chief among them digital video discs (DVDs), digital video recorders (DVRs), flash drives (thumb drives, jump drives), PDAs, optical storage media, Internet and intranet storage, and cell phones. These types of media present users with many advantages, particularly in the amount of information they can store and the convenience, speed, transportation, and cost with which that information may be accessed. But, of course, they represent new opportunities for criminals and fraud. Fraud auditors, and especially forensic accountants, should be aware of, know how to search for, and understand how to handle the various forms of media storage.

Although e-mail does not quite fit the term *media,* it deserves special attention because of its similarities to media. E-mail stores data. Actually, e-mail stores a vast amount of data, sometimes critical to the organization and sometimes revealing a fraud. In several of the noted frauds in the late 1990s and early 2000s, e-mail communications supplied evidence of fraud. To date, fraudsters tend to be less diligent in being clandestine via e-mail than with other activities. With the business world tightly connected and ever communicating, *e-mail will undoubtedly become a critical aspect of fraud auditing.*

AUDIT TRAIL CONCEPT

In every transaction, there is a bigger process occurring than the transaction itself. The accounting cycles described earlier depict the typical processes overlying business transactions. Whether manual or automated systems are in place, a trail exists when transactions move through these processes.

Financial auditors often refer to this trail as the *audit trail,* a series of items of evidence in the recording of a transaction through the accounting information system. Single items of evidence are associated with other evidence and form the path the transaction has taken, such as a sales invoice, cash receipt, and bank deposit. Certain elements connect those documents and verify each other; certain actions are taken involving these documents, like approvals on paper or in electronic form. In fraud audits, the amounts, approvals, and other transactional details found in the audit trail are of critical importance to the audit, as it is self-authenticating, and *one connection can reveal substantial evidence capable of ending the investigation.*

Although computerized systems do not leave physical trails of evidence, the audit trail concept still applies. The data either went somewhere or it did not, was edited or was not, and is correct or it is not. The difficulty in proving either of those in an automated system is that the audit trail can be a bit more complex, vague, or less reliable. However, many systems inherently store attributes that described the data (called *metadata*), such as File Creator or Last Modified Date and various monitoring capabilities exist for detailed logging. The audit trail concept is dependent on one assumption: *some* indication always exists describing transaction details. While records can be erased and certain frauds do not involve manipulations of records, cash is predominantly the root of most audit trails. Determining whether forensic evidence exists in records of accounts, logs, and other audit trail sources requires an objective and investigative mind-set, and a walk down the cash trail.

SUMMARY

One key factor in becoming an effectual fraud investigator is to understand the business processes and controls of the subject entity. But that understanding is based on a foundation of understanding the major accounting cycles. This chapter attempts to explain that foundation. It adds to that some basic concepts about accounting controls for those accounting functions, of which segregation of duties is probably the most important one for fraud prevention and detection. The chapter also addresses some basic information systems concepts because almost all entities have computerized accounting information systems.

CHAPTER ELEVEN

Gathering Evidence

INTRODUCTION

Knowledge of the rules of court, the legal system, and especially evidence are necessary for the effective completion of a fraud investigation by a forensic accountant or fraud auditor. The forensic accountant in particular is normally involved with the final phase of a fraud investigation—prosecution. Forensic accountants also often work with lawyers on cases performing litigation support services. Thus, the forensic accountant must know the basic rules of the judicial system regarding evidence. As was said earlier in the book, every fraud investigation should *assume* it is going to end up in court from the start. Then if it does, evidence will be *forensic*—effective for purposes in court. Ignorance on the front end could easily compromise evidence, impairing the ability of a victim to obtain the best outcome from a civil case, or a successful prosecution in a criminal case.

RULES OF EVIDENCE

A court trial is intended to deduce the truth of a given proposition. In a criminal case, the proposition is the guilt or innocence of an accused person. The evidence introduced to and received by the court to prove the charge must be beyond a reasonable doubt—not necessarily to a moral certainty—and the quantity and quality of evidence must convince an honest and reasonable citizen that the defendant is guilty after it is all considered and weighed impartially.

But what is evidence and how can it be weighed and introduced? In a broad sense, *evidence* is anything perceptible by the five senses and any species of proof—such as testimony of witnesses, records, documents, facts, data, or concrete objects—legally presented at a trial to prove a contention and induce a belief in the minds of the court or jury. In weighing evidence, the court or jury may consider such things as the demeanor of witnesses, their bias for or against an accused, and any relationship to the accused. Thus, evidence can be testimonial, circumstantial, demonstrative, inferential, and even theoretical when given by a qualified expert. Evidence is simply anything that proves or disproves any matter in question.

To be legally acceptable as evidence, however, testimony, documents, objects, or facts must be relevant, material, and competent to the issues being litigated, and gathered lawfully. Otherwise, on motion by opposing counsel, the evidence may be excluded. Therefore, some discussion about evidence being relevant, material, and competent will help one understand how to gather forensic evidence in a fraud investigation.

Relevant

Relevancy of evidence does not depend on the conclusiveness of the testimony offered, but on its legitimate tendency to establish a controverted fact.[1] Some of the evidentiary matters considered relevant and therefore admissible are:

- Motive for the crime
- Defendant's ability to commit the crime
- Defendant's opportunity to commit the crime
- Threats or expressions of ill will by the accused
- Means of committing the offense (possession of a weapon, tool, or skills used in committing the crime)
- Physical evidence at the scene linking the accused to the crime
- Suspect's conduct and comments at the time of arrest
- Attempt to conceal identity
- Attempt to destroy evidence
- Valid confessions

Material

The materiality rule requires that evidence must have an important value to a case or prove a point at issue. Unimportant details only extend the period of time for trial. Accordingly, a trial court judge may rule against the introduction of evidence that is repetitive or additive (that merely proves the same point in another way), or evidence that tends to be remote even though it is relevant. Materiality, then, is the degree of relevancy. The court cannot become preoccupied with trifles or unnecessary details. For example, the physical presence of a suspect in the computer room or tape library or near a terminal on a day when a spurious transaction was generated may be relevant and material. One's presence in a non-computer–related area of the building may be relevant, but immaterial.

Competent

Competency of evidence means that which is adequately sufficient, reliable, and relevant to the case and presented by a qualified and capable (and sane) witness. The presence of those characteristics or the absence of those disabilities that render a witness legally fit and qualified to give testimony in a court applies in the same sense to documents or other forms of written evidence. But competency differs from credibility. Competency is a question that arises before a witness's testimony can be considered; credibility is that witness's veracity. Competency is for the judge to determine; credibility is for the jury to decide.

The competency rule also dictates that conclusions or opinions of a nonexpert witness on matters that require technical expertise be excluded. For example, testimony by an investigating officer on the cause of death may not be appropriate or competent in a trial for murder or wrongful death, because the officer is not qualified by education, study, or experience to make such an assessment. The officer testifying that there were "no visible signs of life" when the body was found may be acceptable, however.

This example demonstrates the difference between a CPA or forensic accountant serving as a "fact witness" versus an "expert witness." When testifying about facts observed, an eyewitness or other witness can testify as to facts that they know about the case. But if the person gives an opinion (e.g., cause of death in the previous example), then that person is acting as an expert witness. The role of expert witness carries more scrutiny, criteria, and credentials than a fact witness. (See Chapters 14–16 for more on expert witnesses.)

When an expert witness is called on to testify, a foundation must be laid before testimony is accepted or allowed. Laying a foundation means that the witness's expertise must be established before a professional opinion is rendered. Qualifying a witness as an expert means demonstrating to the judge's satisfaction that by formal education, advanced study, and experience, the witness is knowledgeable about the topic on which his testimony will bear. The testimony of experts is an exception to the hearsay rule.

Hearsay Rule

The hearsay rule is based on the theory that testimony that merely repeats what some other person said should not be admitted because of the possibility of distortion or misunderstanding. Furthermore, the person who made the actual statement is unavailable for cross-examination and has not been sworn in as a witness. Generally speaking, witnesses can testify only to those things of which they have personal and direct knowledge, and not give conclusions or opinions.

But there are occasions—exceptions—when hearsay evidence is admissible. Some examples are:

- Dying declarations, either verbal or written
- Valid confessions
- Tacit admissions
- Public records that do not require an opinion but speak for themselves
- *Res gestae* statements—spontaneous explanations, if spoken as part of the criminal act or immediately following the commission of a criminal act
- Earlier testimony given under oath
- Business entries made in the normal course of business

Primary Evidence

Photocopies of original business documents and other writings and printed matter are often made to preserve evidence. Investigators use these so that the original records needed to run a business are not removed and to ensure that in the event of an inadvertent destruction of such originals, a certified true copy of the document is still available as proof. Investigators may also use the certified copy to document their case reports. At the trial, however, the original document—if still available—is the best evidence and must be presented. The best evidence in this context means primary evidence, not secondary; original as distinguished from substitutionary; the highest evidence of which the nature of the case is susceptible: "A written instrument is itself always regarded as the primary or best possible evidence of its existence and contents; a copy, or the recollection of a witness, would be secondary evidence."[2] Further, "Contents of a document must be proved by producing the document itself."[3]

Secondary Evidence

To introduce secondary evidence, one must explain satisfactorily to the court the absence of the original document. Secondary evidence is not restricted to photocopies of the document; it may be the testimony of witnesses or transcripts of the document's contents. Whereas the federal courts give no preference to the type of secondary evidence, most other jurisdictions do. Under the majority rule, testimony (parol [word-of-mouth] evidence) will not be allowed to prove the contents of a document if there is secondary documentary evidence available to prove its contents. However, before secondary evidence of the original document may be introduced, the party offering the contents of the substitute must have used all reasonable and diligent means to obtain the original. Again, this option is a matter for the court to determine.

When the original document has been destroyed by the party attempting to prove its contents, secondary evidence will be admitted if the destruction was in the ordinary course of business, or by mistake, or even intentional, provided it was not done for any fraudulent purpose.

HEARSAY EXCEPTIONS

In an idealistic sense, a court trial is a quest to determine the truth. However, the means of acquiring evidence vary. Some means are legal, others are illegal; for example, investigators may violate constitutional guarantees against unreasonable search and seizure, forced confessions, or failure to be represented by counsel. Realistically, therefore, a court trial can result only in a measure of truth and not in absolute truth in the philosophical sense.

Yet in the Anglo-American tradition, witnesses other than experts cannot generally testify as to probabilities, opinions, assumptions, impressions, generalizations, or conclusions (things limited to expert witnesses), but only as to things, people, and events they have seen, felt, tasted, smelled, or heard firsthand (i.e., a fact witness).

Even those things must be legally and logically relevant. *Logical relevancy* means that the evidence being offered must tend to prove or disprove a fact of consequence. Even if it is logically relevant, a court may exclude evidence if it is likely to inflame or confuse a jury or consume too much time. Testimony as to the statistical probability of guilt is considered too prejudicial and unreliable to be accepted.

Testimony as to the character and reputation of an accused may be admissible under certain conditions, even though it would seem to violate the hearsay rule. Such testimony may be admitted when character is an element of the action; that is, when the mental condition or legal competency of the accused is in question.

Evidence of other crimes an accused committed is not generally admissible to prove character. It may be admitted for other purposes, however, such as proof of motive, opportunity, or intent to commit an act.

A witness's credibility may also be attacked by a showing that she was convicted of a serious crime (punishable by death or imprisonment for more than a year) or for such crimes as theft, dishonesty, or false statement. Such conviction should have occurred in recent years—usually within the last 10 years.

Evidence can be direct or circumstantial. Direct evidence proves a fact directly; if the evidence is believed, the fact is established. Circumstantial evidence proves the desired fact indirectly and depends on the strength of the inferences the evidence raises. For example, a letter properly addressed, stamped, and mailed is assumed (inferred) to have been received by the addressee. Testimony that a letter was so addressed, stamped, and mailed raises an inference that it was received. The inference may be rebutted by testimony that it was not in fact received.

The best evidence rule deals with written documents proffered as evidence. The rule requires that the original, if available, and not a copy thereof, be presented at a trial. If the original was destroyed or is in the hands of an opposite party and not subject to legal process by search warrant or subpoena, an authenticated copy may be substituted. Business records and documents kept in the ordinary course of business may be presented as evidence too, even if the person who made the entries or prepared the documents is unavailable.

OTHER RULES OF EVIDENCE

Other than obtaining forensic evidence, the most important aspect of evidence is the ability to present that evidence in court effectively. That goal is helped or hindered by the chain of custody. Other rules of evidence also affect the ability of evidence in a fraud investigation to be effective; that is, forensic.

Chain of Custody

When evidence in the form of document or object (means or instrument) is seized at a crime scene, or as a result of subpoena *duces tecum* (for documents), or discovered in the course of audit and investigation, it should be marked, identified, inventoried, and preserved to maintain it in its original condition and to establish a clear chain of custody until it is introduced at the trial. If gaps in possession or custody occur, the evidence may be challenged at the trial on the theory that the writing or object introduced may not be the original or is not in its original condition and therefore is of doubtful authenticity.

For a seized document to be admissible as evidence, it is necessary to prove it is the same document seized and is in the same condition as it was when seized. Because several people may handle it in the interval between seizure and trial, it should be adequately marked at the time of seizure for later identification, and its custody must be shown from that time until it is introduced in court.

Investigators or auditors who seize or secure documents should quickly identify them by some marking, so they can later testify that they are the documents seized and that they are in the same condition as they were when seized. Investigators might, for instance, write their initials and the date of seizure on the margin, in a corner, or at some other inconspicuous place on the front or back of each document. If circumstances suggest that such marking might render the document subject to attack on the grounds that it has been defaced or it is not in the same condition as when seized, the investigators or auditors can, after making a copy for comparison or for use as an exhibit to the report, put the document into an envelope, write a description and any other identifying information on the front of the envelope, and seal it.

These techniques should be applied any time investigators or auditors come into possession of original documents that might be used as evidence in a trial. If auditors make copies of documentary evidence, they should take steps to preserve their authenticity in case they are needed as secondary evidence if the original documents are not available for the trial.

Privileged Communications

The rule supporting privileged communications is based on the belief that it is necessary to maintain the confidentiality of certain communications. It covers only those communications that are a unique product of the protected relationship. The basic reason behind these protected communications is the belief that the protection of certain relationships is more important to society than the possible harm resulting from the loss of such evidence. Legal jurisdictions vary as to what communications are protected. Some of the more prevalent privileged relationships are:

- Attorney–client
- Husband–wife
- Physician–patient
- Clergy–congregant
- Law enforcement officer–informant

When dealing with privileged communications, consider these basic principles:

- Only the holder of a privilege, or someone authorized by the holder, can assert the privilege.
- If the holder fails to assert it after having notice and an opportunity to assert it, the privilege is waived.
- The privilege may also be waived if the holder discloses a significant part of the communication to a party not within the protected relationship.
- The communication, to be within the privilege, must be sufficiently related to the relationship protected (e.g., communications between an attorney and client must be related to legal consultation).

Under common law, a person cannot testify against his spouse in a criminal trial. While they are married, neither may waive this testimonial incompetency.

Conversations in the known presence of third parties are not protected. Protected communications are those that are in fact confidential or induced by the marriage or other relationship. Ordinary conversations relating to matters not deemed to be confidential are not within the purview of the privilege.

The laws of different states vary widely in the application of the principles of privileged communications. Depending on what protected relationship is involved, different rules may apply regarding what communications are protected, the methods of waiver, and the duration of the privilege.

Whenever an auditor or investigator is confronted with the need to use evidence that consists of communications between parties in one of these relationships, she should consult with an attorney, especially if the evidence is crucial to the case.

Interrogations/Interviews

Crime is a risk for both victim and victimizer. The victim's risk is the loss of something valuable—life, limb, or property. The victimizer's risk is the loss of freedom, social status, and possibly of life, limb, and property too. But criminals intend to gain something as a result of a crime, something to which they are not legally entitled. So criminals, rational ones at least, must concern themselves with weighing the risk of discovery, apprehension, and conviction against the intended gain.

If the risk of discovery and the amount of the possible gain are great, then more time and thought must be spent on planning, disguising, surprising, escaping, and possibly covering up the crime. Fortunately for police authorities, criminals tend to act in haste. Their plans often go awry. They do not anticipate everything that can happen. They usually add to their arsenal of defenses rationalizations for their misconduct, or alibis. "It wasn't me; I was elsewhere." "The devil made me do it." "I am poor and misunderstood, a victim of oppression." "He [the victim] had it coming." "I must have been crazy for doing what I did."

These rationalizations are what police interrogations are intended to sort through. Here again, intuition may play an important role. Criminals usually offer an excuse or justification for what they do. Sometimes they feign ignorance or illness. Sometimes they even feign amnesia. Interrogation cuts through these defenses, excuses, and rationalizations.

During an interrogation, it is important to remain sensitive not only to what the suspect is saying but to the manner in which it is being said, and to observe facial expressions, body and eye movements, word choices, and posture. Verbal fencing with the suspect does not help. Challenging the suspect's comments on the basis of pure logic and rationality does not persuade most criminals to confess. Suspects can stay with a lame excuse forever and almost come to believe it after a while. The reason they persist in lying is that their crimes were not committed out of a sense of logic but mainly for emotional reasons, such as lust, greed, anger, or envy. So when interrogating suspects, one must be prepared to deal with their emotions. "Why did you do it?" is not a very good question early on. It calls for intellectualizing by the suspect, or rationalizing, rather than an emotional response.

The better choice is to ask questions that do not get to the *grava men* (main issue) of the crime at all—questions about a suspect's feelings and emotions:

- How are you feeling?
- Can I get anything for you?

- Do you feel like talking?
- Can I call anyone for you?

The purpose of these innocuous questions is to build rapport, first at the emotional level and later at a rational level. Not all criminal suspects feel compelled to talk about their crimes, but most do, if an interrogator can establish rapport with them. And rapport can be established even after they are advised of their right to remain silent.

An apprehended suspect, or one merely being informally interviewed before arrest, is under great emotional strain. Fears of conviction and incarceration are exacerbated. These fears must be overcome before intelligent conversation can be achieved. The tone and demeanor of the interrogator/interviewer must be reassuring, if not friendly. Intuition enters this process only if the investigator remains calm, dispassionate, and sensitive to the emotional needs and concerns of the suspect or witness. Intuition does not work when the investigator's mind is cluttered with isolated facts or a list of questions about the details of a crime.

Once investigators have learned something about the suspect's history, family, friends, and feelings, they can discern the most appropriate interrogation technique. If the suspect remains cold, aloof, and noncommunicative while innocuous questions are posed, he will be the same when the questions get more serious. In such a case, the investigator needs a command of all the known facts of the crime to gain a confession.

If the suspect responds openly to the investigator's offers of kindness and civility, the latter can lead by general questioning. The investigator will let the suspect describe the crime and not get in the way by verbal bantering, accusation, or sparring. The suspect should be allowed to tell the story in his own way, even if the investigator knows that some of the facts are being distorted. The investigator can always come back and ask for clarification and then compare the conflicts with the testimony of witnesses or confederates.

The importance of confessions and admissions in resolving crime should not be understated. Without such confessions and admissions, many crimes would never be solved. In some fraud cases, accounting books and records do not provide enough evidence to convict a suspect. So a confession from a thief, defrauder, or embezzler makes fraud prosecutions easier. A freely given confession often details the scheme, the accounts manipulated, and the uses to which the purloined funds were applied. The evidence gathered after a confession may corroborate the crime. A confession alone will not support a criminal conviction, however, so the auditor will have to retrieve from the data available within the accounting system and from third-party sources enough corroborating evidence to support the confession.

Admissions and Confessions

The goal of a forensic accountant in a fraud investigation is eventually to obtain a written confession by the fraudster, if a fraud did indeed occur. That goal is why the processes of a fraud investigation deliberately avoid confronting the suspect until the last phase of the gathering of evidence. The last phases may include interviews, but the last process in an investigation is to interview the fraudster. By then the forensic accountant has gathered sufficient forensic evidence to both identify the fraudster and successfully resolve the case. Interviews begin far away from the "target," and gradually the forensic accountant interviews people closer to the suspect. When it finally comes time to interview the target, the purpose of that interview is to obtain a signed confession and is thus referred to as an admission-seeking interview.

SUMMARY

Any fraud investigation has the potential to end up in court in either a civil or criminal court case. Therefore it is important for fraud investigators, forensic accountants, fraud auditors, and even managers to know the facts about the legal rules for evidence in order to be successful in court. In addition, the responsible parties need to understand the proper protocol of gathering, maintaining, and presenting evidence from a fraud investigation. That understanding includes the process itself, such as the proper way to conduct interviews.

NOTES

1. *ICC v. Baird,* 24 S. C.T. 563, 194, U.S. 25, 48 L. Ed. 860.
2. *Manhattan Malting Co. v. Swetland,* 14 Mont. 269, 36, p. 84.
3. *Nunan v. Timberlake,* 85F. 2d 407, 66 App. D.C. 150.

CHAPTER TWELVE

12 Cyber Forensics

If your company has been lucky enough to avoid the need for computer forensics (or so you think), congratulations; it will come soon enough.[1]

INTRODUCTION

In any individual fraud case, the most effectual evidence could come from different sources. It could be the best evidence comes from an interview, or paper documents, or digital information. The latter is becoming more commonplace in frauds, including information in e-mails, notes made in computer files, electronic files the fraudster erased, and many other sources, especially those of a personal nature. One reason for the growing opportunity to find forensic evidence in computers and technology is the exponentially growing presence of technology in our society.

For instance, cell phones have become powerful microcomputers in their own rights, and contain many forms of information including e-mails, contacts, tasks, calendar events, notepads, and text messages. People tend to let their guard down when doing e-mail and text communications, leaving these areas of potential evidence to extract useful investigative information, or to extract "forensic" evidence. At the same time, forensic tools and techniques are growing in the cyber forensic profession. Thus cyber forensics is becoming more important in the antifraud profession, especially in gathering evidence.

Cyber forensics involves the effectual capture, preservation, identification, extraction, analysis, and documentation of digital data and events. One way of viewing the cyber forensic process is like any other type of forensic investigation—the professional is looking for forensic evidence that will stand up in a court of law, if necessary, and will provide something akin to a fingerprint that helps to identify the perpetrator.

EXPECTATION OF PRIVACY

One key element of acquiring cyber evidence, or any other fraud evidence, is the legal policy known as expectation of privacy. This policy is actually associated with—comes from—the Fourth Amendment:

> The right of the people to be secure in their persons, houses, papers, and effects against unreasonable searches and seizures, shall not be violated, and no warrants shall issue, but upon probably cause, supported by oath and affirmation, and particularly describing the place to be searched, and the persons or things to be seized.

As it relates to fraudsters who commit fraud against the entity, expectation of privacy relates to that person's office space and all of the things in it. As it relates to cyber forensics, that would extend to the employee's computer, corporate cell phone (or similar device), USB drives, CDs, DVDs, external drives, and any other source of digital evidence. That is, if the employee has reason to *expect* his or her privacy is respected in the workplace, then a sudden search or seizure of that person's effects, including the company's technologies, could be a violation of that person's expectation, or put another way, a violation of that person's rights under the Fourth Amendment.

Therefore, any fraud investigation that includes the need to acquire sources of potential evidence, especially digital in nature, from an employee's office space needs to first make sure there will be no violation of expectation of privacy. Generally speaking, that can be done in two ways. First, the entity may be able to seek a search warrant (see the "Public Investigations" section in this chapter for more on search warrants). If the suspected offense is a fraud, it may not be easy or possible to establish "probable cause" in the legal process of obtaining a search warrant. If the suspected offense is a violation of policies and procedures instead of a fraud or crime, a search warrant is not necessary.

Secondly, the entity could establish effectual policies and procedures before the need arises. Once the appropriate antifraud policies and procedures have been developed, which include an explicit statement that the employee should have no expectation of privacy over specified things in their office space or on their person, the entity should have all employees read it and sign it to officially recognize their willingness to comply. But the establishment of the appropriate policies and procedures, including a signature of the employee, might not be sufficient if acquiring evidence from a suspect's workspace becomes necessary. For example, if the entity does not monitor the policy by occasionally checking employees at random, reviewing relevant objects in the employee's workspace or person, then the employee who has been with the entity for many years, having never been checked, may still have an expectation of privacy. Therefore, the appropriate policy and procedure should be accompanied by an effective monitoring function, or at least take this into account in dealing with expectation of privacy.

One thing the entity can do related to cyber evidence is to incorporate a logon warning box. When employees log onto the network, a pop-up box could appear with wording similar to this one:

> You should have no expectation of privacy in your use of this network. Use of this network constitutes consent to monitoring, retrieval, and disclosure of any information stored within the network for any purpose including criminal prosecution.[2]

The bottom line here is that the lead investigator needs to make sure the initial acquiring of potential cyber evidence does not violate the person's Fourth Amendment rights, and the person's expectation of privacy.

TYPES OF INVESTIGATIONS

For a cyber forensics investigation to occur, there naturally has to be an event that initiates it. The initiation event and decisions immediately thereafter are critical to the success of the subsequent cyber investigation. Basically, the investigation will take one of two types: a public investigation or a private one. These are different and each puts its own constraints and needs upon the cyber forensic case.

Public Investigations

The public type of investigation involves a potential violation of a law creating a potential criminal prosecution. Because the potential criminal prosecution includes a law and the accompanying criminal court procedures, the investigation needs to be conducted in a way that will be compliant with legal requirements and procedures. For instance, cyber forensic evidence will need to address the violation of the law and legal requirement to prove the criminal offense. Since the event will become public, the victim needs to consider the publicity impact of the event. The investigator will need to understand the constraints of custody of evidence, expectation of privacy, and other critical issues in a public investigation.

Custody of evidence includes knowledge of proper legal protocol for acceptable (i.e., forensic) evidence in the courtroom. Those rules of evidence affect the original capture of the cyber evidence, and all time between then up to and including the hearing of the case in court—what is called a proper chain of custody. Thus when sources of potential cyber forensic evidence are captured, the cyber forensic specialist (CFS) understands what can or cannot be done at the crime scene, and what steps or precautions must be done to preserve the potential evidence. The CFS understands the types of actions or things that will alter or damage the potential evidence according to the legal perspective. For example, if anyone, including a representative of the victim organization, accesses the suspect's computer (assuming it is a Windows system) and browses around looking for evidence, that act will provide defense counsel with grounds to dismiss the evidence. The defense may show the dates accessed in Windows Explorer and make the claim that the last person to access the computer is the one who put the incriminating evidence on the computer.

Secondly, there is the consideration of expectation of privacy, which was mentioned earlier. For a public investigation, the key here is the need for a search warrant. Because it is an incrimination of a violation of a criminal law, and because of the Fourth Amendment rights, a search warrant will need to be obtained before the CFS begins to capture evidence. Skipping this step could lead to a violation of Fourth Amendment rights of the suspect, and cause the potential evidence to be disallowed in court.

But seeking a search warrant is not enough. The CFS and lead investigator from the law enforcement agency need to work together in crafting the warrant to make sure it stipulates explicitly all potential sources of cyber evidence, and to include a caveat for any potential evidence for which they are not aware at the time of seeking the warrant but discover later at the crime scene. Lastly, these two people should review the actual warrant to make sure the actual warrant includes all of the specific things they had stipulated. There are cases where the lead agent did not review the actual warrant and at the scene or later discovered that the legal clerk had not listed anything or mistakenly left items off the list. This oversight would likely lead to the team's inability to legally collect or use any, or key pieces, of that potential evidence.

Perhaps the best source of understanding how to properly acquire cyber evidence in a fraud is the U.S. Department of Justice manual on search and seizure of cyber evidence. The manual is entitled, "Searching & Seizing Computers and Obtaining Electronic Evidence in Criminal Investigations."[3]

In addition to the need to understand federal laws and legal rules of evidence, there is also the complication of differences in states' criminal code in defining computer crimes. For example, a victim corporation that operates in multiple states has to determine which state's criminal code applies, and what state-specific constraints or legal needs apply to this case. The same is true for the legal process in general; legal process depends on the state's local custom, legislative standards, and rules of evidence.

Private Investigations

The cyber forensics investigator will need to understand the constraints and investigative requirements of evidence, expectation of privacy, subsequent litigation, and other issues in a private investigation, which are different from those in a public investigation.

For instance, as already mentioned, in a private investigation, the investigation is not governed directly by Fourth Amendment rights. However, in the case of fraud, one must be careful in conducting an investigation without regard to expectation of privacy because fraud is one type of private investigation that is a crime. Therefore, the investigation should consider expectation of privacy in a fraud investigation as a safeguard.

The private type usually involves a potential violation of, or dispute regarding, the entity's policies and procedures, or a crime such as fraud. In the case of the former, issues might include unacceptable e-mail activity, falsification of corporate data, discrimination, sabotage, or industrial espionage (all of these are beyond the scope of this chapter). In the case of a fraud, it always has the potential to end up in litigation because rarely does the investigation unit or management know fully the extent of the fraud and relevant circumstances at the beginning of an investigation. Thus for fraud, even a private investigation may need to follow the public guidelines because of the possibility of criminal prosecution or civil litigation.

In developing antifraud policies and procedures, the entity should have designated who would lead a fraud investigation in general, and who would lead the cyber forensics aspect of a fraud investigation, when needed (see

Chapter 8). Possible lead investigator for a cyber forensic investigation includes corporate security, internal audit, general legal counsel, legal department, cyber forensics consultant or attorney under retainer, or "boutique" cyber forensics firm.

Because of circumstances or evidence that develop during an investigation, private investigations can become public; that is, the victim may decide to pursue criminal prosecution or civil litigation, during or after the fraud investigation process. In these cases, the attorney or prosecutor often will not understand cyber and digital evidence well enough to present it in court without expert assistance. The CFS can provide value to the private investigation not only by gathering effectual cyber evidence to support the case, but by educating and assisting lawyers or prosecutors in providing a "plain English" explanation of the digital information. Often that is accomplished by creating easy-to-understand graphical representation of the process, data, and results, accompanied by simple childlike explanations of each. The latter is much more effective in court than "geeky" presentations and explanations (see Chapter 16 on the effective tactics and procedures for the expert witness).

However, the communications with the attorney should be kept to a minimum to avoid unnecessary exposure. When working with an attorney, the investigator should be able to employ attorney–client privilege over the work results and communications. The documents communicated should be headed "privileged legal communication: confidential work product" to maintain the attorney–client privilege until it becomes legally required to be forfeited, if it becomes required to do so (e.g., the evidence will be used in litigation).

SOURCES OF DIGITAL DATA

Rich digital sources of information and evidence are available in a cyber forensic investigation. Cyber forensic specialists are familiar with the available and applicable different storage devices. Fraudsters can hide data in many ways by moving it from organizational systems to their own computer or placing it on a removable, portable device; or using nonentity storage devices from the beginning. Such devices include:

- Office computer
- Home computer
- Laptop
- Network servers

- Backups
- Internet service provider (ISP) servers
- Removable external drives
- Flash drives (USB/thumb drives) can be disguised as a normal fountain pen
- CDs
- DVDs
- Digital watches
- Memory chips for digital cameras that are small enough to hide under a postage stamp or in a digital camera in plain sight
- Printer memory
- E-mail accounts: business and personal
- Voice mail
- Personal digital assistants (PDAs)
- Cell phones (including Blackberry, iPhone, Droid, and other smartphones)

Care needs to be taken about distinguishing personal sources of digital data from organizational ownership of digital data. For example, if an employee uses his or her own cell phone and links it to a corporate Outlook system, who owns the data on that cell phone? Can employees secretly take valuable organizational information with them on that cell phone? The same is true about the need for a search warrant, if the victim suspects the perpetrator stored evidence on personal computers or storage devices not located on the premises of the organization.

TYPES OF CYBER DATA

Basically, cyber digital data takes three forms: extractable digital data, metadata, and latent digital data.

Extractable Digital Data

Extractable digital data could be defined as *observable*—observable not with the naked eye but the right technology. For example, digital data stored from an Excel spreadsheet on a hard drive is extractable, but hardly visible to the eye. However, if one uses the right version of Excel, and can locate and access the digital file, it clearly becomes visible to the eye. Extractable data then is subject to knowing the tools and techniques to locate and convert it to observable data and information.

In addition to bringing stored information back to visible view, extractable data includes data files that can be "mined" to uncover anomalies that, for all intents and purposes, are hidden in the morass of data. Data mining tools[4] can be used on accounting data files to look for evidence of a fraud. By combining the knowledge about fraud schemes (see Chapter 3) with knowledge of the red flags of fraud schemes (see Chapter 4), a digital investigator (or fraud auditor) has the possibility of uncovering any on-the-books fraud. For instance, the fraud auditor may look for evidence of a shell company scheme in the vendor file by data mining for known red flags of a shell company[5] in the master vendor file, accumulate the red flags by vendor, and develop a list of suspicious vendors for further review. This scenario is another level of extractable data.

Metadata

Metadata is generally stored by applications or developers and are a potential source of valuable information or evidence. *Metadata* can be defined as data about data. For example, a formula behind a cell in Excel is metadata, describing how the data being displayed was developed. All Microsoft Office products have properties metadata that contain a wealth of user-defined metadata about the file, but also include data added as defaults. For example, the author field in properties defaults to the user's name added at installation of the product. It also includes the dates associated with the file (created, last modified, and last accessed), file name, file location, and certain stats. Metadata can be embedded internally to the digital file, or a separate file external to the object file. Either way, the default information in metadata can be helpful in extracting useful evidence. A list illustrating some of the types of metadata include:

- E-mail headers and routing information
- Spreadsheet data sources and formulas
- Database structure and relationships
- Microsoft Office properties
- Word processing editing history (e.g., track changes, deletions/undo)
- System logs of users' activities
- Windows NTFS/FAT library files (directories of files, sectors, and hard drive facts)
- Certain HTML code
- Certain aspects of XML files

Latent Digital Data

Latent digital data could be defined as undiscovered, concealed, misplaced, missing, or hidden data. Under normal operating circumstances, latent data is not easily converted to observable information by some common application or subject to data mining tools, and is generally transparent to operating systems and file managers. It takes special cyber knowledge, tools, and techniques to find and extract this type of cyber data.

Latent data is easily altered or destroyed because of its nature. Extra precautions are needed to prevent alteration to it. Latent data also requires special tools and equipment. It requires one or more specialized subject matter experts (SMEs) who have the requisite training and experience in order to extract any potential evidence.

Latent data includes digital data on hard drives that is not accessible by applications or visible by the operating system but were handled by the operating system. For example, when a user deletes a file using the operating system's delete command, the file is not actually deleted, but rather marked as available for future use by the library function (e.g, NTFS/FAT). For years, cyber forensics have had an "undelete" tool available to locate deleted files, and unless the space was used to record data subsequent to the delete, that digital data is fully recoverable. Examples of this type of latent data include:

- Deleted files
- Slack space (temporary files for downloads of files or images)
- RAM data
- Temporary files
- Unused space (may still contain traces of previously existing files)
- Interpartition space
- Windows swap files
- Stored printer images

Another type of latent digital data is the deliberate and covert embedding of data in unexpected places by a cyber-savvy criminal. There are numerous ways to place digital data on storage drives in a sophisticated manner that makes it difficult for even a CFS to locate and recover. Basically, the criminal hides application data on storage media or TCP/IP packets in places where the standards suggest it does not belong.[6] Stenography is one way to accomplish this covert method of hiding data, which means the data is hidden in plain view of data that is recognized by applications, observed by the operating system, or retrievable in some manner (extractable data). As cyber crooks become more sophisticated, latent data will become more and more difficult to find.

Latent data can be a source of potential evidence in a fraud investigation. It takes a CFS to locate and extract most of this type of data. Most of the latent data will likely not be relevant to a case, but investigators should be cognizant in data discovery planning to consider all potential latent data sources.

CYBER FORENSICS INVESTIGATION PROCESS

The process of the cyber forensic investigation is naturally critical to a successful investigation. Some of those steps have been referred to already (see Exhibit 12.1).

The process begins when the investigation is initiated by a tip or other event. The victim, having asked a CFS to be involved, will ask that person to evaluate the situation for potential evidence. It is the job of the cyber forensic expert to accurately identify all potential sources of evidence and information that could potentially be valuable to the investigation.

The next step is not the responsibility of the CFS, but the team needs to resolve expectation of privacy. If it is determined that a search warrant is necessary, the CFS will need to assist in developing search items to list on the warrant, and to review the actual warrant for accuracy once it is created.

EXHIBIT 12.1 Typical Cyber Forensic Investigation Process

Identify all potential digital sources of potential evidence of sources of information.
Resolve/consider expectation of privacy issue (search warrant details, if necessary).
Acquire and authenticate digital/cyber evidence (without alterations).
Secure original evidence (bag, tag, establish chain of custody).
Transport evidence to secure forensics lab.
Create copies of original device (without alterations to original).
Authenticate copies.
Develop specific cyber forensics tests, procedures, and overall plan (use *formal* procedures).
Execute the plan using applicable forensic tools.
Convert digital data into presentable form (e.g., graphs).
Complete and file a report on evidence, analysis, and conclusions.

Next the CFS will actually go with the lead investigator or team to the crime scene and acquire the devices or equipment that contain the sources identified in the first step. It is critical that the CFS authenticate the objects captured by the appropriate means, and then secure them.

The investigator must immediately establish a chain of custody for the evidence. The objects need to be tagged and placed into bags or wrapped with tape (for those too big to bag). He or she must write on the bags/tape the identification information. The CFS knows to take care as to what type of bag to use. For example, antistatic or cushioned bags would be needed for certain types of devices to prevent unintended alteration of the evidence. The CFS also needs to immediately record all items of evidence on a chain of custody form designed for cyber forensic investigations. Exhibit 12.2 shows a cyber forensic evidence chain of custody form for a single piece of evidence. If the investigation includes multiple items, a similar document would be used for each piece of evidence. Note that all subsequent activities associated with the original evidence are recorded in the "Processed by" section near the bottom of the form, creating an audit trail of custody.

Next, the CFS would transport the original evidence to a secure forensics lab, where a closet or locker is used to store the original evidence securely. The lab has the tools and equipment necessary to perform the appropriate tests and

EXHIBIT 12.2 Sample Chain of Custody Form for Cyber Forensic Evidence

Cyber Forensic Expert Evidence Custody Form *Single piece of evidence*			
Case No.:		Unit Number:	
Investigator:			
Desc. of Case:			
Location:			
Item ID	Description of Item	Vendor	Model/Serial No.
Locked up by:		Date/Time	
Locked up by:		Date/Time	
Processed by:	Activity:		Date/Time
			Page _____ of _____

procedures. Circumstances may prevent the equipment from being moved to the lab, and thus sometimes the CFS will need to acquire digital images on site.

The CFS cannot perform tests or procedures on the original objects, so the CFS knows to create copies of the original without tampering with or altering the originals. The CFS takes the originals one by one and makes working copies from which tests will be performed. The CFS also documents that process on the chain of custody form (see Exhibit 12.2, near bottom of form). For hard drives, a bit streaming software is needed to make sure the working copy is an *exact* replica of the original because of latent digital evidence that would not get copied with normal copy procedures. During this process, the CFS would need to authenticate the copies as being exact replicas before performing any tests.

At that point, the CFS needs a plan of exactly what tests and procedures to perform. If that plan was not created beforehand, it should be *formally* documented at this step. That would include the tests, tools, techniques, and objectives. Then the CFS executes the plan, using the appropriate tool, and documents any evidence extracted.

Courts and judges want to see professionalism used in handling evidence presented to the court. Part of that would be evidence that the expert used formal procedures, such as a checklist, and industry standard best practices in extracting data, handling data, and analyzing data—just like courts do with valuation experts and other experts.

Finally, the CFS takes the analysis and conclusions and turns the digital data into useable, effective objects for the lead investigator, attorneys (if applicable), and especially for the court, if applicable (i.e., judge and/or jury). Usually, that would be plain English, effectual graphs or a slide show file to facilitate the ability of a reader to assimilate the facts without abstract terms, geeky discussions, or highly technical graphs. Obviously, the CFS may be called to be a fact or expert witness if a trial becomes necessary.

The U.S. Department of Justice (USDOJ), especially the Computer Crime and Intellectual Property Section (CCIPS), and FBI, especially the Computer Analysis Response Team (CART), have been leaders and pioneers in cyber forensics. CCIPS has its own prescriptive cyber forensic process defined in three steps: prepare/extract, identify, and analysis.[7]

VARIETY OF SPECIALISTS IN CYBER FORENSICS

Clearly, a CFS is a subject matter expert (SME) with a specialized set of skills, knowledge, and abilities. However, the cyber forensics profession actually has a variety of specialists within it. The aforementioned CART unit has at least three different specialists that it uses:

- Digital evidence collection specialist (seize and preserve digital evidence)
- Computer investigator (Internet, networks, tracing computer communications)
- Computer forensic examiner (extracts data for investigators)

This list illustrates the need to know a variety of cyber forensic specialists, and the possibility of the need for multiple CFS on an investigative team, and how complex the whole cyber forensic world actually is.

There are a variety of organizations, many from the government, that support the field of cyber forensics. There are also several certifications, including CART's own. The most common certification at present is probably the Certified Information Systems Security Professional (CISSP) sponsored by ISC.[8]

SUMMARY

It is likely that some fraud cases have suffered from the absence of cyber forensics considerations that may have been able to find valuable evidence embedded in cyber sources. The effective use of cyber forensics is predicated on the type of investigation, the cyber sources of evidence available, an SME, and a CFS who can even identify when his work could prove to be beneficial. An adequate evaluation of potential cyber sources can provide the most effective evidence in a fraud investigation.

The process of collecting that evidence is predicated on dealing with expectation of privacy, the right tools, and a proper extraction of potential evidence. The process is also affected by the fact that much, if not all, of the cyber evidence is more or less invisible, and being guarded by the perpetrator who is trying hard to keep it secret. Furthermore, it may take more than one type of CFS to extract all of the potential evidence and information.

All fraud cases should at least consider the possibility of cyber/digital evidence, and the potential value it could bring to the case.

NOTES

1. Taken from Bill Nelson, Amelia Phillips, and Christopher Steuart, *Guide to Computer Forensics and Investigations*, 4th ed. (Florence, KY: Course Technology/Cengage Learning, 2010).

2. Ibid.
3. Access the 3rd edition, September 2009, at www.cybercrime.gov/ssmanual/index.html.
4. Data mining tools include products such as ACL, IDEA, Active Data, and many others.
5. Examples would include a post office box but no physical address, missing contact data, missing or incorrect EIN, and so on. See Chapter 4 for a list of red flags for a shell company scheme.
6. One method is to add data between the end-of-file and the end of the associated cluster in which the file was placed, called file slack or slack space. See http://camouflage.unfiction.com for an illustration.
7. See www.cybercrime.gov/forensics_chart.pdf for more information.
8. See www.isc2.org/cissp/default.aspx for more information.

CHAPTER THIRTEEN

13 Obtaining and Evaluating Nonfinancial Evidence in a Fraud Examination

INTRODUCTION

Evidence in a fraud can potentially come from a variety of sources both financial and nonfinancial. Generally speaking, the focus on fraud investigation tends to be mostly, if not solely, financial. Fraud investigators and auditors should consider the possibility of valuable evidence that is nonfinancial. Nonfinancial sources include interviews, document examination, handwriting analysis, and physiological aspects of the fraudster. The latter refers to something the fraudster reveals in behaviors, physical expressions, or communications that can be cues as to the veracity of the fraudster's statements about his or her involvement in the fraud in question.

The primary purpose of the physiological techniques and concepts presented in this chapter is to detect deception. If a fraud is being perpetrated, the fraudster is certainly being as clandestine as possible including using deception in appearance and communications. Secondarily, these techniques and concepts also could be helpful in gathering useful information.

From an educational background perspective, interviewing and legal aspects are taught in arts and sciences colleges, while forensic accounting is taught in business schools. Therefore, generally speaking, an accounting major has had little to no relevant education in the areas of sociology, psychology, and anthropology to assist in these techniques and tools. This chapter is an introduction to some of those concepts.

INTERVIEWS

Auditors ask questions in the course of most audits, whether they are internal or external. But there is a big difference in asking questions in an audit and asking questions in a fraud investigation. To ask questions effectively in a fraud investigation, one must employ best practices for interviewing techniques in that context. According to Joe Wells, founder of the Association of Certified Fraud Examiners (ACFE), "The best clues usually don't come from the books but from the people who work with them."

Questions used in interviews could be (1) introductory, (2) informational, (3) closing, (4) assessment, or (5) admission-seeking. [1] Experts agree that open-ended questions are far superior to questions that can be answered with a simple "yes" or "no."

One of the problems about interviews in a fraud investigation is the possibility the investigator is not trained or experienced in proper interview techniques (i.e., best practices) or worse yet, unfamiliar with the legal protocol of interviews. In the case of the latter, the case could be frustrated from a successful conclusion or even end in a counter lawsuit for some legal cause.

Best Practices

Joe Wells wrote an article describing common best practices for interviews (see a summation of it in Exhibit 13.1). The list begins with an appropriate level of preparation, and ends with getting a signed statement, especially when the interview is the suspect who confesses during the interview.

The second step is "think as you go." Although it seems intuitive that the interviewer should write down questions for the interviewee, actually the best thing to do is *not* write them down. Instead, the interviewer should have a list of key points and allow the conversation to take its natural course. Besides, you do not want the astute fraudster to get a peek at the questions and prepare an answer.

EXHIBIT 13.1 Top Ten Steps in a Top-Notch Interview

1.	Prepare.
2.	Think as you go.
3.	Watch nonverbal behavior.
4.	Set the tone.
5.	Pace your questions.
6.	Do more listening than talking.
7.	Be straightforward.
8.	Take your time.
9.	Double-check the facts.
10.	Get it in writing.

Source: Copyright 2002 American Institute of Certified Public Accountants, Inc. All rights reserved. Reprinted with permission.

Next, the interviewer should watch for nonverbal behavior. Usually, humans have a different body language when under stress. The trained fraud investigator knows how to watch for signs of stress in a process called calibration. This process is used to assess a witness's truthfulness (most of the rest of this chapter addresses techniques that could be used in calibration).

Fourth, the interviewer sets the tone. That includes dressing properly, using good social skills, introducing himself or herself appropriately, and especially developing a rapport with the interviewee. Next, the interviewer should pace the questions to keep the interviewee comfortable with the interviewee and the process—not too fast, not too slow, and not too long! The hard questions should follow a few easy questions and ease up to the harder ones. Sixth, the interviewer should listen more than talk, allowing the interviewee to become stressed, if he or she is being deceptive, and eventually provide the interviewer cues of his or her deception. Besides, the more the investigator talks, the more the interviewee learns, which could be a strategic mistake for an interviewer.. Next, the interviewer should be straightforward. Approach the process in an open way, and be as honest as possible without compromising the process. Trying to be too secretive or aggressive can cause the interviewer to become defensive, and that would likely lessen the effectiveness of the interview process.

Next, the interviewer needs to take his time. Honest people usually do not mind follow-up questions when the interviewer's instincts say he did not get all of the facts. Guilty people, however, typically get impatient. Another obvious step is to double-check supposed facts gathered, and start that process during the interview. Nothing damages an investigation more than having testimony contradicted by the very person who gave it. Tape recording is an option, but the downside to that tactic is the probability of losing rapport with the interviewee. Guilty persons tend to clam up or be evasive when a tape recorder is on.

The primary purpose of the interview process in a fraud investigation is to interview the suspect, last in the investigation process, and to obtain a signed confession in that interview: known as an admission-seeking interview. There is little evidence more reliable in court than a written confession signed by the perpetrator's own signature.

Perhaps no one is considered more of an expert than Dan Rabon on effective interviews. Don provides deception indicators in his books,[2] such as dry mouth, excessive sweating, and so on that are obviously useful in an interview, and are more calibration cues.

Legal Issues

Fraud investigators do not necessarily require legal authority to interview or inquire into fraudulent matters. If the interviewer represents herself as an investigator, however, some states do require a license for investigators. Sometimes you can actually use deception to legally gain information from a suspect, as long as the interviewer does not use deception that will likely cause an innocent party to confess. Promises of leniency, confidentiality, monetary rewards, or other advantages should be approved by an attorney first.[3] The interviewer should also avoid any statement that could be taken as extortion (e.g., "Either tell us the truth or we will turn you over to the IRS to investigate you for tax evasion.").

BODY LANGUAGE

A person's body movements usually indicate emotions he is experiencing through adapters or symptoms. Generally, the person is not aware that she is exhibiting body language at the time. The body behaviors could be certain movements, pitch of the voice, speed of talking, crossing legs or arms, or other body movements.

Some body language cues are related to anxiety or stress, and thus could be related to deception. Those cues include: speech hesitations, increase in vocal pitch, speech errors, pupil dilation, excessive blinking, hand or shoulder shrugs, and unusual or excessive touching hands or face. But body language cues are not absolutes.

Some other interesting facts about body language are: legs are farther from the brain and harder to control than other extremities, feet will point in the direction the person subconsciously wishes to go, ankle on knees is associated with stubbornness, and tilting the head is a sign of friendliness.

However, body language varies depending on the individual. And there is a tendency to read body language as deceptive by people who are already suspicious. The latter would include auditors and forensic accountants using professional skepticism. Therefore body language is fraught with circumstances that cause it to be unreliable as a means to detect deception consistently, and it is inadmissible in court.

DECEPTION CUES

In addition to body language cues, there are other cues that are used to identify lies.[4] A list of some areas of cues and an example of each follow:

- *Interpersonal interactions.* Shakes head "yes" *after* the point is made, inconsistent gestures.
- *Emotional states.* Deceitful people tend to avoid touching the person questioning them.
- *Verbal content.* Reflects question back as the answer immediately after the question; "Did you write a check to yourself?" "No, I didn't write a check to myself."
- *How comments are made.* Disassociating people, events, and so on by replacing the *pronoun*—"the equipment" versus "my equipment."
- *Psychological frames.* Deceitful statements almost always omit what went wrong in describing events, except concerning delays or cancellations.

As interesting as these signs are, again, there is enough inconsistency to create problems. Yet it would be helpful if a fraud investigator at least was aware of these signs. In addition, some are the same basic cues as those used in more reliable deception detection methodologies (e.g., SCAN).

EYE LANGUAGE

A more reliable indicator of truthfulness is eye language.[5] Experts believe the eyes are the most communicative part of the human body. The eyes do have a language and the principles that follow are referred to as visual accessing cues (VAC). The eye movement cues and interpretations, however, are true only for right-handed persons. So have the interviewee sign something before starting any use of VAC because the cues are opposite for left-handed people; that is, you would be interpreting responses as truthful versus deceitful or vice versa!

According to experts such as Don Rabon, when interviewees are asked questions for which they need to recall something to respond, the eyes give away whether the mental process is deceptive or truthful. Here are the combinations:

- *Eyes to the left and up.* Retrieving visual images from the past—"What color was your first car?"
- *Eyes to the left toward the ear.* Retrieving auditory memories, remembering a sound—"What was your ring tone on your first cell phone?"
- *Eyes to the left and down.* Associated with internal dialogue, a direction people usually stare when talking to themselves.
- *Eyes to the right and up.* Visually constructing images—"What would your next house look like?"
- *Eyes to the right toward the ear.* Creating a sound—"Can you create a new song and sing it for me?"
- *Eyes to the right and down.* Associated with feelings or kinesthetic—"Can you remember the smell of a campfire?"

Eye language principles also include aspects of blinking. Under normal circumstances, a person blinks about 20 times per minute, each blink about a fourth of a second. Under stress, a person usually blinks considerably more than normal, and typically faster than normal. Some benign circumstances lead to unusual blinking. If being filmed, or on TV, a person would blink about twice as fast as normal. But a sleep-deprived person also blinks more often.

Other eye language cues:

- *Gaze downward.* In American culture, this equates to defeat, guilt, or submission.
- *Raising eyebrows.* Uncertainty, disbelief, surprise, or frustration.
- *Raising one eyebrow and head tilted back.* Disdain, arrogance, or pride.
- *Dilation of pupils.* Interest in the thing.

Too much can be made of eye language, and the use of best practices in interviews would lead to more reliable results and interpretations.[6]

STATEMENT ANALYSIS

Statement analysis is a technique used to detect deceit in statements that individuals make. According to German psychologist Udo Undeutsch, supposedly the father of statement analysis, "Statements that are the product of experience will contain characteristics that are generally absent from statements that are the product of imagination."[7]

Statement analysis uses a word-by-word examination of statements. It determines truthfulness by an analysis of the words rather than focusing on whether the stated facts are truthful. Subconsciously, the deceitful person reveals the conflict with which they are struggling in the *way* they communicate. Basically, statement analysis looks for cues that the person is trying to distance themselves from the issues or facts (e.g., the pronoun replacement cue mentioned earlier).

Some specific red flags to look for in statement analysis include special attention to "I"; any deviation is a red flag (e.g., the person starts out referring to "I" and switches to "we"). Subconsciously, deceitful people will try to distance themselves from the issues or facts. This red flag is true of possessive pronouns as well. Any change in noun usage is a red flag (e.g., "my computer," to "the computer"). The technique works on written statements, audio-recorded statements, or videotaped statements. Examples of deceitful words are described for each type in Exhibit 13.2 (the first factor is truthful; the 2nd/vs. is deceitful).

Another statement analysis red flag is the actual balance of a written statement. When asked to describe what happened before the event in question (e.g., a fraud), the event, and what happened after the event, the way the person *balances* the *amount* of content on these three sections is

EXHIBIT 13.2 Statement Analysis

Written	Pronoun analysis: I vs. them Noun analysis: Joe/Susie vs. they/it Verb analysis: past tense vs. changing tenses (will often change subconsciously in a statement) Extraneous information analysis: missing vs. present Organizational analysis: chronological vs. disorganized Handwriting analysis: (a bonus technique)
Audio	<same>
Video	Body language deviations Body language analysis

an indicator of truthfulness. An honest person tends to balance equally the content of the three time frames. A deceitful person's account will be out of balance because she wants to distance herself from the bad event (wanting to be disassociated with a fraud)—specifically the middle time frame, the adverse event; the account of that middle time frame will contain substantially fewer words than the other two.

SCAN

Scientific content analysis (SCAN) is a technique that is similar to statement analysis. Like statement analysis, SCAN does not try to look for the truthfulness of the facts but rather the reflection of deception in the way statements are made. SCAN is cross-cultural, which increases its applicability. Deceitful people tend to lie indirectly, and not tell blatant lies. The indirect lies involve hedging, omitting critical facts, feigning forgetfulness, pretending ignorance, and distancing oneself from the adverse event in the choice of words. Deceitful people are reluctant to commit themselves to deceptions, and instead use "verbal trickeration" to avoid making damaging statements. In order for SCAN to be effective, the analyst needs a clean truthful statement from the suspect.

SCAN, like statement analysis, looks for a shift in the use of pronouns. It also looks for gaps in the narrative, which portray deception. The "I don't remember" phrase often is an attempt to conceal something. A change in tense also indicates a strong emotional response to the context. There are a number of other cues that experts in SCAN use.

According to one expert, SCAN is as reliable as a polygraph examination. But both SCAN and polygraph are investigative tools and not legal evidence.[8]

SUMMARY

There are many nonfinancial sources of potential evidence in a fraud investigation. One of those key areas is people; interviews, casual conversations, and physical cues of deception or guilt. There has been a lot written about these physiological aspects, or profile, of fraudsters. Books have been written on discourse analysis, SCAN, and other techniques used to determine the presence of deceptive behavior. Thus almost all fraud investigations can benefit from understanding these principles of the physiological behaviors of fraudsters.

The physiological arena of nonfinancial information is limited in its ability to provide evidence that courts will allow. Some of the methods are not even reliable enough for serious use in a fraud investigation, and should be used with great caution (e.g., body language and lies cues). In fact, of the ones described in this chapter, the only one that would be "forensic" enough for evidence is interview.

By combining some of the common cues across the tools/techniques described, there are some common cues that come to one's attention. One example is the fraudster distancing himself from the accusation or adverse event; true in several of the techniques discussed.

NOTES

1. For details on the types of questions and their role in an effective interview, see the ACFE article, "Interview Preparation: Before You Ask the First Question," located at the ACFE web site, members only.
2. For example, Don Rabon and Tanya Chapman, *Interviewing and Interrogation*, 2nd ed. (Durham: Carolina Academic Press, 2009).
3. See "Interview Preparation: Before You Ask the First Question," taken from the ACFE web site. http://www.acfe.com/login.asp?redirect=http://www.acfe.com/resources/view.asp?ArticleID=248, last accessed April 28, 20101.
4. For the full list of cues and examples, read David J. Lieberman, *Never Be Lied to Again* (New York: St. Martin's Press, 1998).
5. For a full description of this technique, see Don Rabon, "Interviewing: Achieving Rapport"(Part One), taken from the ACFE web site, members only. Rabon is considered a leading expert on interviewing principles, including eye language.
6. This conclusion was given to the authors by Alton Sizemore, 25-year veteran of the FBI, and currently a fraud examiner for Forensic/Strategic Solutions in

Birmingham, AL. Alton is considered a leading expert on how to conduct successful interviews.

7. Undeutsch, Udo. *Statement Reality Analysis.* In ArneTrankell (Ed.): Reconstructing the past: The Role of Psychologists in Criminal Trials. (Stockholm: Norstedts, 1982).
8. For examples of SCAN, see "Technique Sets the Truth Free," *Orlando Sentinel*, September 23, 1991; "Analysts Probed 911 Caller's Every Word," *The Standard*, St. Catharines, Ontario, August 19, 1992; "Ramsey Trapped by His Own Words," *Globe*, March 11, 1997. Also read more about SCAN, "SCAN: Deception Detection by Scientific Content Analysis," *Law and Order*, Vol. 38, No. 8 (August 1990), by Tony Lesce.

14

CHAPTER FOURTEEN

General Criteria and Standards for Establishing an Expert Witness's Qualifications[1]

INTRODUCTION

Determining that a given person is sufficiently knowledgeable and capable of serving as an expert depends on two factors. First, does the candidate possess the objective qualifications for the job? Does he have the appropriate credentials, relevant prior experience, and critical information that bear on successful resolution of the case?

Second, does the expert, even if sufficiently qualified, have the personal characteristics to function effectively as part of the investigative team? Is the individual a team player? Do her professional reputation and the quality of previous work recommend using her in the case at hand? Can the expert explain technical complexities in such a way that both the criminal justice practitioners—investigators, prosecutors, and judges—and the jury can clearly understand his meaning and importance? Does the expert project a professional manner? Can she build and keep rapport with others? The sections that follow address in detail both the requisite formal credentials and the essential personal characteristics that effective consultants and expert witnesses must display.

CREDENTIALS

Credentials and standards vary for assessing the knowledge of out-of-court experts, depending on the area of expertise. Even with regards to laying the foundation at trial for the court to accept a witness as an expert, the criteria, although generally standardized between fields of expertise in the eyes of the law, are not inflexible and are subject to some variation. With these caveats in mind, there are several broad areas in which experts are expected to have credentials and qualifications that distinguish them from laypeople.

These include:

- Professional licensure, certification, or registration by a recognized professional body in the field of expertise in question
- Undergraduate, graduate, and postgraduate academic degrees that are either in the field of expertise or serve as a suitable background to it
- Specialized training and/or continuing professional education beyond academic degrees that indicate up-to-date familiarity with the latest technical developments in the subject area
- Writings and publications that display technical opinions and are available as part of the general body of knowledge in the subject area
- Relevant teaching, lecturing, and/or other consultancies that indicate that one is held in high professional esteem in the subject area
- Affiliation with professional associations
- Directly relevant prior experience gained through similar assignments, whether as technical advisor or expert witness, in the subject area
- Special status, or access to privileged information, peculiar to the case at hand, which renders the individual an expert

Professional Licensure, Certification, or Registration

Most professional organizations, to some degree, regulate their members and feature mechanisms for reviewing a practitioner's qualifications—often at periodic intervals. Endorsements about competence—a license to practice the profession, a certification in a specialty area, or registration at a central professional regulatory authority in the jurisdiction—are all common practices. A professional license, certification, or registration is an important factor in assessing the level of basic competence for technical advisors in most areas of expertise useful in financial and computer-related crime investigations. Establishing an individual has a license or certification in the profession, or is registered in the jurisdiction as a practitioner of that profession, is a standard step in laying the foundation at trial for the court to accept the testimony of such a person as an expert.

Standards used to qualify a practitioner in a given profession can easily be determined by inquiring of the professional licensing or certifying body in question. In addition, many jurisdictions require practitioners in a wide variety of professions, who may have acquired their credentials elsewhere, to register with a central government authority if they want to practice their profession locally. The central registering authority can be a useful source of information on professional licensing standards locally and perhaps a source of expert referrals.

Many of the more traditional professional organizations supply experts in crime cases. Those include lawyers, engineers, and forensic chemists. Most states have laws that dictate the criteria for professional licensing in these broader professions.

Academic Degrees

Traditionally, the academic degrees professionals hold have been a key to determining whether they will qualify as expert witnesses. Even when experts are used only behind the scenes in the investigation of computer-related crimes, their backgrounds can be investigated by the defense and their credentials will be considered. This consideration is particularly true because as technical advisors they become potential expert witnesses.

Despite the strategic importance of appropriate academic credential for experts whose credibility the defense may challenge, it is important not to rely too heavily on academic qualifications alone. Many universities do not have well-developed courses about computer-related crime, especially on the postgraduate level, and because the field is changing so rapidly, the courses they do have may not be current. Therefore, knowledgeable sources agree that when an expert witness's academic credentials are considered, how recently the degrees were awarded and whether she has continued to take courses in the field should be considered as well.

Training and Continuing Education

Developments in computer programming, electronics, telecommunications engineering, information technology auditing, computer security, and other specializations are increasing rapidly. Training and continuing education in these areas, and such fields as combating white-collar crime, economic crime, and computer crime, are being offered widely. Professional associations and regulatory bodies frequently offer certificates of completion and other objective indicators of ungraded skills for attending such courses.

How many current, relevant training courses and continuing education courses has the prospective technical expert attended? How up to date is he on the state of the art in this technical field? A showing of such currency is generally a corollary to the presentation of academic credentials to the court when an expert witness's qualifications are reviewed. The absence of such current educational updates would not only have a strong effect on the quality of the expert advice given to the government, but it can lead to the government's expert witness being impeached on cross-examination and the technical accuracy of aspects of the government's case being challenged.

Writings and Publications

Whether prospective expert witnesses have published in the field of their purported expertise is traditionally an important factor to review when laying the foundation at trial for the technical advisor to take the stand as an expert witness. Prior publications may be less relevant when experts are used as technical advisors to the investigative or prosecutorial team during the case preparation stages. However, this situation is not necessarily the case. The prior publications of computer-related crime scholars/researchers retained to assist in profiling the computer felon(s) and determining the modus operandi in complex computer fraud cases will be directly relevant. Their availability could greatly assist the team by providing them with an orientation, and such published views could be challenged if the technical advisor's identity is discoverable during pretrial.

What books or articles has the technical advisor written on the subject in question? Were they published, and if so, how recently? How were the expert's works received by professional peers? Are the expert's works considered authoritative? Do other published works in the same field challenge or contradict the expert's published views? Are the expert's published views consistent in all of his writings? Are her published views, while consistent among themselves, congruent with her current views on the case at hand?

These are all critical questions to be addressed when selecting an expert. Especially if there is to be an established or prolonged professional relationship with the expert, the consultant's published works must be analyzed and monitored during pretrial preparation to avoid significant discrepancies that may arise between the expert's present planned testimony and past, possibly contradictory, positions taken.

Teaching and Other Consultancies

Activities that show a consultant's prior acceptance as an expert advisor or instructor go to the issue of her reliability and credibility as part of the government's team. Teaching or consulting in a given field traditionally is considered when an expert's credentials are presented to the court before the person takes the stand as an expert witness. Because of the newness and rapid evolution of computer-related technology, such credentials may hold more weight in a computer-related crime case than academic degrees or publications. A careful check with past users of the prospective experts' service—trainees or clients for whom they have consulted—can be an excellent way to assess their reliability and stature, plus the currency and nature of their views before retaining them in a given case.

Government experts' extensive prior teaching and/or consultancies, if they have been retained for a fee, sometimes can work to the detriment of the prosecution. For example, experts who for a fee have done extensive training of investigators and prosecutors of computer crime, and/or who have for a fee testified frequently for the prosecution in such cases, but not for the defense, could be impeached for bias and/or financial interest if the government calls them as expert witnesses.[2] Especially when a substantial part of an expert's income derives from such services to law enforcement, his comparative usefulness as an expert witness may be compromised.

Even if such experts are not potential expert witnesses, their identity and involvement in preparing the case may prove discoverable by the defense and lead to allegations of bias in the technical advice rendered at the investigatory stage. These considerations aside, retention of an expert who has extensively trained and consulted for only one side in such cases can lessen the fundamental value of having an outside expert on the investigative team in the first place.

Professional Associations

As in the case of professional licensure, prospective experts' certification or membership in professional associations adds to a presumption of competence and is routinely included in the proffering of an expert's credentials to the court before presenting expert testimony. As with the matters of licensure, academic degrees, continuing education, and prior consultancies, membership in professional associations is subject to verification checks and to the gathering of references from the expert's professional peers. This verification is an important and useful quality-control check.

Previous Similar Experience

Because the various computer technology fields are new and new developments in computer technology occur so quickly, formal credentials are less important in computer-related crime cases than direct prior experience with the victim company's computer operations, the brands of hardware or software the victim used, and the software applications involved. In addition, prior experience in investigating computer-related crimes, providing computer security, or computer-related crime research can be the critical element that renders a particular party an expert advisor. Identifying trustworthy and objective advisors who have such direct prior experience can be the most important factor in selecting an expert. Despite traditional criteria, such as formal credentials, by which a proffered expert's qualifications to testify as an expert witness are normally assessed, the trial judge has broad discretion to base a decision that an individual is an expert qualified to testify on a given subject primarily—or even solely—on that person's prior relevant experience.

There are pitfalls in overreliance on technical advisors with extensive prior experience in a subject area. Maintaining control over the overall management and direction of the case can be difficult. Susceptibility to defense charges of partisanship and bias against experts with extensive prior experience disproportionately on the government's side only is another hazard. Regardless, past experience remains the single most important qualification of experts in computer-related crime.

Sole Access to Privileged Information or Facts

Employees of the victimized agency or of the manufacturer, vendor, or service organization whose computer products the victims used can be among the most useful technical advisors when investigating a computer-related crime case or preparing one for trial. The background, education, and other credentials of such people can vary tremendously; this group can include top management at the victim organization, in-house computer technologists, data providers, equipment operators, and others who handle relevant data or are in sole possession of facts about the victim's operations. As a result, these people's qualifications in their own fields, while important, will prove secondary to their familiarity with aspects of the victim's operations and equipment. For the narrow purpose of laying out what such operational practices routinely were or what equipment capabilities and vulnerabilities are, courts can be expected to admit expert testimony from such people, if the prosecution is able to demonstrate their familiarity with such factors and their general competence.

The greatest pitfalls in using such individuals as pretrial technical advisors or as expert witnesses at trial are: (1) distinguishing the true area of competence and (2) bias. Employees or service personnel may be qualified to speak authoritatively on only very narrow points and be completely unqualified on other related points. In addition, loyalty to the employer, job security considerations, or a grudge against the employer or another employee may taint the individual's objectivity and hence her utility. And, of course, the investigative team must be especially circumspect about bringing such persons in as technical advisors, unless and until their possible complicity in the crime is completely ruled out.

PERSONAL QUALITIES OF THE EXPERT

The other standards in deciding whether to use a particular person as a technical advisor or expert witness are the personal qualities of the prospective expert. Because this area is primarily subjective, as distinguished from the relative objectiveness of credentials, it is difficult to say what the key factors are and how they should be assessed. However, eight considerations hold true for the use of technical advisors or expert witnesses in any major case, whether it is computer related or not. The sections that follow present these considerations.

Ability to Work as Part of a Team

Regardless of the area of their professional competence, many individuals are not temperamentally or attitudinally geared to working as part of a team. Doubtless this problem is more prevalent with certain professions than with others because of the nature of the work and other factors. Assessing whether a prospective expert will be a team player is a critical decision that must be made very early in the relationship, before the expert is retained. Reference checks and personal interviews help in making this determination. Effective management of the expert in the case, the security of sensitive investigative data, and the effectiveness of the expert as a witness on the stand are only a few of the overriding considerations that dictate using only team players in expert roles.

Trustworthiness and Integrity

Despite the advisability of limiting a technical advisor's access to casework on a need-to-know basis, the expert invariably will be exposed to sensitive information during the course of the case. At the very least, this exposure will extend to knowledge of her own role in the case, of those aspects of the investigation where she has been providing input, and the identities of others on the investigative team. The trustworthiness and discretion of the expert must be assured and maintained. Similar to the problem of ensuring that the expert is a team player, detailed reference checks and personal interviews must be used to check the expert's trustworthiness and integrity.

Professional Reputation and Recognition

An expert's stature and reputation among his peers are as important as academic degrees and publications. While this reputation will be partly a product of the authoritativeness of his views and credentials and experience in the field, it will also be reflective of his qualities. Many of the qualities will be directly relevant to whether the expert will be able to establish a harmonious working relationship with others on the case.

Experts' reputations can cut both ways with regard to their credibility as expert witnesses on the stand: If their views are controversial or even contested, the greater the experts' fame, the more likely the defense will be able to identify counterexperts familiar with the views and at odds with them. However, increased fame can go to the issue of stature and authoritativeness, by which opposing expert opinion can be overshadowed.

Reference checks and a review of the literature in the field to accurately gauge experts' professional stature and reputation are important steps to take before retaining them. Even if they are not retained as potential expert witnesses, the nature of their role in the case or the nature of the retainer agreement can make experts' identities discoverable by the defense at the pretrial stage, and thus their reputations are open to attack.

Quality and Timeliness of Previous Work

It is critically important to assess the quality of experts' work before retaining them. Most directly, the quality of their prior consultancies and service as expert witnesses must be checked out in great detail. The professional community's perception of the quality of the experts' work, publication, teaching, or lectures should be determined. If the government's expert is a potential expert witness, assume that the defense will make a thorough assessment in this area and will attempt to impeach the witness. The investigative and prosecutorial team cannot afford surprises on cross-examination in this regard. Employers, prior clients, professional references, and professional and regulatory agencies, among others, should be contacted for an assessment of the quality and timeliness of the prospective experts' work.

Professional Bearing and Demeanor

Perhaps subtle, but always significant, is the professional bearing and demeanor of the technical advisor. The ability to speak authoritatively, to sustain composure under vigorous cross-examination, to avoid argumentativeness with opposing counsel, and to simplify for the judge and jury without condescension are essential characteristics. The absence of any of these should exclude the admitted expert from consideration as an expert witness. Moreover, the behind-the-scenes technical advisor must also possess these qualities, because she must work closely with the other members of the investigative team, often under pressure.

Determining professional bearing and demeanor can be complicated. Initial impressions during interviews and preliminary discussions about the case are important, as are assessments by references and other outsiders. However, all of these observations are of limited utility. Engaging in role play early in the process with other investigators or prosecutors simulating an interrogation or cross-examination will provide useful information about the experts' reactions under pressure and in response to challenges to their expertise. Playing devil's advocate in a discussion with experts about their views or opinions on technical issues, or asking them to discuss the weaknesses in their own positions, or probing them on subjects beyond their area of expertise to assess the degree to which they are opinionated by nature are also useful techniques. In short, stress interviews for experts, whether they are viewed as potential expert witnesses or not, are essential tools to gauge bearing and demeanor.

"Presence" before a Group

The ability to present ideas effectively to a group is a learned skill. However, many individuals in all areas of endeavor lack this skill. An expert whose knowledge of a technical area is sound and who can effectively advise investigators behind the scenes may or may not possess an effective presence before a group. This skill is critical in any expert witness; for potential expert witnesses, advance screening for the presence of this skill and practice sessions to enhance it for trial are a must. However, the ability to make effective presentations to groups may also be a necessary attribute of the behind-the-scenes technical advisor; this situation should be considered when retaining any expert.

Advisors at the investigative or pretrial stages of complex cases may be called on to give orientation sessions on technical aspects of the case to a large group of investigators and other technical advisors. This circumstance requires experts to be effective at group presentation. In addition, should the identity of the technical advisors become known to the defense at the pretrial stage, depending on the nature of their relationship with the government and their role in the case, they may be subpoenaed to testify. This case would require them to have the same ability to effectively command the attention of a group as if they had been designated by the government as potential expert witnesses.

Ability to Explain Technical Issues in Lay Terms

A thorough grounding in their field of expertise and the ability to make an effective group presentation are undercut if technical advisors are unable to simplify complex technical matters so that intelligent laypeople can understand them. Indeed, this ability is the most fundamental skill technical advisors or expert witnesses must possess. The ability to make technical points understandable to the members of the investigative or prosecutorial team is critical to their ability to erect a sound theory of the case and to implement an effective strategy to break the case and/or obtain a conviction. Similarly, the ability to bring important technical points home to the judge and jury, without confusion or condescension, will have a direct impact on the likelihood of a favorable verdict.

If the experts have performed other consultancies in the past or served previously as expert witnesses, it should be easy to determine whether they have this skill by performing a thorough reference check. However, in the absence of these prior experiences, an effective technique would be to have prospective experts explain to a group of lay office staff the meaning of a few technical terms or concepts the interviewer selects. If the office staff cannot grasp the expert's explanation, chances are that other laypeople on the investigative team or the jury will not readily understand either. The presence or absence of strong interpersonal communications skills in experts is universally acknowledged as a key factor in the advisability of retaining them.

Mannerisms and Idiosyncrasies

Distinctions distract. Peculiar mannerisms, unusual modes of dress, and other aspects of experts' personalities tend to deflect attention from their message. The use of vulgarity or excessive humor at inappropriate times and derogatory remarks about professional rivals alienates listeners and turns them against the speaker and thus against the message. Such distractions must be eliminated at all costs in the case of potential expert witnesses, by either modifying their behavior or replacing them. Again, because behind-the-scenes technical advisors can under certain circumstances be subpoenaed to testify, these caveats are not limited solely to designated expert witnesses.

SOURCES FOR LOCATING EXPERT WITNESSES

Technical advisors for use in crime cases can be selected or drawn from a number of sources. These include:

- In-house sources
- Other law enforcement agencies
- Other agencies of state or local government
- State and local licensing, certifying, and registering bodies
- Law enforcement professional associations
- Professional associations in the subject area of expert knowledge sought
- The victimized organization
- Manufacturers/vendors and serving organizations that supply equipment or interface services to the victim
- Other organizations in the victim's field of activity or industry
- Area universities and research centers
- Private consulting firms specializing in the subject area
- Prior experience at obtaining experts
- Preexisting relationships with other agencies and referral sources
- Facts and circumstances of each case

Determining which source(s) to use for a particular sort of expert will be dictated by a mix of factors (see Exhibit 14.1).

EXHIBIT 14.1 Likely Sources of Technical Advisors in Computer-Related Crime Cases, by Type of Experience

	In-House Resources	Other Agencies of Government	Licensing Bodies	Professional Associations in Subject Area	Law Enforcement Professional Associations	Victim Company or Organization	HW/SW Manufacturer Vendor/Servicers	Other Organizations in Victim's Industry	Area Universities, Research Centers	Private Consulting Firms	Other Law Enforcement Agencies
Computer Scientists		X	X	X		X	X	X	X	X	
Electronic Engineers		X	X	X		X	X	X	X	X	
Telecommunications Engineers		X	X	X		X	X	X	X	X	
Computer Crimes Scholars			X	X	X				X	X	X
Subject Matter Experts from Victim's Industry				X		X	X	X			
Computer Users						X	X	X			
Data Providers						X	X	X			
Computer Operators						X	X	X			
Noncomputer Personnel Who Interface in Victim's Operation						X	X	X			
Computer Programmers	X	X	X	X	X	X	X	X	X	X	X
Systems Analysts	X	X	X	X	X	X	X	X	X	X	X
Database Managers				X		X	X	X			
IT Auditors	X	X	X	X	X	X	X	X	X	X	X
Computer Security Specialists	X	X	X	X	X	X	X	X	X	X	X
Experienced Computer-Related Crime Investigators	X	X	X	X	X		X		X		
Forensic Scientists	X	X	X	X	X		X		X		X

DISTINGUISHING THE ACTUAL AREA OF COMPETENCE

A concluding consideration when selecting an expert is offered as a caveat: Be certain precisely for which area(s) of expertise the investigative team needs other advisors, and carefully distinguish between these various areas of technical expertise when selecting a given consultant. For example, the decision to retain a computer programmer, an information technology (IT) auditor, and a computer security specialist as a core team of outside technical advisors when undertaking a complex computer-related crime case will be a common decision. However, selecting a programmer who is proficient in the programming language of the victimized company will be equally essential. Selecting a programmer and an IT auditor who are familiar with business applications of computer technology within the victim's field or industry will be necessary. When selecting a computer security consultant, one must decide whether a physical security specialist or a data security specialist is needed, or both. (Most computer security consultants are not expert in both.) These examples could be expanded almost infinitely.

Distinguishing the area(s) of specialized expertise needed must be coupled with distinguishing the true area(s) of a given consultant's expert competence from other areas in which he is not truly expert. This process is made more difficult because experts in one area are often unaware, or unwilling to admit, the limitations of their expertise. In such situations, representatives of the victimized organization or the manufacturers or vendors of the computer hardware or software equipment involved in the crime may be the best sources of guidance as to precisely what outside expertise is needed and what types of people would be likely to have the requisite capabilities. Consultation with experienced computer crime investigators or prosecutors, whether local or from other jurisdictions, can provide helpful information about the legal ramifications of securing outside technical advice.

SUMMARY

What constitutes a qualified expert witness in a fraud case? One must be more than an auditor or accountant. This chapter covers the best practices of assessing qualifications for an expert witness and identifying those credentials deemed indicative of an expert in this field. Although *The Computer Crime Expert Witness Manual* was written in 1980, the content of the original government document is just as valid today as it was then in determining the qualifications of an expert witness in a fraud case.

Larry Crumbley, editor of *The Journal of Forensic Accounting* and a pioneer in forensic accounting, provided some helpful points for forensic accountants who are thinking about being expert witnesses. First, he must be realistic about whether he is the right expert for the job. Second, she should review her qualifications and resume or vitae. They must make sure they have the competencies necessary to serve as an expert witness in a particular case. Third, they must get their credentials in order. Federal rules of civil procedures require that experts disclose their identity, the issues their opinions will address, their professional qualifications (including their publications of the last 10 years and all cases in which they provided expert testimony in the last four years), and who is paying them. Fourth, once a forensic accountant has been retained, she should prepare in depth. Do not let the attorney mold conclusions. The forensic expert must practice beforehand, possibly recording one's own testimony and reviewing the audio recording.

NOTES

1. Excerpted from the Bureau of Justice Statistics and Koba Associates, Inc., *Computer Crime Expert Witness Manual* (Washington, DC: Bureau of Justice Statistics, 1980). Reprinted with permission of the Bureau of Justice Statistics, U.S. Department of Justice. This document was written before the *Daubert* case and the resulting legal rules and guidelines for evaluating experts, their methodologies, and their conclusions. *Daubert,* therefore, supersedes the information in this chapter, as it is a ruling of the U.S. Supreme Court on how lower courts are to be gatekeepers in that evaluation, and provides legal guidance for that process. See Chapter 15 for an explanation of *Daubert* and its ramifications on the *legal* standards for evaluating an expert's qualifications and testimony.
2. Michael H. Graham, "Impeaching the Professional Expert Witness by a Showing of Financial Interest," *Indiana Law Journal.* (Winter 1977), p. 198.

15

CHAPTER FIFTEEN

The Legal Role and Qualifications of an Expert Witness

INTRODUCTION

Based on the definitions used in this book, one of the distinguishing differences between a fraud auditor and a forensic accountant is the role played *after* the fraud investigation or audit is completed, competent and sufficient evidence has been gathered (i.e., forensic evidence), the fraudster has been identified, and the fraudster is being prosecuted. Generally speaking, conducting the audit and gathering evidence is the extent of the fraud auditor's work. Regardless, the auditor involved in gathering the evidence is likely to be involved in the court case that follows, should one occur, typically as a fact witness; or the fraud auditor, having worked under the direction of a forensic accountant, helps to prepare evidence for presentation in court where the forensic accountant does the testifying as an expert witness regarding that evidence. A forensic accountant, in terms of the last stage of fraud investigations, is a specialist in serving as an expert witness in the subsequent trial, where he or she generally expresses an opinion about the accounting evidence. This chapter provides information about the legal role of the expert witness in a fraud case, the legal qualifications for the expert and his evidence.

ROLE OF A FORENSIC ACCOUNTANT AS A WITNESS IN COURT

Lay witnesses in civil and criminal cases generally are restricted from giving legal testimony consisting of opinions, conclusions, and characterizations, although they may estimate the speed of a moving vehicle, approximate temperature and distances, identify common smells, and testify in matters of physical description such as age, height, and weight. However, qualified experts may give their professional opinions, including forensic accountants serving as expert witnesses. Consider the Michigan Supreme Court Rules of Evidence on this point:

> RULE 702: TESTIMONY BY EXPERTS
>
> If the court determines that recognized scientific, technical, or other specialized knowledge will assist the trier of fact to understand the evidence or to determine a fact in issue, a witness qualified as an expert by knowledge, skill, experience, training, or education, may testify thereto in the form of an opinion or otherwise.
>
> RULE 703: BASES OF OPINION TESTIMONY BY EXPERTS
>
> The facts or data in the particular case upon which an expert bases an opinion or inference may be those perceived by or made known to him at or before the hearing. The court may require that underlying facts or data essential to an opinion or inference be in evidence.
>
> RULE 704: OPINION ON ULTIMATE ISSUE
>
> Testimony in the form of an opinion or inference otherwise admissible is not objectionable because it embraces an ultimate issue to be decided by the trier of fact.
>
> RULE 705: DISCLOSURE OF FACTS OR DATA UNDERLYING EXPERT OPINION
>
> The expert may testify in terms of opinion or inference and give his reasons therefore without prior disclosure of the underlying facts or data, unless the court requires otherwise. The expert may in any event be required to disclose the underlying facts or data on cross-examination.

RULE 706: COURT-APPOINTED EXPERTS

(a) Appointment

The court may on its own motion or on the motion of any party enter an order to show cause why expert witnesses should be appointed, and may request the parties to submit nominations. The court may appoint any expert witnesses agreed upon by the parties, and may appoint expert witnesses of its own selection. An expert witness shall not be appointed by the court unless he consents to act. A witness so appointed shall be informed of his duties by the court in writing, a copy of which shall be filed with the clerk, or at a conference in which the parties shall have opportunity to participate. A witness so appointed shall advise the parties of his findings, if any, his deposition may be taken by any party, and he may be called to testify by the court or any party. He shall be subject to cross-examination by each party, including a party calling him as a witness.

(b) Compensation

Expert witnesses so appointed are entitled to reasonable compensation in whatever sum the court may allow. The compensation thus fixed is payable from funds which may be provided by law in criminal cases and civil actions and proceedings involving just compensation under the Fifth Amendment. In other civil actions and proceedings the compensation shall be paid by the parties in such proportion and at such time as the court directs, and thereafter charged in like manner as other costs.

(c) Disclosure of appointment

In the exercise of its discretion, the court may authorize disclosure to the jury of the fact that the court appointed the expert witness.

(d) Parties' experts of own selection

Nothing in this rule limits the parties in calling expert witnesses of their own selection.

RULE 707: USE OF LEARNED TREATISES FOR IMPEACHMENT

To the extent called to the attention of an expert witness upon cross-examination or relied upon by him in direct examination, statements contained in published treatises, periodicals, or pamphlets on a subject of history, medicine, or other science or art, established as a reliable authority by the testimony or admission of the witness or by other expert testimony or by judicial notice, are admissible for impeachment

> purposes only. Expert witnesses may be cross-examined as any other witness and especially as to qualifications, bases of opinions, and compensation for testifying.
>
> Expert witnesses may express opinions in response to hypothetical questions, if the hypothesized facts in the questions are supported by the evidence of the case.
>
> Accountants and auditors are often called upon to provide testimony in litigation support matters and criminal prosecutions in which their services are utilized to support investigations of such crimes as financial frauds, embezzlement, misapplication of funds, arson for profit, bankruptcy fraud, and tax evasion. Accountants and auditors may also be utilized as defense witnesses or as support to the defendant's counsel on matters that involve accounting or audit issues.[1]

The last section is of particular importance in identifying both accountants/auditors and their role in fraud cases.

Daubert and Standards for Admissibility of Expert Witness Testimony

Over the years, the legal standards for acceptance of expert testimony have changed. The current U.S. standard is the *Daubert* case (1993) standards that were determined by the U.S. Supreme Court, and which in 2000, were used to modify Rule 702 to include Daubert challenges. These standards are critical in the determination of an expert's qualifications and, more important, her testimony.

Brief History of Legal Standards on Expert Testimony[2]

The courts used a "general acceptance" guideline for admitting expert testimony. This guideline was the result of *Frye v. United States.*[3] It stated that an expert opinion that was based on scientific technique is not admissible unless the technique is generally accepted as reliable within the relevant scientific community.

In 1975, the U.S. Congress adopted the Federal Rules of Evidence (Rule 702), establishing rules rather than common law as the basis for determining the acceptance of evidentiary issues. Rule 702 was designed so that more expert testimony would come before triers of fact.[4] The rule does not state that evidence is admissible only if it is generally accepted, and therefore it was in conflict with the previous standard established in *Frye*. Under Rule 702, trial judges rarely disqualified expert witnesses or testimony, but did limit the area where expert testimony could be offered.[5]

Daubert *Ruling*

In 1993, the U.S. Supreme Court empowered trial judges to be gatekeepers regarding expert witness testimony by making them specifically responsible for excluding unreliable expert witness testimony in *Daubert v. Merrell Dow Pharmaceuticals Inc.*[6] The Court also discussed limitations that Rule 702 placed on admissibility. One conclusion was that scientific evidence needed to be relevant and reliable. The Court also mandated a flexible approach in determining the admissibility of expert testimony. Four key factors to be considered are:

1. The credentials and/or experience that indicate an expert
2. The testimony's basis in fact
3. The testimony relevance and reliability
4. Other factors

In addition, the Court established five nonexhaustive factors to aid judges in assessing the reliability of expert testimony:

1. *Testing.* Can the theory or technique be tested, or has it been tested?
2. *Peer reviews.* Has the theory or technique been subjected to peer review or publication that aids in determining flaws in the method?
3. *Error rates.* Are there established standards to control the use of the technique? Is there a high rate of error or potential rate of error in the chosen method?
4. *Acceptability.* Is the theory or technique generally accepted in the relevant technical community?
5. *Time.* Did the theory or technique exist before litigation began?

While the *Daubert* ruling codified factors in evaluating the qualifications of expert witnesses, it also created some problems of its own. The most important to the topic of this book is the applicability of *Daubert* to nonscientific testimony, such as forensic accountants.

Cases That Amplified the Daubert *Ruling*

Some courts applied the *Daubert* ruling only to scientific testimony, while other courts interpreted it more broadly. The U.S. Supreme Court resolved this predicament in *Kumho Tire Company, Ltd. v. Patrick Carmichael.*[7] The Court extended trial judges' exclusionary responsibility to the testimony of nonscientific, technical, and other specialized experts (e.g., forensic accountants). In the same case, the Court reasserted a critical finding from *General Electric Co. v. Joiner*[8] that district courts hold the gatekeeper responsibility and circuit courts should overturn an admissibility decision only when there is clear abuse of discretion by a trial judge.

The second problem created in *Daubert* is that courts were inconsistent in the type of test employed in determining admissibility of an expert, which was the result of the flexibility in *Daubert*. Some judges interpret the *Daubert* ruling as close to the *Frye* test as possible, while others adopt the more liberal approach in Rule 702. Each judge is likely to employ his own criteria. Forensic accountants need to work closely with the attorneys to prepare testimony that will ultimately be considered appropriate and admissible in a specific court or by a specific judge.

Whether the *Daubert/Kumho/Joiner* principles extend to state courts is within the discretion of the various individual states.[9]

Implications for Forensic Accountants

The challenges allowed by *Daubert* apply to the expert testimony of forensic accountants. Because of *Daubert*, and the subsequent rulings in *Kumho* and *Joiner*, any errors leading to the exclusion of testimony by a forensic accountant have little hope of being reversed.

Forensic accountants must be careful to meet *Daubert* challenges successfully when being engaged as an expert witness. Since *Daubert*, an increasing number of testifying experts have been subjected to challenges by opposing counsel in an attempt to prevent the expert from testifying. In fact, several trial courts have applied the *Daubert* factors to exclude valuation-related expert testimony. For example, in *Andrew J. Whelan, et al. v. Tyler Adell, et al.*, the judge excluded the financial valuation expert testimony of a Big Four CPA.[10] The expert used only one valuation method, a discounted cash flow method that relied on speculative financial projections. In *Target Market Publishing, Inc. v. ADVO, Inc.*, the same thing happened: Another Big Four CPA had his testimony excluded because he used only one method and speculative assumptions.[11]

Reilly provides these guidelines for forensic accountants serving as expert witnesses:

- Know the relevant professional standards.
- Apply the relevant professional standards.

- Know the relevant professional literature.
- Know the relevant professional organizations.
- Use generally accepted analytical methods.
- Use multiple analytical methods.
- Synthesize the conclusions of the multiple analytical methods.
- Disclose all significant analytical assumptions and variables.
- Subject the analysis to peer review.
- Test the analysis and the conclusion for reasonableness.[12]

According to Parfitt, there are six things attorneys should do to make sure the expert (forensic accountant) is "*Daubert*-proof":

1. Examine the forensic accountant's curriculum vitae (CV) for general qualifications, such as research in a relevant field, number of relevant publications, and publication bias.
2. Question the forensic accountant to ascertain whether there are any misrepresentations, inaccuracies, or significant omissions in the CV.
3. Examine positions the forensic accountant has taken in publications to identify consistent, or inconsistent, opinions.
4. Review copies of the forensic accountant's prior testimony on the subject to determine if opinions have been stricken in other trials.
5. Educate the forensic accountant fully on forensic accounting issues relevant to the case.
6. Prepare materials to support an argument to include your forensic accountant's testimony, including Rule 702 and *Daubert* case law, and relevant judicial opinions.[13]

LEGAL QUALIFICATIONS FOR A FORENSIC ACCOUNTANT AS AN EXPERT WITNESS

When accountants and auditors are called by the prosecution, they generally testify about their investigative findings. When they are called by the defense, they may testify about the quality of the findings or the opinions expressed by the prosecution's accounting expert, in order to create doubt in the minds of jury members about the credibility or weight to give to the prosecution's expert.

Qualifying accountants and auditors as technical experts generally is not a difficult task. Questions are posed to them concerning their professional credentials—education, work experience, licensing or certification, technical training courses taken, technical books and journal articles written, offices held in professional associations, and awards and commendations received.

Defense lawyers usually are not prone to challenge the expertise of accountants and auditors, assuming they meet at least minimum standards of professional competence. To do so might give these experts an opportunity to fully highlight their professional credentials and perhaps make a greater impression on the jury or judge, thus adding more weight to their testimony. So defense attorneys often pass on the opportunity to challenge these expert witnesses.

The question of whether being a CPA or chartered accountant (CA) is sufficient to qualify oneself as an expert often arises. Generally, persons may be experts in their particular field of expertise if they have sufficient experience and are members of their institute. This situation does not mean that CPAs/CAs are automatically experts. However, this credential passes the first hurdle. To be considered an expert, it is helpful to have prior experience with litigation or criminal matters. This qualification is primarily a result of the knowledge and skills that are gained during the testifying experience.

Further, it is often beneficial to have been accepted as an expert in other matters, thereby easing current acceptance. A danger exists, however, of appearing to be an expert at being an expert witness.

Often, the counsel introducing the witness will read the expert's qualifications or ask specific questions of the witness to establish her credentials. On occasion, the qualifications of the expert witness are read directly into the court record. Although the expert's qualifications are not often contested, it is a distinct possibility. Over and above being accepted by both parties, it is most important that the expert witness be accepted by the court.

An extract reproduced from the proceedings in *Regina v. Scheel* shows how the accountant's qualifications as an expert witness can be established and how accounting exhibits might be introduced (see Appendix 15A).[14]

QUALIFICATION AND ADMISSIBILITY OF ACCOUNTING EVIDENCE

Documentary accounting evidence may be presented in a court of law in two forms: (1) primary, including original, individual accounting documents obtained from the parties concerned or other sources, and (2) secondary, including summaries and schedules based on the original documents. An accountant produces these secondary documents based on an examination of the primary evidence.

The admissibility of such evidence is well established in the United States. In *Hoyer v. United States*, the court held that in a prosecution for attempting to evade income taxes, summaries prepared from documentary and oral evidence were admissible to show the defendant's correct net income. In delivering the judgment of the court, Chief Judge Gardner said:

> . . . these exhibits so compiled and prepared purported to show the correct net income of the defendant for the years covered by the indictment. They were prepared by experts from documentary evidence introduced and from oral testimony. As the documentary evidence had already been introduced, counsel for the defendant had ample opportunity to examine it and to cross-examine the expert as to the basic testimony and his calculations based thereon. The evidence was clearly admissible.
>
> The documentary evidence presented a complicated situation and required elaborate compilations which could not have been made by the jury. It is also to be noted in this connection that the Court advised the jury that the testimony of the experts was advisory and need not be accepted by them as a verity.[15]

In *Daniel v. United States*, District Judge Hunter, delivering the judgment of the court, said:

> The rule is that a summary of books and records is admissible, provided cross-examination is allowed and the original records are available. Here the records of which the exhibits are summaries were in evidence, and the man who prepared them was available for cross-examination.
>
> It is perfectly proper that litigants be permitted the use of illustrative charts to summarize varying computations and to thus make the primary proof upon which such charts must be based more enlightening to the jury. The district judge did not abuse his discretion by permitting the use of these summaries.
>
> I would also observe that in the present case the summaries were helpful to the appellant, with respect to some of the counts.
>
> The introduction of the summaries did not offend against the rule that requires the production of original documents, since the documents which were the primary source of the summaries were in evidence. It is accordingly unnecessary in this case to

invoke the exception to the rule referred to by Wigmore in the following passage:

Where a fact could be ascertained only by the inspection of a large number of documents made up of very numerous detailed shipments . . . as the net balance resulting from a year's vouchers of a treasurer or a year's accounts in a bank ledger—it is obvious that it would often be practically out of the question to apply the present principle by requiring the production of the entire mass of documents and entries to be perused by the jury or read aloud to them. The convenience of trials demands that other evidence be allowed to be offered, in the shape of the testimony of a competent witness who has perused the entire mass and will state summarily the net result. Such a practice is well established to be proper.

Most courts require, as a condition, that the mass thus summarily testified to shall, if the occasion seems to require it, be placed at hand in court, or at least be made accessible to the opposing party, in order that the correctness of the evidence may be tested by inspection if desired, or that the material for cross-examination may be made available.

Accordingly, we were of the view that the learned trial judge did not err in admitting the summaries previously described.[16]

EXPERT'S ROLE IN THE LITIGATION TEAM

The accountant may be called on to give a different opinion from that reached by an equally credible expert accountant on the other side. This situation may arise because of different interpretations of the facts of the case or various alternative accounting techniques that might be available under the circumstances. In some cases, given equally plausible alternatives, the case often is decided on based on whichever side has the most credible expert witness.

PRETESTIMONY ACTIVITIES

One important problem in preparing reports and accounting summaries for the trier of facts arises from the delegation of tasks to junior accountants. If the person giving evidence has not had direct knowledge or has not examined the specific documents or prepared the accounting summaries, it may be possible that the expert will be trapped under the hearsay rule. If tasks are delegated, it is important that the review process entail review of all work to original documentation on a 100 percent basis.

It is also important to know the effect of other assumptions on the conclusion or opinion reached in the report. It is often possible to trap an expert into giving alternate opinions, based on other assumptions that had not been considered. Generally, working papers supporting the report and accounting schedules should not show contradictory conclusions to the report, as they are producible in court. This suggestion does not advocate that working papers should be deleted or amended subsequent to preparation; rather, it is a caution that these papers should be prepared with the precept that they could ultimately be submitted to the court and, as such, should take the appropriate form when they are prepared.

Another aspect of pretrial preparation relates to the availability of all notes that the witness intends to use or rely on. These notes may be requested in evidence for the court or may be producible during examination.

Further activities could consist of determining whether sufficient material is present to support the report. It may be necessary to derive information from other witnesses to support the expert's conclusions. This information normally is communicated by reference to discoveries or earlier will-says. Unfortunately, the witness cannot refer to these unless he has direct knowledge of their contents. If the accountant has relied on opinions or information presented by other witnesses, then he must either hear that evidence in court or have the transcript or agreed statement of facts available. Otherwise, that information and any opinions drawn from it would not be allowable.

SUMMARY

There is much about being an expert witness in a fraud investigation that most auditors would not know. This chapter details the legal role and legal qualifications of the expert witness, and the rules that will be used to admit expert testimony. It is likely that if an auditor serves as an expert witness that the opposing counsel will challenge that person's qualifications using *Daubert*. Therefore, it is extremely important to understand the *Daubert* challenge and to be prepared for it from the beginning of the case.

NOTES

1. Michigan Supreme Court Rules of Evidence: Rules 702, 703, 704, 705, 706, 707.
2. Raymond E. Figlewicz and Hans-Dieter Sprohge, "The CPA's Expert Witness Role in Litigation Services: A Maze of Legal and Accounting Standards," *Ohio CPA Journal* (July–September 2002), pp. 33–38.
3. *Frye v. U.S.*, 293 F. 1013 (D.C. Cir 1923).
4. V. M. Hansen, "Rule of Evidence 702: The Supreme Court Provides a Framework for Reliability Determinations," *Military Law Review* 162 (1999).
5. R. F. Reilly, "Accountants Consideration of *Daubert*-Related Decisions in Expert Testimony," *National Public Accountant* 45, No. 8 (2000), p. 12f.
6. 509 U.S. 579 (1993).
7. 526 U.S. 137 (1999).
8. 522 U.S. 136 (1997).
9. L. L. Kruschke, "Expert Opinion Testimony in State Courts," *Judges & Lawyers Business Valuation Update* 2, (June 2000).
10. D.C., U.S. District Court, civil action nos. 87-442 and 87-1763.
11. 136 F. 3d 1139, U.S. App. Lexis (1998).
12. Reilly.
13. Michelle A. Parfitt, "Daubert-Proof Your Expert," *Trial* (July 2005), p. 88.
14. Ontario Court of Appeals, *Regina v. Scheel*, May 12, 1978.
15. *Hoyer v. U.S.*, 8 Cir. 223 F.2d 134, 1955, p. 138.
16. *Daniel v. U.S.*, 5 Cir. 343 F.2d 785, 1965, Hunter District Judge, p. 789.

APPENDIX 15A: TRANSCRIPT OF TYPICAL COURT TESTIMONY OF EXPERT WITNESS

The following is an extract from the proceedings in *Regina v. Scheel.* It is an illustration of how the accountant's qualifications as an expert witness can be established and how accounting exhibits might be introduced.

Robert John Lindquist: Sworn Examination-in-Chief by Mr. Hunt (Crown):

Q: *Mr. Lindquist, where do you reside, sir?*

A. I live in Toronto, Ontario.

Q: *And what is your occupation?*

A. I am a chartered accountant.

Q: *And do you practice on your own or with someone else?*

A. I practice in partnership with other chartered accountants under the firm name of Lindquist, Holmes, and Company.

Q: *And how long have you been operating the partnership as a chartered accountant?*

A. Close to six years now.

Q: *And prior to that were you associated with any other firm?*

A. Yes, prior to that I worked for a period of six years with a national accounting firm where I studied after my graduation from University.

Q: *And in what year did you qualify as a chartered accountant?*

A. In 1972.

Q: *And since that date have you had occasion to testify in court with respect to accounting matters?*

A. I have.

Q: *And on approximately how many occasions would that have occurred?*

A. An estimate of some 50 occasions.

Q: *Your Honor, I tender Mr. Lindquist as a witness who should be classified as an expert witness on the basis of his qualifications that I have elicited.*

Mr. Hermiston: I am content with the qualifications, Your Honor.
His Honor: Thank you.

Mr. Hunt: Mr. Lindquist, I understand that you have prepared a number of documents relating to various transactions dealing with Metro Pallet Repair?

A. Yes, I have.

Q: *Could I see Exhibit A? I am presenting to you a document, a rather large document, marked Exhibit A on the Voir Dire. I would ask you to look at that document and tell me if you recognize that?*

A. Yes, I do.

Q: *And did you prepare that document yourself?*

A. Yes, I did.

Q: *And I wonder if, so the jury can see it, you would hold it in such a way that the jury will be able to see the structure of the document. It appears to consist of a number of columns, vertical columns; am I correct?*

A. That's correct.

Q: *And the document is headed what?*

A. It's headed "Analysis of Sales for the Period August 1, 1973, to October 3, 1973."

16

CHAPTER SIXTEEN

Effective Tactics and Procedures for the Expert Witness in Court

INTRODUCTION

Getting a fraud examination to a prosecuting agency is only half the battle against a crime of fraud at best. If the prosecuting agency proceeds with legal charges, then the forensic accountant becomes vital to the success of the case. Some high-profile cases, and many not so high-profile, have been lost due to blunders by the person serving as the expert witness. There are many cases where the expert witness was ineffective or the evidence was mishandled by the forensic accountant, resulting in a "not guilty" verdict in a criminal case; usually followed by a civil case where the parties switch roles! That scenario could be seen as "double dipping," where the fraudster successfully defrauded a victim organization for a huge sum, then pursues a civil case award of even more money. Thus the tactics and procedures of the expert witness are critical to the successful outcome of a fraud examination and court case. This chapter provides information about successful tactics and procedures, along with some of the subtleties of the court processes, such as the strategies of the opposing attorney on cross-examination.

EFFECTIVE PROFILE

Expert accounting witnesses must have a thorough knowledge not only of generally accepted accounting principles (GAAP) but also of the current promulgations of their institution. Often the expert's expertise may involve special knowledge of a specific industry, such as construction accounting or accounting in a stock market environment. In this case, the expert should be aware of recent developments and any important accounting issues within that area.

Experts must also be analytical and possess the ability to work with incomplete data; however, they may not always be able to recognize when data are incomplete. As a result, experts may make various assumptions that would then be open to interpretation or attack. If all data have not been made available, then it is quite possible that the opposing counsel may be able to offer alternate scenarios that are more plausible under the circumstances, thus discrediting the expert.

Experts must have the ability to simplify complex issues. It is helpful if they can communicate very directly and simply, keeping in mind that they are talking to nonaccountants and that the expert's role is to clarify complex issues so that everyone can understand them. In view of this, some background or experience in teaching often is helpful.

BEING A CREDIBLE EXPERT WITNESS

The goal of forensic accountants is to make their findings understandable to counsel, judges, and juries, and to avoid resorting to jargon and academic polemics about accounting rules and standards. The facts, stated simply and briefly, are all the audience needs or cares to hear. Anything beyond that only makes accounting and auditing more obscure.

To be a credible expert witness, accountants and auditors should be knowledgeable in their own fields by education and experience and members in good standing of the profession or of some specialized aspect of practice that would be pertinent to the case at hand. But there are other considerations as well to make an expert witness credible. Experts will appear credible when they follow these suggestions:

- Speak clearly and audibly.
- Refrain from using professional jargon.
- Use simple rather than complex terms to describe findings and opinions.

- Address the specific questions asked; do not go off on tangents or volunteer more than a question asks.
- Do not verbally fence with the defense attorney or prosecutor.
- Look directly at the question poser (prosecutor or defense counsel).
- Maintain a professional demeanor; do not smile gratuitously at the judge, the jury, the lawyer who hired you, or the opponent's counsel.
- Be calm and deliberate in responding to questions; speak neither too slowly nor too rapidly.
- Dress conservatively.
- Have a neat appearance including attire.
- Use graphs, charts, and other visual aids if they help to clarify a point.
- Do not read from notes if it can be avoided. (If the expert does read from notes, the opposition lawyer will probably demand to see them, and then the expert will appear to have rehearsed her testimony.)
- If you have documents to introduce, have them organized so that they can be retrieved quickly when asked to do so by the counsel for whose side you are testifying.
- Do not hem and haw or stammer. Retain your composure when a tough or complex question is posed.
- Ask for repetition or clarification if you do not fully understand the question.
- If you do not know the answer, say so—do not guess.
- In cross-examination, do not respond too quickly. Counsel for your side may wish to interpose an objection to the question.
- If the judge elects to ask a question, respond to it by looking at her.
- Do not stare off into space or at the floor or ceiling.
- Be friendly to all sides.
- Do not raise your voice in anger if the opponent's lawyer tries to bait you.
- Be honest. Do not invent. Do not inflate. Do not evade.

EXPERT'S ROLE IN THE LITIGATION TEAM

Generally, experts play an ongoing part in the litigation team. In particular, their involvement may be at various stages throughout the development of the case, most notably in:

- Case assessment
- Identification of documentation required to support the case, both additional and currently available

- Evaluation of the scope of work
- Preparation of initial financial assessment and analysis
- Consultation with counsel on legal issues and approach
- Preparation of report and accounting schedules and, if necessary, a document brief
- Negotiations between parties
- Assistance to counsel in court
- Expert evidence in court

Thus the expert witness function includes activities beyond those on the witness stand and preparation for testifying. The forensic accountant should make sure he is qualified to do these ancillary functions adequately, and be prepared to be a part of the litigation team outside the courtroom.

PRETESTIMONY ACTIVITIES

Pretestimony activities generally encompass preparing the report of the expert witness to a final stage. Without stating that the list is all-inclusive or appropriate in all circumstances, reports should include a discussion of these financial aspects:

- Issues
- Reliance on data to achieve conclusion
- Assumptions made in arriving at conclusion
- Restriction on assumptions
- Date of information cut-off
- Opinion and conclusion based on the available documentation
- Limitations of opinion and sensitivity to assumptions
- Detailed schedules and documents supporting the opinion and conclusion

It often is useful to have a list of all other witnesses including the witnesses for the other side. This information is important so that the expert is not surprised by the existence of other experts or reports. The expert can then determine if it is necessary that he be present for the testimony of those witnesses and obtain the related court approval. If another expert will be present, then it is incumbent on the expert witness to examine the alternate reports and assess whether reasonable points are brought by the other side that may affect the credibility of the expert's report.

Other pretestimony activities encompass ensuring that any required graphic displays are ready and available, that all important discussions with the lawyer have been held as part of the pretestimony meetings, and that the expert completely understands the report and all other relevant issues in the trial, whether accounting related or not. Most important, the expert must ensure that he agrees with counsel as to the sequence of the expert's evidence and the strategy for presenting it. It is often useful to have a dry run at the direct testimony, with counsel posing all the questions to the expert witness in order to avoid surprises during trial.

At pretestimony meetings, it is often appropriate to discuss the witness's qualifications again to assure that they are current, to discuss the strengths and weaknesses of the case, and to discuss and agree on which parts of the expert's reports, if not all, are to be entered into court as exhibits.

TRIAL AND TESTIMONY

The expert witness needs to understand the process and protocol of being involved in a court case, and to understand all of the measure an expert witness should take in order to add forensic value to the evidence that is being presented. For those who have never testified, they may be surprised to learn that demeanor, appearance, and other personal factors are sometimes as important as the evidence. In reality, what it means is the ability to convince a judge or group of jurors that you as the expert witness are credible, and therefore your testimony is credible.

On the Stand

Judges and juries often base their assessments of expert witnesses at least in part on how the witnesses look. Therefore, it is important that witnesses be well groomed and neatly dressed. In the case of an accountant, a dark business suit is the expected image. This appearance may enhance the image to psychological advantage. In the witness box, the witness should maintain a poised, alert appearance, stand still, and be ready to take the oath. It is important to control the hands, avoid fidgeting, and maintain eye contact with the questioner. As the judge will be taking notes, the witness should speak slowly enough to ensure that the judge does not fall behind. The voice should be strong and directed to the questioner. The witness should enunciate clearly.

Several things should be avoided in giving evidence. These range from drinking five cups of coffee immediately before testifying or chewing bubble gum while giving evidence, to small physical mannerisms that may affect one's appearance. These physical mannerisms, which might be as simple as rubbing the hands together continually, looking down at one's hands, continually moving in the stand, or jingling coins in a pocket, could quickly become irritating to the judge.

Direct Examination

The purpose of direct examination is to enable counsel for the side the expert represents to draw out the financial evidence to prove the case. Most likely, this examination will be only a reiteration of what has been discussed previously with counsel outside of the courtroom. It is still very important, however, for the expert to refresh her memory by reference to anything she may have read, written, or given in evidence on the case beforehand.

Direct examination is the most organized aspect of the trial; it is the stage in which the expert's credibility must be established with the judge or jury. According to the concept of the primary memory feature, people remember best what they hear first and last. This fact is often a useful idea to employ in giving or structuring evidence. A further noteworthy point is that the jury often has a limited attention span in a long trial; thus, it is often useful to use a "grab/give/conclude" method of presenting evidence.

For a witness, the interpretation of questions and the ability to listen are crucial skills. Even though the witness already may have gone through a mock direct examination, it is critical that each question be evaluated carefully again; the witness should reflect on the questions asked and not anticipate them. (They may have been changed since the time of rehearsal.) Throughout, it is useful to remember that this aspect of testimony was rehearsed in advance and so is the easiest part of examination.

It is necessary to be honest in answering questions. Less obvious, however, is the need to avoid bias and prejudice when answering. The answers to all questions should be clear and concise, and when complex terms are used, they should be clarified. Use of notes should be limited as much as possible in order to maintain eye contact with both the judge and the rest of the court.

Accounting schedules should be described accurately and succinctly in layperson's terms. Schedules are by their nature concise documents and should be described in that manner. If opinions are given, they should be given with conviction once the appropriate groundwork has been laid.

Cross-Examination

Cross-examination is truly the highlight of the adversarial court system; it is geared to allow counsel either to clarify or to make points at the witness's expense. As such, it is generally the most difficult part of the trial process for any witness. Anything unexpected can turn up that might refute or embarrass the witness, whose credibility is constantly called into question.

The goals of the opposing counsel during cross-examination are threefold. The first is to diminish the importance of the expert testimony just presented. The second might be to have the expert testify in support of the opposing position by providing a series of assumptions. The third is to attack the opinion itself or to show the inadequacies of the expert's work in arriving at her opinion, thereby discrediting the opinion, the report, and the witness in the eyes of the court.

The opposing counsel can attack or question anything that was said or entered into court. This cross-examination includes notes, working papers, affidavits, will-says, reports, and preliminary trial or discovery transcripts. Often cross-examination is conducted in an atmosphere of confrontation and contradiction. At all times, financial expert witnesses must remember that, however crucial to the case they may be, they are merely a piece of the puzzle. Most important, witnesses must not take attacks or attempts to discredit them personally. There are many ways to discredit an expert witness. Throughout the process, it is important for the witness to maintain pride and professional integrity. An adage to remember is that "even mud can be worn well."

In general, proper attitude and demeanor during direct examination are also applicable to cross-examination, except that opposing counsel wants to reduce or limit the impact of the witness's evidence. It is natural to feel a certain amount of apprehension at this stage, and this stress does a great deal to keep the witness alert.

The jury often watches the judge, and therefore the expert often can take a clue as to the tempo and reaction of the jury and the judge to the evidence being presented. Slight changes in style and presentation can be made accordingly.

The opposing counsel usually has a plan of cross-examination in mind, and an expert witness should be able to establish this direction to prevent falling into a trap or erring. A danger of this mental logic, of course, is that the witness will spend as much time planning ahead as answering the questions and may not be giving appropriate weight to the immediate questions. Further, in attempting to anticipate questions, the witness may misunderstand the one being asked.

When asked questions, the expert should evaluate them carefully and take time to consider the answers. The witness should be calm and pause before answering, and tread very carefully toward the answer, knowing exactly how it relates to both the question and the issues before the court.

When answering, it is important to be honest and to avoid the appearance of bias and prejudice. It is equally important not to exaggerate, ramble, allow oneself to be baited, or attempt to be humorous. One of the most devastating blows to a litigation or defendant is having an expert witness make a transparent attempt to hide errors or lose his temper.

Generally, it is a rule of thumb for an expert witness not to give away or volunteer information. Further, during her responses, often it may be extremely difficult to avoid being trapped in various assumptions, what-if scenarios, and generalities presented by counsel during cross-examination. If this entrapment attempt occurs, the expert should retrench by asking for the question to be rephrased in smaller components.

Never underestimate the accounting expertise of the opposing counsel. Often opposing counsel underplay their understanding of the issues in order to lull the expert into a sense of security. Obviously, this tactic can lead the expert into a difficult situation.

In general terms, opposing counsel's golden rule is to cross-examine only if the cross-examination would benefit a case. In questioning the witness, opposing counsel will generally ask either simply worded short questions or leading questions. Usually counsel knows the answers to her questions in order to eliminate any surprises and to allow her to lead the witness along. Several techniques are also available to destroy witnesses without touching their evidence.

Opposing counsel generally will evaluate answers and then take a specific approach that furthers their arguments. Usually a witness will not be allowed to explain or elaborate on answers at that time as that would allow the witness to alter the thrust of the carefully orchestrated cross-examination. Opposing counsel is also continually questioning or evaluating how its last question and answer could be used against the witness. If the question has raised new ground, can it be developed and used to enhance the opposing counsel's position?

Opposing counsel will often prepare by reading all of the witness's earlier testimony and publications. Opposing counsel might also speak to other lawyers about the witness's earlier performance in court. This preparation may indicate specific weaknesses a witness may have. If any are discovered, the questioning of the witness will probably be directed to that area.

Opposing counsel may also attempt to take psychological control of a witness by:

- Using their physical presence to intimidate
- Maintaining nonstop eye contact
- Challenging the space of the witness
- Posing fast-paced questions to confuse the witness
- Not allowing the expert to explain or deviate from the exact question

Opposing counsel often uses physical domination. Opposing counsel will quickly discover the expert's response pattern and might take an aggressive stance to lead the expert to the point where he or she is unsure, with devastating results.

Opposing counsel might use these strategic methods to discredit witnesses or to diminish the importance of their testimony. These methods could be used singly or in conjunction with one another, and are not an all-encompassing list. In cross-examination, a good counsel will quickly discover the witness's weak areas and employ any possible techniques to achieve his or her goal. Thus, it is often useful to have an overall understanding of some of the more common methods employed, which include:

- Myopic vision
- Safety/good guy
- Contradiction
- New information
- Support opposing sides theory
- Bias
- Confrontation
- Sounding board
- Fees
- Terms of engagement
- Discrediting the witness

Myopic Vision

Myopic vision entails getting the expert to admit to excessive time being spent in the investigation of a matter, then highlighting an area of which the expert is unsure or in which he or she has not done much work. This area may not be central to the issues in the case but must be relevant to conclusions reached. Then the opposing counsel will make a large issue of it and prove that the expert's vision is myopic in that the work was limited in extent or scope and, as such, substandard. At the same time, the question of fees could be drawn in to show that large sums were expended to have this "obviously incomplete" work done.

Safety/Good Guy

Often opposing counsel will begin a cross-examination gently, not attacking the expert and so lulling her into a feeling of false security. Then opposing counsel might find a small hole that could be enlarged quickly. Many times opposing counsel appears friendly and conciliatory, so that the jury becomes sympathetic to their cause. Opposing counsel may also attempt to achieve a rapport with the witness that will make her want to help the opposition to bring out information in the matter. Doing so might result in the witness volunteering information that otherwise would not have been given. With this additional information, it might be possible for opposing counsel to find a chink or hole in the evidence and develop it further.

Contradiction

Opposing counsel might use leading questions to force the witness into a hard or contradictory position. Alternately, counsel can establish in court the credibility of a potentially contradicting document or quote from other articles written by other experts in the field. If these documents or articles contradict the expert, then the expert might admit to that contradiction. If the contradiction exists, the expert might be drawn into an argument as to who is the most appropriate or experienced expert in the circumstances. Instances also have occurred when witnesses have contradicted themselves or their own articles written several years earlier merely because they have forgotten or have become confused by the attack.

New Information

Opposing counsel may introduce new information of which the expert might not be aware, or refer to a specific relevance in the conclusions the expert witness reaches. This tactic is normally done to confuse witnesses so that they might contradict themselves or develop a series of alternate scenarios, given the new information that shows that their report and opinions are no longer of value.

Support Opposing Sides Theory

This approach establishes and recognizes an expert's qualifications and evidence. The same information the expert uses is then used and interpreted by opposing counsel in a different way to support an alternate theory. By getting the expert to agree to the alternate interpretation of the facts and theory, opposing counsel has in effect made the expert a witness for the other side. This technique is useful to obtain concessions from witnesses that would damage their conclusions and, ultimately, their credibility.

Bias

This method draws the expert's counsel and the expert together to show possible collusion in the evidence being presented in testimony, and hence show bias. This bias can be shown if opposing counsel determines that the expert's counsel had instructed the witness about what to say or by limiting the expert's scope and hence conclusions. This approach can also focus on the question of whether the expert was told by the client what to do and look for. With this approach, opposing counsel can attempt to show that the expert overlooked important documentation in an effort to assist their client.

Confrontation

This very simple method is the continued use of a confrontation of wills to put witnesses into a situation in which they might lose control and become angry. Once a witness has exploded, credibility disappears.

Sounding Board

This method uses the witness as a sounding board to reacquaint the jury with the favorable aspects (to opposing counsel) of the case. This technique often uses the "Is it not true" and "Would you agree with me" approach. Constant nonstop agreement is useful to browbeat the expert. To the judge and jury, agreement with various questions the opposing counsel raises may also be interpreted as a general concurrence with the opposing counsel's position. This tactic is often a valuable psychological tool.

Fees

This method attacks the witness for taking an inordinate amount of time to achieve the result. Further, the attack may indicate incomplete work and may be correlated to the fees charged. This method is often related to "bias" and "myopic vision." Because of high fees or reoccurring engagements with a client, it may be suggested that the witness and his opinion are biased for the client. This technique often builds to a conclusion in which opposing counsel shows that the work was superficial and unprofessional, but the expert received a great deal of money for this and other areas of service to the client; the direct implication is that the testimony was purchased or that the expert was paid to overlook facts contradictory to his or her conclusions.

Terms of Engagement

This technique normally starts by opposing counsel obtaining the original engagement letter and examining the terms of engagement, then showing that the expert intended to examine only items in support of his or her client and glossed over any alternative theories, generally to the detriment of the opposition. Therefore, the witness could be portrayed as partial.

Discrediting the Witness

Discrediting the witness is the concept of proving that the expert is unworthy to be a credible witness. This strategy often is accomplished by showing that the expert currently is, or has previously been, grossly biased, prejudiced, corrupt, convicted of criminal activities, shown to engage in immoral activities, made inconsistent statements, acquired a reputation for a lack of veracity, and/or exaggerated his qualifications. Discrediting might also look at the quality of the experts' educational background to reveal any other unusual activities that might bias them or exclude them from the court as experts.

SURVIVAL TECHNIQUES

When deciding to become or serve as an expert witness, there are some issues one should consider. An expert witness must be prepared and willing to deal with the unexpected. It is also likely opposing counsel will present challenges to the expert witness. Larry Crumbley and Keith Russell make these suggestions to forensic accountants regarding being an expert witness.[1]

Use Visual Aids

Simplify the presentation of accounting matters that are often difficult for the general public even when they are simple to the accountant, but also can be sophisticated in the case of testimony in court. Use PowerPoint charts, graphs, or related illustrations.

Do Not Answer an Ambiguous Question

If you are unable to respond to a question, say so and request clarification.

Maintain Your Composure

Opposing counsel will attempt to discredit you and destroy your self-confidence if your testimony could have a detrimental impact on their client's case. The more effective your testimony is for your side, the more intense the attack from opposing counsel is likely to be.

Be Patient

There will be many delays, motions, recesses, sidebars, and so forth. On the stand, you must remain calm in demeanor in what will sometimes feel like a chaotic or turbulent scene. Your client, the judge, and the jury will expect you to be professional at all times.

Maintain a Careful Sense of Humor

Well-timed, natural humor is fine, in the right circumstances. It actually can help an expert witness to appear natural and spontaneous. However, a joke can backfire. Make sure not to use cruel jokes, and do not force one.

Know Your Limitations

Do not try to bluff when you do not know an answer. Successful expert witnesses claim expertise only in those areas where they are justified in doing so. The other side has access to its own accounting experts who can validate or refute your testimony. Opposing counsel will normally try to build a case around its own experts rather than attack a witness who is poised and objective.

Do Not Become Argumentative or Defensive

Avoid displays of negative behavior, even though it may be hard to hide your feelings at times. If the opposing attorney appears to have gained the upper hand during cross, remember that your attorney has the option to redirect testimony to examine the points necessary.

Do Not Forget Who Is Deciding the Case

Direct your replies to the judge and jury. You are speaking to people who will base their understanding and acceptance of your testimony on your professionalism. They must trust you in order for you to be effective. Much of what you say will be accepted or rejected according to whether you speak clearly, project self-confidence, and communicate a strong sense of ethics, a positive attitude, and enthusiasm. These factors may have a greater influence on the outcome than the actual testimony.

Summary For the Expert Witness

Here are 10 points for the expert witness to remember both in preparing for and in giving evidence at trial. Remember to:

1. Prepare your material completely.
2. Know your material thoroughly.
3. Plan your testimony in advance.
4. Be alert.
5. Listen carefully.
6. Carefully consider each answer, and pause before answering.
7. Be honest and avoid bias.
8. Clarify—use simple words.
9. Keep your cool.
10. Maintain professional pride and integrity throughout.

SUMMARY

Once the auditor is on the witness stand, the protocol for successful testimony goes far beyond telling the truth or having good forensic evidence. The auditor must convince a judge or jury, who are laymen in terms of accounting, and put forth a good image socially. This chapter conveys best practices to perform well on the witness stand, which many consider to be more important than the evidence itself.

NOTES

1. D. L. Crumbley and K. A. Russell, "So You Want to Be an Expert Witness," *Journal of Accountancy* (October 2004), pp. 23–30.

CHAPTER SEVENTEEN

17 Fraud and the Public Accounting Profession

 INTRODUCTION

The public accounting profession has become more and more involved with fraud over the twentieth century and the first decade of the twenty-first. The involvement includes roles and responsibilities, and in particular a significant increase in auditor liability related to financial audits. The roles have been expanded as the need for forensic services by entities have seen a substantial increase. Those services sometimes cause independence issues. The auditor's responsibilities have changed, and basically seen expansion as well, over the last century. Court decisions, new laws, and new standards have led to new responsibilities.

 HISTORY OF FRAUD AND THE AUDITOR: A SUMMARY

Many of the standards and significant events in the history of the audit profession and public accounting in particular are related to a fraud. Exhibit 17.1 presents a recap of some of the more significant frauds and court cases.

EXHIBIT 17.1 Significant Events in History of Fraud and Public Accounting

Year	Event	Significance
1720	South Sea Bubble	Major financial statement fraud, perhaps the first one. First occurrence of an external audit.
1920	Charles Ponzi	Ponzi created a pyramid scheme to defraud investors. He was not the first to do this kind of fraud, but has since been referred to as a Ponzi scheme.
1931	*Ultramares v. Touche Niven*	Auditor negligence. Attempted to extend auditor's liability to third-party financial statement users. Limited auditor liability for ordinary negligence to those with privity. (Only two states still do: VA, PA.)
1932	Ivar Kreuger Scandal	Major financial statement fraud associated with stock trades. Largest fraud to date in history. Led to SEC acts 1933 and 1934.
1933	*McKesson Robbins v. PW*	$19 million in inventory and A/R accepted at management's word, but was fraudulent. Resulted in new standards: (1) Observation of inventory, and (2) Confirmation of receivables.
1967	*1136 Tenants Corp v. Max Rothenberg*	CPA firm was sued for negligent failure to detect an embezzlement. Firm was held liable and fined $237,000; audit fee was $600! Resulted in new audit standard—engagement letters.
1968	*Yale Express v. Peat Marwick*	Fraudulent statements were knowingly made by management. Peat Marwick hired and found material

		misstatements and fraud. Court held them liable to inform those relying on statements about the resulting changes to financials. Resulted in new standard—subsequent events, SAS No. 41.
1969	*Continental Vending v. Simon*	Defendant contended reporting of fairness should be separate from report on compliance with GAAP. Criminal liability found when court determined auditors knew audited statements were falsified. Three auditors were convicted of violating SEC 1934 and fined.
1973	*Equity Funding v. Weiner*	Equity Funding used computers to perpetrate a multi billion dollar fraud in receivables. Stock price was motivator. Criminal liability found on part of some auditors; three were convicted of criminal offenses and went to prison. Various CPA firms paid $44 million in related civil cases.
2001	Enron	Financial statement fraud at Enron became public. Largest fraud to date.
2002	WorldCom	Financial statement fraud. Largest to date, approximately $13 billion. Congress already considering legislation following Enron, but accelerates and passes SOX on July 30, 2002.
2008	Bernie Madoff	Ponzi scheme by man of celebrity status. Approximately $65 billion, lasted about 30 to 40 years. Largest fraud to date. Led to major changes at SEC.

1933/1934: SEC Acts

Auditors had been sued before the stock market crash of 1929, the Securities Act of 1933, and the Securities Exchange Act of 1934. However, the Securities and Exchange Commission (SEC) acts added more responsibility and liability to the independent financial auditor and, more important, established a public perception of accountability. The acts were most likely influenced more by a fraud than by the stock market crash of 1929.

By the time of that stock market crash, external auditing had become a somewhat standardized profession, but not a particularly large one. Since bankers were the primary users of financial statements, the only companies needing audits were those that depended on banks for capital. Companies that depended on stockholder financing were not required to have audits. Consequently, often even companies listed on the New York Stock Exchange did not issue audited financial statements. That situation would change because of Ivar Kreuger—one of the greatest swindlers the world has ever seen (see Chapter 1 for more on the Kreuger scandal).

Newspaper articles kept U.S. citizens aware of the extent of Kreuger's fraud; meanwhile, Congress had been and was considering the passage of the federal securities laws. Thus, the timing of the bankruptcy and the corresponding media coverage made it politically expedient to pass laws that would make similar schemes difficult in the future.

1977: SAS No. 16

The Auditing Standards division of the American Institute of Certified Public Accountants (AICPA) summarized auditors' responsibilities regarding fraud and illegal acts under generally accepted accounting standards (GAAS):

> The auditor's responsibility to detect and report fraud is set out in Statement on Auditing Standards (SAS) No. 16, *The Auditor's Responsibility for the Detection of Errors or Irregularities* (1977) and SAS No. 17, *Illegal Acts by Clients* (1977). The standards were developed as a direct result of problems in the business community in the mid-1970s. The disclosure of client frauds, such as Equity Funding, and questionable payments, primarily in foreign countries, stirred the profession to adopt more specific standards in the area of client misconduct.

SAS No. 16 established an affirmative requirement for auditors; the auditor is required to plan the examination to search for material errors and irregularities and to carry out the search with due skill and care. If auditors discover an error, irregularity, or illegal act, they are required to report it to management and, depending on its significance, possibly to the board of directors or its audit committee. Auditors were also required to assess the effect on the financial statements and, if material, to insist on adjustment or additional disclosure in the statements or to qualify the audit report.

SAS No. 16 recognized that although there was an affirmative responsibility to search for material errors and irregularities, there was a chance that they would not be found. Auditors test selectively; that is, they usually sample accounts rather than examining 100 percent of the accounts. Thus, if the sample does not identify a fraudulent transaction, the auditor will be less likely to suspect one in the unsampled portion of the financial statements. Auditors, of course, control this sampling risk, but to eliminate it would require them to examine all of the entity's transactions for the year, which would result in astronomical audit costs and still would not necessarily detect cleverly forged or unrecorded transactions.

1977: Foreign Corrupt Practices Act

The Foreign Corrupt Practices Act of 1977 (FCPA) not only prohibited illegal payments but also addressed issues related to fraud, such as internal controls. Specifically, the FCPA required SEC registrants to establish and maintain financial books, records, and accounts. It also required the establishment of internal accounting controls sufficient to meet these objectives:

- Transactions are executed in accordance with management's general or specific authorization.
- Transactions are recorded as necessary to prepare financial statements (i.e., generally accepted accounting principles [GAAP]) and to maintain accountability.
- Access to assets is permitted only in accordance with management authorization.
- The recorded assets are compared with existing assets at reasonable intervals.

After the passage of the FCPA, many corporations established internal and information technology (electronic data processing, [EDP]) audit functions or bolstered the staffs of these organizational units only to discover no decrease in the number of defalcations—frauds, thefts, and embezzlements—by corporate employees. Researchers tested the hypothesis that an increase in the perceived aggressiveness by internal and external auditors in detecting corporate irregularities would function as a deterrent.[1] Their study concluded that managers contemplating acts of management fraud are not deterred by the presence of internal and external auditors; neither does an increase in the perceived aggressiveness of the internal or external auditor significantly decrease the occurrence of corporate irregularities. Thus these tenets may benefit the corporation only in terms of asset misappropriation and corruption, but not fraudulent statements (see Chapter 1).

1984: Professionalism

In *United States v. Arthur Young & Co.* (March 21, 1984), the Supreme Court tried to define *professionalism* in the accounting profession in the loftiest terms. In a unanimous decision the Court stated:

> By clarifying the public reports that collectively depict a corporation's financial status, the independent auditor assumes a *public* responsibility *transcending any employment relationship* with the client. The independent public accountant performing his special function owes *ultimate allegiance to the corporation's creditors and stockholders,* as well as to the investing public. This "public watch-dog" function demands that the accountant maintain *total independence from the client at all times* and requires *complete fidelity to the public trust.* To insulate from disclosure a certified public accountant's interpretations of the client's financial statements would be to ignore the significance of the accountant's role as a *disinterested analyst charged with public obligations.* [Emphasis added.]

The Court continued:

> It is therefore not enough that financial statements be accurate; the public must also perceive them as being accurate. *Public faith* in the reliability of a corporation's financial statement depends upon the *public perception* of the outside auditor as an independent professional. [Emphasis added.]

1986: Financial Fraud Detection and Disclosure Act

The public furor in the United States about the liability of external auditors for detection of fraud continued through the 1980s. In the United States, the Financial Fraud Detection and Disclosure Act of 1986 was one manifestation of the public's concern. The congressional history and details of that bill follow.

The regulatory system established by the federal security laws is based on the concept of complete and fair disclosure of important information to investors and other users of corporate financial reports. This regularity system is administered by federal agencies, such as the SEC, working in concert with private, independent auditor firms, which check corporate financial records and certify the reports given to the public. Over the past several years, numerous cases of massive financial fraud have occurred where the independent auditors failed to either detect or to report the fraudulent activities at the companies being audited. These include E.F. Hutton, United American Bank, General Dynamics, E.S.M. Government Securities, Inc., Home State Savings and Loan of Ohio, American Savings and Loan of Florida, Saxon Industries, San Marino Savings and Loan of California, and many others. The costs of these frauds have been enormous both financially and in terms of public confidence in the soundness of the nation's economic system.

The AICPA, a private trade organization, establishes GAAS, which are used by independent auditors and accepted by the SEC. Under present GAAS rules, independent auditors do not include as part of their audit significant procedures to detect management fraud, and their consideration of fraud is restricted to its material impact on a corporation's financial statements. In a large corporation, financial fraud amounting to millions or even hundreds of millions [of dollars] could go unreported because such amounts would not be considered material to the total financial condition of the corporation.

Even when actual fraud and illegal acts are discovered, the GAAS rules only say that the auditor should inform the company's management and consider resigning from the audit account. There is no requirement that auditors report fraud or illegal acts to the appropriate government authorities. In addition, auditors rely on the internal control systems of a corporation, but do not issue an opinion regarding the adequacy of management's internal controls. Thus, financial fraud has occurred in many corporations which have been allowed to operate with substandard or nonexistent internal controls because the independent auditor did not report on the adequacy of internal controls.

The AICPA and the SEC were criticized on this issue ten years ago by the Senate Subcommittee on Reports, Accounting and Management. That subcommittee's final unanimous report stated that auditors should look for illegal acts and report them to government authorities. The AICPA appointed its own study group, the Cohen

Commission, which failed to recommend active detection and reporting of illegal acts. The SEC and the AICPA did nothing further until the Subcommittee on Oversight and Investigations began its accounting hearings on February 20, 1986.

At the March 6, 1985 hearing, Chairman Dingell was joined by other members in expressing his concern about an audit rule that merely suggested that the auditor, as the public watchdog, only consider leaving the premises if he or she found a criminal, instead of reporting the criminal to the proper authorities. In response, the AICPA established a new group, the Treadway Commission, to further study the issue. Neither private accounting organizations nor the SEC have the authority to grant independent auditors immunity from legal action that could arise as a result of fraud detection and disclosure responsibilities, so legislation is the only way to fully protect auditors performing their duties in good faith.

Chairman William Seidman of the Federal Deposit Insurance Corporation, who formerly headed a large audit firm, agreed with Chairman Dingell and Congressman Wyden at the Subcommittee's April 28, 1986, hearing that auditors should look for fraud and report it to regulators.[2]

The Financial Fraud Detection and Disclosure Act of 1986 amends the federal securities laws to provide reasonable assurance that fraudulent activities at companies covered by these laws will be discovered and reported to the proper authorities. The act does not apply to small businesses or other companies that are exempt from the securities laws. The act was necessary because the SEC and the accounting profession lacked the authority to provide full legal protection for auditors who report fraudulent activities.

The act strengthened the regulatory system of federal agencies working with private audit firms by establishing clear standards for the detection and reporting of financial fraud as well as the tools necessary to meet those standards and fully protect auditors performing their duties. The act has several basic provisions:

- The act requires that auditors include specific and substantive procedures for detecting financial fraud as part of the audit plan. Current audit standards regard fraud detection as incidental to the financial audit. Therefore, many auditors either fail to recognize indications of fraudulent activities or else convince themselves that such activities are not within the scope of the audit and that they have no responsibility to act on such matters.

- The act requires that auditors evaluate the internal control systems established by corporate managers in order for auditors to determine whether those internal controls assure that corporate assets are being handled properly and lawfully. Existing audit standards on reviewing internal controls were not strong enough in this regard.
- The act requires auditors to issue a written report that: (1) gives the auditors' opinion regarding the adequacy of internal control systems; (2) identifies any weaknesses in those systems; and (3) states that the audit was conducted in a manner that provides reasonable assurance that fraudulent activities have been detected and reported. The auditors' written report is the place where auditors give opinions on the results of the audit. Current standards did not require that auditors issue an opinion on fraud detection or the adequacy of internal controls.
- The act requires that the individuals actually responsible for the audit sign the audit opinion on behalf of the firm conducting the audit. Existing audit opinions bore only the name of the audit firm conducting the audit, even though the firms auditing most SEC registrants were giant organizations with hundreds of partners and thousands of staff. It also provided personal recognition for the individuals doing good work and enabled the public and regulatory authorities to determine if auditors identified with problem audits were being made responsible for other audit engagements. The practice of individuals signing work product personally on behalf of their firm is commonplace in the legal profession and others.
- The act requires public disclosure of known or suspected fraudulent activities and gives auditors a responsibility for assuring such disclosure. Current standards do not provide adequate disclosure of fraudulent activities, and auditors had no responsibility for assuring disclosure. Under existing rules, the corporate managers who are often involved in the fraud were given sole responsibility for reporting to the public. In most cases losses are magnified and irrevocable by the time legal proceedings are completed. This provision meets the requirement of the securities laws to give fair and complete disclosure of important information to the public in a timely manner, so that the financial markets will operate efficiently.
- The act requires that auditors report known or suspected illegal activities to the appropriate government, regulatory, or enforcement authorities. Existing standards required only that auditors report such activities to corporate management (who may be involved) and then consider

resigning the audit engagement if the corporate managers do not take appropriate action. This provision also improves the efficiency of government regulatory and enforcement authorities by giving them the information that can be found only through the work of on-site auditors.

- Finally, the act provides complete legal protection for auditors who perform their duties under the act in good faith. This provision is consistent with the legal protection given to officials acting in good faith on the public's behalf in other areas.[3]

1986–1995: Treadway Commission, COSO, SAS No. 78

In the early 1980s, the number of savings and loan (S&L) scandals and frauds stirred the U.S. Congress and audit profession to action. Once again the public asked how those responsible for auditing these companies could give them "clean" audit opinions while a significant financial statement fraud was going on. A committee, officially the National Commission on Fraudulent Financial Reporting, was formed to analyze the frauds and what could be done to mitigate them, chaired by James C. Treadway, Jr. (Executive Vice President and General Counsel, Paine Webber, and a former commissioner of the SEC). It became known as the Treadway Commission. The charge was to come up with recommendations to prevent or detect financial statement frauds going forward.

The commission recommended that publicly-traded companies should employ better internal controls. Based on those recommendations, the work continued under the Committee of Sponsoring Organizations (COSO), which was sponsored by the American Accounting Association (AAA), the AICPA, the Institute of Management Accountants (IMA), the Institute of Internal Auditors (IIA), and the Financial Executives International (FEI). COSO developed a model for internal controls that has become known as the COSO Model, officially released to the public in 1992.

The COSO Model focuses on five areas of internal controls: risk assessment, the control environment, information and communication, monitoring, and control activities. Generally speaking, the latter had been the focus of internal controls up until then.

After its introduction in the early 1990s, the COSO Model was widely adopted by the accounting and business world. In 1995, the AICPA adopted the COSO Model officially by incorporating it into the auditing technical literature as SAS No. 78, *Consideration of Internal Controls in a Financial Statement Audit.*

2002: Sarbanes-Oxley Act

In 2001, the financial fraud being perpetrated at Enron became public, partly due to whistleblower Sherron Watkins. The fraud was the largest in history at that point. In the preceding decade, several other significant financial frauds had occurred such as Waste Management, Sunbeam, and Phar-Mor. As we know, the Enron fraud caused a significant number of activities in Congress and the profession.

In June 2002, Congress was working on a bill to address the issues in the Enron scandal. Arthur Levitt and others had provided input to Congress in developing a reform bill that was sponsored by Senator Paul S. Sarbanes and Representative Michael G. Oxley. In June, the WorldCom fraud was exposed mostly because of the courage of internal auditor Cynthia Cooper. It was the largest fraud to date. Upon news of the new debacle, Congress moved the bill up to debate after the July 4 recess. On July 30, 2002, Congress passed the Sarbanes-Oxley Act of 2002 (SOX). All of the prior standards or regulations pale in comparison to the effects of the passage of SOX.

Related to fraud and auditor liability, some of the major points in SOX are:

- Financial audit firms are prohibited from providing certain services in conjunction with financial audit fees (i.e., independence—similar to Arthur Levitt's original proposal at the SEC).
- A more independent board (Public Company Accounting Oversight Board [PCAOB]) was established to issue auditing standards for SEC companies (at least two of the five-member board are from the public—that is, these two members are *not* CPAs or former CPAs).
- PCAOB was given oversight of financial auditors for SEC companies (to "police" those who should or should not be auditing SEC companies).
- Section 404: Management is required to assess the effectiveness of the system of internal controls within 90 days of the audit report date and *must* identify any material control weaknesses; concomitantly, the financial auditors must opine on that evaluation. This new requirement could be seen as more exposure or liability for the financial auditors.
- The financial auditor is to be hired and have its audit fees set by the audit committee.
- Financial auditors must be rotated.

2002: SAS No. 99

In 1997, the AICPA adopted SAS No. 82, *Consideration of Fraud in a Financial Statement Audit*. The next year, the AICPA established a task force to revise it.

This revision was part of a bigger project that would become the risk-based standards (SAS No. 104-111) adopted years later, and represented a significant change in the way in which financial audits are to be conducted, as prescribed by technical standards. After the scandals at Enron and WorldCom, that revision process picked up speed at the AICPA while the U.S. Congress was busy on the same subject.

In December 2002, the AICPA adopted SAS No. 99, *Consideration of Fraud in a Financial Statement Audit*, which superseded SAS No. 82. The most significant differences between SAS No. 99 and its predecessor are the process itself and the auditor's responsibility for immaterial frauds.

FRAUD AND THE AUDITOR'S LIABILITY

Auditor liability has never been a crystal-clear issue to the public, regulators, or even auditors themselves. Few people in the general public know that financial statement audits are aimed at providing reasonable assurance as to whether a *material misstatement* in the financial statement exists and whether financial transactions are recorded and financial statements are presented in conformity with GAAP. That language is nearly synonymous with the financial audit "opinions" issued for financial statement audits mandated by GAAS as promulgated by the AICPA. In addition, GAAS states that the "The auditor has a responsibility to plan and perform the audit to obtain reasonable assurance about whether the financial statements are free of material misstatement, whether caused by error or fraud."[4] This view is complicated by the fact that over 90 percent of frauds are immaterial, the fact that material financial statement frauds are being perpetrated by an executive who is being clandestine in his efforts, and that financial audit procedures are designed to detect material misstatements in the financials—not fraud.[5]

One source for insight on the financial auditor's standard of care and responsibility for fraud detection is *American Jurisprudence*. Under the general heading "Accountants," that volume offers this:

> It is generally recognized that a public accountant may be held liable on principles of negligence, to one with whom he is in privity, or with whom he has a direct contractual relation, for damages which naturally and proximately result from his failure to employ the degree of knowledge, skill, and judgment usually possessed by members of that profession in the particular locality.

But Section 17, page 366, reads:

> An accountant is not an insurer of the effectiveness of his audit to discover the defalcations of frauds of employees but may be found liable for fraudulent or negligent failure to discover such defalcations because of lack of compliance with proper accounting procedures and accepted accounting practices or by his contract in the light of circumstances of the particular case. . . . And the employer may be precluded from recovery because of his own negligence when it has contributed to the accountant's failure to perform his contract and to report the truth.[6]

The second excerpt gives auditors a breather. Obviously they should not be held liable for not detecting fraud when their clients deceive them.

FRAUD AND THE AUDITOR'S RESPONSIBILITY

Primarily, the auditor's responsibility regarding fraud involves compliance with SOX, PCAOB rules and standards, and compliance with SAS No. 99. Auditors still walk a fine line in performing financial audits because of the possible repercussions of finding fraud. For example, if an auditor finds a fraud that has been going on for 24 months, then it was going on during the last financial audit and if this audit firm performed that audit, the situation could be difficult.

SAS No. 99 changed the prior guidance, SAS No. 82, in several ways, but perhaps the most notable is the brainstorming required in the planning stage. Auditors are required to brainstorm the specific fraud schemes that might be perpetrated and the level of risk for each. Accordingly, the high risks that can lead to a material misstatement must be addressed in the audit procedures themselves. Second, the auditor basically assumes that a revenue recognition (financial statement) fraud is going on. The AICPA argues that the risk assessment process used in SAS No. 99 is very different, including many more elements than previously required, and follows a top-down, risk-based approach that is more effective in detecting material fraud.

Under SAS No. 99, financial auditors must do the following regarding financial audits and their responsibility for fraud:

- Understand the characteristic causes and signs of fraud.
- Assess the risks of a material financial statement misstatement due to fraud.

- Plan and perform the audit to obtain reasonable assurance about whether the financial statements are free of material misstatement, whether caused by error or fraud.
- Exercise due care in planning, performing, evaluating, and documenting the results of audit procedures and instances of fraud.
- Possess the proper degree of professional skepticism, assuming neither dishonesty nor unquestioned honesty of management.
- Assign significant engagement responsibilities to audit personnel with the experience and training indicated as needed by the risk assessment (i.e., personnel experienced in antifraud).
- Report all instances of fraud to the appropriate level of management.
- Insist that financial statements affected by a material fraud be modified to reverse the affects of the fraud or provide a qualified opinion.
- Inform the company's audit committee of fraud, except those that are clearly inconsequential.

In those instances when a misstatement is or may be the result of fraud, and the effect is either material or cannot be determined, the auditor is required to take certain specific steps:

- Attempt to obtain additional evidence.
- Consider the implications for other aspects of the audit.
- Discuss the matter and the approach for further investigation with an appropriate level of management that is at least one level above those involved and with senior management and the audit committee, if appropriate.
- Consult legal counsel.

In those instances when a misstatement is or may be the result of fraud, and the effect is either material or cannot be determined, SAS No. 99 suggests that the auditor *should*:

- Consider consulting legal counsel.
- Consider the need for a separate fraud audit.

Auditor liability can be seen in a common occurrence in a financial audit. Suppose an auditor is examining accounts payable (A/P) transactions and performing substantive procedures on audit objectives such as authorization and accuracy. Because of sampling techniques, the auditor pulls a few dozen samples of transactions. In the process of examining the documents, the auditor finds a check made out to an accounts payable clerk, endorsed by the clerk as a deposit to his bank account. Further suppose that the entity does not reimburse employees for travel or purchases on behalf of the company through accounts payable. Then the auditor may conclude that the check is suspicious regarding potential fraud. The check is for $2,000 and materiality of the A/P account is $250,000. This transaction is the only one that is suspicious. What should the auditor do? Take a larger sample and look for another "anomaly"? Statistically, that is not likely to occur. Ignore it because of materiality? Some auditor managers would recommend this action. Or call upon a subject matter expert (SME), a forensic accountant, who is expert at detecting fraud. That person is likely to "drill down" on the transaction to look for more similar checks in order to ascertain whether the check is fraud. Although that takes time and resources, it also protects the firm against liability should the check be fraud and be dismissed as being immaterial, but the actual extent of the fraud exceeds tolerable misstatement or material misstatement level, and the fraud becomes public (something that the authors call "iceberg theory").

An example of the iceberg theory is the Koss fraud. In December 2009, the Vice President of Finance, Sujata Sachdeva, was fired after the CEO of the company discovered she had been embezzling funds for the previous four years to buy furs, jewelry, and pay credit card debt. The original estimate of the fraud loss was about $4 million, but the amount escalated each week thereafter until it reached $31 million! For the fiscal year ending June 30, 2009, Koss had sales of $38.2 million and profits of $2 million; the prior year's figures were $50 million and $4.5 million respectively. Considering the VP stole almost $8 million a year, it seems logical to conclude the theft was material. The audit firm during those years, Grant Thornton, was fired by Koss. Sachdeva claimed oniomania as the reason for her embezzlement—that is, she was a shopaholic, spending about $650,000 per week! This example again shows the auditor's responsibilities and the potential liability and risk in failing to find a fraud.

One key point about auditor liability, and the time during which SOX was passed, relates to the audit firm of Enron (2001), World Com (2002), and Waste Management (1995)—all big financial statement frauds audited by the same public accounting firm, Arthur Andersen. The pressures surrounding Arthur Andersen and its decisions and activities in these and other audits led to the demise of one the top five worldwide audit firms. This fact is a reminder of how far reaching the auditor's responsibility is, and how far liability can go under the wrong circumstances.

FRAUD AND THE AUDITOR'S ROLE

The discussion to this point has focused on the CPA's responsibility and liability related to fraud, but there are also opportunities for the CPA to provide valuable services. There is a role the CPA plays in fighting fraud. Forensic accounting services involve the application of special skills in accounting, auditing, finance, quantitative methods, certain areas of law, research, and investigative skills to collect, analyze, and evaluate evidential matter and to interpret and communicate findings, and may involve either an attest or consulting engagement.[7]

Litigation Support

It is customary for attorneys who take on fraud-related cases to hire an SME to assist them in trying the case. That SME would be a Certified Fraud Examiner (CFE), Certified in Financial Forensics (CFF), or CPA depending on the need. For example, if the attorney wanted someone to serve as an expert witness for his client, the attorney may be looking for a CPA who has experience or special knowledge that would help win the case. But attorneys often need other help, such as understanding and interpreting auditing services, standards, and reports. Sometimes the attorney will hire an SME to assist in doing statistical work. But as the title implies, the CPA would be hired to support the case in some accointing-related role on behalf of the attorney and her client.

Litigation support takes on the roles of fact witness, expert witness, consultant, and other related roles.

Fact Witness

If an auditor finds a fraud, and the client decides to pursue litigation, criminal or civil, the auditor who found the fraud would likely be in a position to serve the client as a witness. Certainly the auditor could serve as a fact witness, and testify as to what was discovered and how. The AICPA defines a fact witness as, "A person who provides relevant testimony based on his or her firsthand knowledge."

Expert Witness

The CPA may also serve as an expert witness. An expert witness differs from a fact witness in that the expert witness gives an opinion. The CPA may be called upon without any prior knowledge or experience with a certain fraud but rather called upon specifically to express an opinion about fraud based on accounting/auditing evidence in a trial on behalf of a plaintiff, or to testify that fraud does not exist on behalf of a defendant.

The AICPA defines *expert witness* as:

> A person qualified and, if required, disclosed to render an opinion in litigation. If the practitioner is formally designated as an expert witness, all work that the practitioner has performed and all written materials and communications (including e-mails, hand-written notes, and draft reports) related to the litigation are potentially subject to being produced to opposing parties through discovery.[8]

Basically, the expert witness works with an attorney to express an opinion on whether a fraud has occurred in a particular case, based on the evidence accepted in court.

Professional standards do present one complication. The CPA firm cannot express an opinion on the financial statements and express an opinion in court on a fraud case during the same time period of the financial audit. Thus if a CPA finds a fraud while performing a financial audit, that CPA firm will not be able to serve as the client's expert witness.

Consultant

The CPA may also serve a client as a consultant. A victim may want to hire a CPA to examine controls and make a recommendation to improve them regarding fraud prevention. Or a victim may hire a CPA to perform a fraud investigation whereupon the CPA may choose the consulting standard to perform that service. The AICPA defines *consultant* in the context of fraud as:

> A person retained to advise about facts, issues, strategy, and other matters. The consultant does not testify unless the consultant's role subsequently is changed to an expert witness. The consultant's work is generally protected from discovery by legal privilege.

As can be seen, the CPA can perform a variety of fraud-related services in the role of consultant. It is also self-evident that should a CPA take on this role, an appropriate engagement letter would be essential to the process.

Valuation

A growing need in fraud-related cases is for an expert to develop a forensic valuation regarding a loss, in a manner that would stand up to debate in a court of law. A subset or crossover role a CPA can serve is to provide this expertise, specifically those who are Accredited in Business Valuation (ABV—AICPA) or

Certified Valuation Analyst (CVA—National Association of Certified Valuation Analysts [NACVA]). Valuation services may be performed stand-alone or as part of another engagement.

The independence of the CPA would be impaired in providing valuation services if the results of the service, individually or in the aggregate, would be material to the financial statements and the appraisal or valuation involves a significant degree of subjectivity, and the CPA performed attest services on those financials.

The types of cases vary from divorce (e.g., hidden assets, reconstruct income), mergers and acquisitions gone bad (e.g., acquires entity, subsequently finds the entity acquired is not nearly as valuable as led to believe), insurance (e.g., loss by fire, where insurer believes amount filed is fraudulent), and other similar situations.

Other

The CPA may also serve in other roles. The AICPA defines these roles as:

> In addition to the roles of expert witness and consultant, the practitioner may serve without limitation as a trier of fact, special master, court-appointed expert, referee, arbitrator, or mediator.

SUMMARY

The role and responsibilities of the CPA are varied and somewhat complicated by standards, laws, guidelines, and legal protocol. The responsibilities include not only certain technical standards, such as SAS No. 99, but laws such as SOX. It also extends to consideration for the auditor's liability as it relates to fraud. The roles include fact witness, expert witness, valuation expert, litigation support SME, consultant, and other fraud-related roles. Thus the CPA can provide a valuable service to victims of fraud and their clients in general by performing their responsibilities and by providing fraud-related services to the public.

NOTE

1. Wilfred C. Uecker, Arthur P. Brief, and William R. Kinney, Jr., "Perception of the Internal and External Auditor as a Deterrent to Corporate Irregularities," *The Accounting Review* (July 1981), pp. 465–478.

2. Financial Fraud Detection and Disclosure Act, H.R. Doc. No. 4886, 99th Cong. 2d Sess., 1986.
3. Ibid.
4. "Generally Accepted Accounting Standards," *AICPA Professional Standards*, Vol. 1, AU Sec. 110 (New York: American Institute of Certified Public Accountants, November, 1972), pp. 322–323. [Sources include SAS No. 78 and SAS No. 82.]
5. Annette Stalker and Michael Ueltzen, "An Audit versus a Fraud Examination," *CPA Expert* (Winter 2009), pp. 1–3.
6. *American Jurisprudence*, 2nd ed., Vol. 1, Sec. 15 (Rochester, NY: The Lawyers Cooperative Publishing, 1962), pp. 365–366.
7. Quoted from the AICPA Special Report 08-1, "Independence and Integrity and Objectivity in Performing Forensic and Valuation Services," p. 9.
8. See AICPA Special Report 09-1, "Introduction to Civil Litigation Services," for definitions and standards regarding these roles.

About the Authors

Tommie W. Singleton, PhD, CISA, CPA (inactive), CITP, CMA, CFF, CGEIT, is an associate professor in the Accounting and Finance Department of the University of Alabama at Birmingham. He is the Marshall Scholar and Director of Forensic Accounting Program. Tommie has published numerous articles on topics related to IT, IT audit, and fraud in publications such as the *Bank Fraud and Security* newsletter, *EDPACS*, *Information Systems Control Journal*, *White-Collar Crime Fighter*, and *Issues in Accounting Education*. His articles have twice been awarded outstanding paper at conferences. He also coauthored three books: *Managing the Internal Audit Function*, *IT Audit and Assurance*, and two editions of *Fraud Auditing and Forensic Accounting*.

Singleton's experience includes 11 years as president of a small value-added dealer of turnkey computer systems. He has also provided consulting services over the last 13 years in various aspects of fraud and IT audit. Since 2008, Dr. Singleton has been a scholar-in-residence at Carr, Riggs & Ingram, a large regional public accounting firm, with responsibilities in IT audit, fraud, and SAS 70 audits.

He is currently serving a two-year term on the Council for the Alabama Society of CPAs, and a three-year term as a member of the AICPA's Information Technology Executive Committee.

Dr. Singleton is a frequent speaker and provider of CPE, having offered more than 50 seminars on fraud. He also provides training to internal audit departments and public accounting firms on fraud and IT audit.

Tommie earned his PhD in Accountancy from the University of Mississippi.

Aaron J. Singleton, CISA, CPA has worked for five years at a global public accounting firm performing information technology, financial statement, and regulatory compliance audits. Aaron's prior experience includes managing accounting and systems for a small wholesale business, and experience in systems development, installation, and support. Aaron has published articles related to fraud and forensics in journals including the *Information Security Journal* and the *Journal of Corporate Accounting and Finance.* Aaron earned his Master's of Accountancy from Bowling Green State University and Bachelor's Degrees in Accounting and Management from the University of Alabama at Birmingham.

Index

accountant, 3–5, 8–25, 31–36, 53, 69–70, 75, 80, 88, 90–92, 94–95, 110, 112, 123, 137, 158, 173, 191, 198, 206, 208, 210, 218, 237, 255–258, 260–269, 271–272, 274–275, 282, 290, 294, 296–297, 299
accounting, 3–6, 10, 12–17, 19–36, 54–56, 73, 76, 78–79, 83–85, 91, 93, 95, 97, 104, 108–109, 111, 113–114, 118, 121–122, 125, 135, 137–140, 142, 145, 153, 155–158, 161, 168, 173, 176–177, 179, 190–191, 193–194, 197–199, 202, 206–207, 217–218, 226, 234, 256–257, 260, 263–264, 266–269, 272, 274–276, 278, 282–286, 289–292, 294, 296–297, 299–300
accounting cycle, 138–140, 190–191, 206–207
admission, 211, 217–218, 235–236, 259
American Institute of Certified Public Accountants (AICPA), 9–11, 34–35, 69, 95, 113, 126, 288, 291–292, 294,
anomaly, 22, 32, 66, 93, 109, 142, 299
asset misappropriation, 20, 47–48, 61, 63–64, 70, 72–78, 82–83, 90, 95, 97, 102, 117, 145, 193, 195, 290
Association of Certified Fraud Eximaners (ACFE), 2, 7, 12, 16, 19–20, 33–35, 40–41, 44–47, 52, 54, 61–64, 60–72, 75–76, 81, 83–84, 86–90, 95, 102, 113–114, 117, 124, 133, 135–136, 142–144, 151, 154, 156, 160–161, 163, 234,
audit, 4–8, 10–23, 25–27, 29, 30, 33, 35–36, 45–48, 50, 55, 61, 63, 65–66, 69–70, 72–73, 75–80, 85, 95–96, 100–101, 104, 107, 109, 112–114, 117, 118, 123, 126–127, 129–133, 135–138, 142–147, 149–150, 155, 157–159, 172–173, 179–181, 191, 194, 198–199, 201–207, 214, 224, 229, 234, 257, 260, 285–286, 289, 291–299, 301
audit committee, 11, 30, 63, 76–78, 118, 123, 129–130, 145, 164, 289, 295, 298
auditing, 7, 9–17, 21, 25–26, 28–30, 34–35, 45, 47–48, 54, 95–96, 112–113, 129, 144, 153,

auditing (*Continued*) 158, 172–173, 206, 246, 272, 288, 293–296, 300
auditor, 4–23, 25–36, 45–46, 50, 61, 63, 69–70, 75–81, 88, 91–92, 94–99, 102, 104, 107–110, 112–113, 123, 126–127, 129–130, 133, 136–138, 140, 142, 145, 158, 172–173, 191, 198–199, 206, 208, 214–215, 217–218, 226, 233–234, 237–238, 254–255, 257, 260, 263–264, 267–268, 272, 284–302

best practices, 10, 30, 113, 117, 133, 138, 187, 200, 202, 230, 234, 239, 255, 284
bid rigging, 91
body language, 236, 237
bribery, 7, 25, 55–57, 59, 61, 64, 74, 77, 81–82, 108, 150

certification, 26, 33–35, 37, 144, 231, 244–245, 247, 264
Certified in Financial Forensics (CFF), 33, 300
Certified Fraud Examiner (CFE), 33–34, 47, 114, 157–158, 300
Certified Public Accountant (CPA), 4–5, 34–35, 158, 210, 262, 264, 286–287, 295, 300–302
check tampering, 84, 87, 139, 148, 149
compliance, 11, 13, 22, 25, 27, 47, 78, 117, 131, 134, 156, 287, 297
Computer-Assisted Auditing Techniques (CAATs), 96, 144, 146–147
confession, 8, 22, 32, 209, 211–212, 217–218, 236
conflict-of-interest, 30, 81, 108
conviction, 32, 45, 136, 216–217, 252, 276
corporate governance, 30, 111, 129–130, 137
corruption, 4, 6–7, 20, 47, 56–57, 59–64, 70, 72–74, 76–78, 81, 95, 97, 99, 108, 117, 150, 290
COSO, 9–11, 45–46, 111, 129, 140, 294
court, 5, 8, 12–13, 17–18, 21–24, 26, 32–33, 40, 67, 154, 158, 208–210, 212–214, 218, 220, 222, 224, 230, 236–237, 241, 244–249, 256–262, 264–267, 271, 274–278, 280, 282–283, 285, 287, 290, 301–302
credentials, 210, 243–250, 255–256, 261, 264
Cressey, 33, 42, 43, 45, 74, 114 (see fraud triangle)
custody, 32, 148, 165, 213–214, 222, 228–230

deception, 37, 38
demeanor, 15, 18, 209, 217, 251, 273, 275, 277, 283
detection, 8–9, 15, 23, 26, 30, 38, 47–49, 51, 72, 75, 94–94, 96, 99, 106–108, 117, 123, 126–128, 132–134, 136–145, 153, 158, 163, 172, 193, 207, 238, 288, 290, 292–293, 296
disclosure, 9, 23, 40, 80, 101, 118, 124, 221, 258–259, 288–293
discovery, 7, 12, 66, 101, 107–108, 149, 173, 216, 228, 277, 301

e-mail, 21, 133, 173–174, 184–185, 205–206, 219, 223, 225–226, 301
embezzlement, 21, 25, 41–43, 55–57, 59–60, 64, 83, 113, 116, 134, 180, 260, 286, 289, 299
Enron, 1, 6, 35, 55, 62, 73–74, 79–80, 111, 130, 173, 287, 295–296, 299
evidence, 5, 8, 10, 12–16, 22–26, 28, 32–33, 35–36, 41, 53, 66–67, 77, 80, 82, 92, 100, 103, 109–110, 131, 135–136, 155–159, 173, 181, 192–194, 206–231, 233, 236, 240–241, 257–258, 260–261, 264–267, 271, 274–278, 280–281, 284, 298, 300–301
expert witness, 5, 8, 12–15, 17, 21, 23, 25, 34, 36, 67, 210, 212, 224, 230, 244–253, 255–278, 280, 282–284, 300–302
eye language, 238, 239

Federal Bureau of Investigation (FBI), 2, 26, 173–174, 180, 230
financial statement fraud, 1, 36, 40, 44, 46–47, 55, 63–65, 71–80, 95, 97, 99, 117, 160, 194, 286–287, 294, 296–297, 299
forensic accountant, 3, 5, 8, 11–25, 31–36, 70, 90–92, 158, 191, 206, 208, 218, 237, 256–258, 261–263, 271–272, 274, 282, 299
forensic accounting, 3, 5–6, 8, 12–13, 16–17, 19, 21–22, 24, 31, 33–36, 109, 155–158, 161, 234, 256, 263, 300
forge, 32, 57, 70, 80, 87, 104–105, 166, 177, 284, 289
fraud auditing, 7, 9–17, 25–26, 29–30, 35, 54, 169, 206
fraud auditor, 8, 12, 14–16, 20, 23, 25–27, 29–30, 32, 35–36, 70, 91–92, 94, 99, 107, 110, 127, 133, 137–138, 191, 199, 206, 208, 218, 226, 257
fraud investigation, 8, 12–13, 22, 26, 31, 33–34, 36–37, 40–41, 53, 66, 73, 93, 111–112, 141, 155, 157–159, 161, 208–209, 213, 218, 220, 223–224, 228, 231, 233–234, 236, 241, 257, 267, 301
fraud risk, 10–11, 36, 47, 76, 111, 114, 118–119, 125–127, 194, 205
fraud survey, 19–20, 46, 53, 64, 73, 76, 162
fraud theory, 22, 31, 37, 66, 91, 94, 141, 180
fraud tree, 20, 35, 47, 61–63, 67, 69–72, 75, 78, 83, 93–95, 97, 124, 141, 175
fraud triangle, 26, 31, 35, 38, 43–45, 67, 93–95, 111, 114, 130, 136–137, 141, 175, 177
fraudulent disbursements, 83, 84, 87, 139

Generally Accepted Accounting Principles (GAAP), 13, 16, 23–24, 78, 80, 100, 102, 145, 272, 287, 296
Generally Accepted Auditing Standards (GAAS), 13–14, 19, 24, 288, 291, 296

Ghost employee, 86, 87, 140, 147, 148
government, 1, 3, 6, 11, 22, 25–26, 29, 35, 53, 58–59, 61, 73, 77, 82, 89, 114, 117, 157, 171, 173, 180,
government (*Continued*) 200, 231, 245–248, 251–254, 256, 291, 293–294
Government Accountability Office (GAO), 26, 85, 104, 173
guilt, 33, 41, 155, 181, 208–209, 213, 236, 239, 241, 271

hand writing analysis, 240

Information Systems Audit and Control Association (ISACA), 35, 69, 95–96, 113, 126
Institute of Internal Auditors (IIA), 35, 69, 95–96, 113, 294
insurance, 2, 9, 13–17, 18, 21, 28, 55, 57, 59, 63–64, 67, 79, 86, 126, 135, 161, 172, 302
intent, 15, 17, 24, 27, 30, 32, 39–41, 44, 54–56, 65, 79, 82–83, 87, 163, 177, 182, 184, 212–213, 226
internal control, 8–13, 20, 23, 27, 30–32, 36, 45–48, 50, 56, 66, 75–76, 94, 97, 100, 104, 107, 109, 111–113, 120, 124, 126–127, 135, 137–138, 143, 168, 175–176, 179, 289, 291, 293–295
Internet Crime Complaint Center (IC3), 2, 174
interviewing, 8, 15, 22, 35, 90, 158, 234
interviews, 12–14, 22, 33, 43, 120, 157, 159, 165, 216–219, 233–236, 238–239, 241, 250–251, 253
irregularities, 27, 30, 41, 96, 109, 113, 126, 150, 155, 163–165, 172

kickback, 21, 25, 57, 64, 70, 77, 81, 108

lapping, 89, 90, 139, 146, 149, 150
larceny, 41, 56–57, 83–84, 91, 102, 139, 145, 177
litigation, 12–13, 15, 17–18, 21, 24, 31, 34–35, 154–158, 160–161, 168, 173, 208, 223–224, 260–261, 264, 266, 273–274, 278, 300–302

material misstatement, 13–14, 19–20, 30, 57, 76, 296, 298
materiality, 14, 17, 24, 63, 70, 74, 76, 109, 210, 299
motive, 8, 24, 30–31, 39, 43–44, 51, 61, 73–74, 175–176, 209, 213

opportunity, 8, 24, 31–32, 43–45, 56, 61, 65, 95, 119, 130, 137, 161, 177–178, 209, 213, 215, 219, 259, 264–265
predication, 31, 36, 66
prevention, 15, 26, 30–31, 36, 38, 45, 70, 72, 75, 92–93, 99, 106, 110, 117, 120, 122–123, 126–127–129, 131–134, 136–140, 153, 162–163, 207, 301
profile, 35, 38, 48, 52, 67, 72, 93, 107, 181–182, 184, 241, 272

prosecution, 8, 67, 132–133, 155, 157–158, 161, 208, 217, 221, 223–224, 247, 249, 260, 263, 265
public accounting, 13, 26, 35, 109, 285–286, 299
Public Company Accounting Oversight Board (PCAOB), 10–11, 13, 111–112, 126, 295, 297

rationalization, 31, 42–45, 65, 95, 130, 136–137, 175, 216
red flag, 9, 14–15, 26, 31–32, 35, 66, 92, 93–111, 122, 124, 126, 128, 140–141, 144, 146, 148, 151, 159, 226, 232, 239
Report to the Nation (RTTN), 2, 7, 19, 44–45, 47, 52–53, 72–73, 75–76, 81, 83–84, 86–90, 113–114, 117, 136, 142–144, 151, 160–161
response (to fraud), 153, 156–161
risk assessment, 9, 36, 47, 111–114, 117–118, 123–125, 128, 153, 161, 181, 294, 297–298

SAS No. 99, 10–11, 76–78, 95, 99, 112, 126, 145, 295–298, 302
SCAN, 240
SEC, 5, 26, 46, 111, 129, 172, 286–289, 291–295
segregation of duties, 53, 65, 75, 108, 135, 137, 139, 191, 197–198, 200, 207
shell vendor (company), 84, 85, 139, 146, 147, 158
SOX, 7, 10, 11, 12, 14, 15, 31
statement analyis, 239, 240
suspect, 7, 12, 27, 32–34, 37, 48, 123, 155, 158, 163–166, 181, 209–210, 216–218, 220–222, 225, 234, 236, 240, 289, 293
Sutherland, 33, 42, 43 (see white-collar crime)
systems, 14, 25, 35, 112–113, 121, 131, 139, 155, 159, 170, 175–181, 184–187, 190–193, 198–207, 224, 227, 231, 291, 293

tips, 47–48, 90, 103, 110, 129, 132–133, 142–144, 155, 158
trial, 15, 18, 28, 33, 51, 57, 67, 133, 208–215, 230, 244–250, 252, 257, 260–263, 266–267, 275–277, 284, 300

white-collar crime, 21, 26, 29, 33, 35–36, 38, 41–42, 45, 48, 50–52, 117, 132, 157, 246